Midlife in Context

McGRAW-HILL SERIES IN DEVELOPMENTAL PSYCHOLOGY

CONSULTING EDITOR: ROSS A. THOMPSON

1. **Carole Beal:** *Boys and Girls: The Development of Gender Roles*
2. **Fredda Blanchard-Fields and Thomas Hess:** *Perspectives on Cognitive Change in Adulthood and Aging*
3. **Sandra L. Calvert:** *Children's Journey Through the Information Age*
4. **Virginia Colin:** *Human Attachment*
5. **Celia Fisher and Richard Lerner:** *Applied Developmental Psychology*
6. **Matthew Merrens and Gary Brannigan:** *The Developmental Psychologists: Research Adventures Across the Life Span*
7. **Rolf E. Muss:** *Theories of Adolescence, 6/e*
8. **Edward F. Zigler and Nancy W. Hall:** *Child Development and Social Policy: Theory and Applications*

Midlife in Context

K. C. Kirasic

University of South Carolina

Boston   Burr Ridge, IL   Dubuque, IA   Madison, WI   New York
San Francisco   St. Louis   Bangkok   Bogotá   Caracas   Kuala Lumpur
Lisbon   London   Madrid   Mexico City   Milan   Montreal   New Delhi
Santiago   Seoul   Singapore   Sydney   Taipei   Toronto

Higher Education

MIDLIFE IN CONTEXT
Published by McGraw-Hill, a business unit of The McGraw-Hill Companies, Inc., 1221 Avenue of the Americas, New York, NY 10020. Copyright © 2004 by The McGraw-Hill Companies, Inc. All rights reserved. No part of this publication may be reproduced or distributed in any form or by any means, or stored in a database or retrieval system, without the prior written consent of The McGraw-Hill Companies, Inc., including, but not limited to, in any network or other electronic storage or transmission, or broadcast for distance learning.

Some ancillaries, including electronic and print components, may not be available to customers outside the United States.

This book is printed on acid-free paper.

Domestic   1 2 3 4 5 6 7 8 9 0 DOC/DOC 0 9 8 7 6 5 4 3

ISBN 0-07-245839-9

Vice president and editor-in-chief: *Thalia Dorwick*
Publisher: *Stephen D. Rutter*
Senior developmental editor: *Rebecca H. Hope*
Developmental editor: *Sienne Patch*
Marketing manager: *Melissa Caughlin*
Project manager: *Mary Lee Harms*
Production supervisor: *Enboge Chong*
Media technology producer: *Ginger Bunn*
Senior designer: *Violeta Diaz*
Cover image: *David Young-Wolff/PhotoEdit*
Manager, Art: *Robin Mouat*
Illustrator: *Rennie Evans*
Compositor: *Carlisle Communications, Ltd.*
Typeface: *Palatino*
Printer: *R. R. Donnelley/Crawfordsville, IN*

Library of Congress Cataloging In-Publication Data

Kirasic, K. C.
   Midlife in context / K. C. Kirasic.
      p. cm.
   ISBN 0-07-245839-9 (alk paper)
      1. Middle age—Psychological aspects. 2. Middle aged persons—Psychology. 3. Aging—
      Psychological aspects. 4. Middle age. I. Title

BF724.6.K55 2003
305.244—dc21

                                                                                    2003048842

The Internet addresses listed in the text were accurate at the time of publication. The inclusion of a website does not indicate an endorsement by the authors or McGraw-Hill, and McGraw-Hill does not guarantee the accuracy of the information presented at these sites.

www.mhhe.com

Dedication
This book is dedicated to
Gary for every possible reason;
Rachael, Sarah, and Evan for their encouragement
during the tough times;
My American and Canadian friends for
their unwavering support;
The students, past, present, and future of The
Psychology of the Midlife Woman class;
And finally to Chubby for the constant source of
humor and love.

About the Author

K. C. Kirasic is a life span developmental psychologist. Trained at the University of Pittsburgh in the Learning-Developmental Program, Dr. Kirasic established an expertise in the area of aging and spatial cognition. During this period in her career, she established herself as one of the foremost researchers in that domain.

Dr. Kirasic finds her recent interests in midlife to be an extension of her early interest in the field of aging. The period of midlife has become central to her current research and teaching efforts. As an associate professor at the University of South Carolina, Dr. Kirasic has been able to broaden her interests to include attachment-related issues as they impact midlife self-esteem and multigenerational attachment relations in female family members of African American, European American, and Peruvian families. This multigenerational, cross-cultural research endeavor was sparked by her popular university course, The Psychology of the Midlife Woman.

In addition to her continued work in attachment and her teaching of life span courses, Dr. Kirasic is working on an interdisciplinary effort to develop a clearinghouse for the establishment of midlife women and elderly women mentors. She considers the period of midlife to be pivotal to success in the later stages of one's life. Midlife, and its many dimensions, deserves recognition and thorough investigation. For this reason, *Midlife in Context* is offered as a first step in that direction.

Brief Contents

PREFACE TO SECTION III

Table of Contents

PREFACE TO SECTION II

PREFACE TO SECTION III

11. Relationships at Midlife

Preface

A book is a tool. Like every tool, there was a specific purpose for which it was designed. This book was designed as a tool to aid the student build a better understanding of the period of the life span known as midlife. The presentation of the material was crafted with the student as the primary consumer. The format is congenial and conversational without sacrificing rigor in content or demands for critical thinking skills.

This book was designed for use by individuals in a variety of fields as an upper level undergraduate or first-year graduate course. Students in a variety of psychology courses, developmental, clinical, or life span, social work, nursing, women's or men's studies could use this as the primary or secondary text. Other audiences in sociology, human relations, cultural anthropology, ministerial training, or human social services could also employ this text in their training. This book is meant to serve as an introduction to a relatively new domain of academic and social investigation. Anyone interested in humans or the process of human development will benefit by familiarizing themselves with this content.

A field sample of approximately 100 students, both undergraduate and graduate, have read and commented upon a variety of aspects of this text. The material, in general, was considered to be accessible and useful in a practical everyday sense. The text insert boxes were said to give the student greater perspective on midlife individuals familiar to them. The miniexercises also gave the student the opportunity to view life from an interactionist perspective. However, the unquestionable favorite section of the text was the "Voices of Our Parents" essays found at the end of each chapter in sections 2 and 3. Students couldn't get enough of these readings. The essays were rated as rich in diversity, eye-opening in experiences, and clearly honest and unguarded. These writings forced the students to realize the many layers that constitute the individual. From these, the students gained a sense that as the world continues to change, so does the realization of one's goals.

The impact of culture, when mentioned where appropriate and if available, forced the student to develop a greater appreciation of cultural diversity. Culture's impact on the many aspects of midlife development became increasingly apparent. It helped the student understand the relative nature of age and the manner in which it is enacted.

This text should also be considered as a pedagogical tool for the instructor. Considerable flexibility is provided to allow the instructor to organize and introduce the material congenial to the course and student needs. In this way, the professor and the student can engage in coconstructive examination of midlife. The chapters are written to afford the creative instructor the latitude to shape particular chapters in the manner most agreeable to their domain of study.

Most important, however, is the recognition of the period of midlife. It is hoped that it will become apparent that this period of the life span is critical to the design of the individual's present and future. The introduction provides the student with the rationale for the development of this book.

Overview and Structure of the Text

This book is divided into fifteen formal chapters with an introduction (Chapter 1) and conclusion section (Chapter 15). The focus of section 1 is theory (chapters 2 and 3), empirical approaches to midlife (chapter 4) and cultural influences (chapter 5). Section 2 focuses on the perception of men and women currently experiencing midlife (chapter 6), physiology and health and fertility and menopause (chapters 7 and 8), and cognitive processing (chapter 9). Section 3 emphasizes relationships with others and one's self—in the family (chapter 11), in the workplace (chapter 12), in educational settings (chapter 13), and in the community (chapter 14). The conclusion (chapter 15) attempts to provide an integrative statement regarding the impact of gender, culture, and history on the life of the maturing adult. Throughout the text, theoretical statements and empirical findings will be presented separately for women and men. This intentional division of the sexes is being used to highlight the fact that although all of the previously mentioned issues are experienced by both men and women, they experience each differently. These differences should be clearly noted and understood, not merely relegated to a footnote.

Also, important terms will be highlighted in each chapter and defined in a glossary at the end of the book. Critical thinking boxes will be selectively placed within certain paragraphs to encourage discussion and reflection. Finally, the appendix has been included to provide the reader with a listing of the questions asked of those responding to the "Voices of Our Parents" essays.

Acknowledgements

The author wishes to thank the editors of McGraw-Hill, as well as the reviewers of this manuscript for their invaluable help. Without the following reviewers the development of this book would not have been possible.

Deborah S. Carr,
University of Michigan

Gypsy Denzine,
Northern Arizona University

Lauren E. Duncan,
Smith College

Tracy X. Karner,
University of Kansas

Jan Sinnott,
Towson University

Perry G. Thompson,
University of Arkansas

Bonnie Wolkenstein,
Antioch University, Los Angeles

Elaine Worthington,
Cornell University

CHAPTER 1

Introduction—Hey, Read This Section!

"Middle age is a state of mind."

—FISKE, 1979.

"Middle age is a period in which some hopes are blighted, some opportunities are seen as forever lost."

—CLAUSSEN, 1986.

Why a book on midlife and not just adulthood? For many years, the primary focus of developmental psychology was the child. In the late 1970s, the period of adolescence was given greater coverage in the standard developmental textbook. The next age group to rise in prominence within the field was that of the elderly adult, thereby leading to an approach called *life-span development*. As the name implies, life-span development as an approach allowed for and invested in the study of human development from conception to death. However, most developmental scientists remained focused on the usual age groups—childhood, adolescence, and older adults. Eventually, researchers and theorists realized the obvious: The period of *adulthood*, the largest and arguably the most important period in the life span, was being ignored. As more attention was focused on adulthood, it became clear that this period could be differentiated into subperiods.

You should be asking two questions.

1. *How appropriate are theories of child development to the study of adulthood?*
2. *When we speak of adulthood, aren't we talking about a long period?*

As a result, there is a growing awareness that *middle age* is critical in understanding the overall picture of adulthood and, by extension, the life span.

Traditionally, the beginning of the life span is divided into the prenatal period, infancy, childhood, and adolescence (spanning approximately 18–20 years), followed by adulthood (potentially spanning 100 years). Contemporary young adults have grown up hearing terms like middle-age spread and midlife crisis. However, middle age as a distinct period of life has only recently become a reality for most humans. Individuals born in the 1780s could expect to live to the ripe old age of 28 years. During the twentieth century, the average *life expectancy* had markedly increased. In 1900, men and women only lived to about 50 years of age. By the end of the century that followed, the average life expectancy had increased to 72 for men and approximately 78 for women (Riley, 1985).

Why was this happening?

This increase during the twentieth century reflected gains in life expectancy equivalent to the preceding 5,000 years (Lemme, 1999a). The emergence of midlife as a part of the life span is a consequence of this increased life expectancy.

As the twentieth century progressed, two *demographic trends* became apparent. First, there was the growing awareness that the average age of the population of the United States was increasing, and second, the largest cohort in the history of the United States (*baby boomers*) was quickly approaching the middle of their life expectancy. In 1996 the first baby boomers turned 50. Between 1960 and 1985, there was a 24 percent increase in individuals between the ages 45–64 resulting in approximately 45 million people in that group. A 72 percent increase, to approximately 80 million, is expected in that age group by the year 2015 (U.S. Bureau of the Census, 1992). A change of this magnitude naturally generates scientific interest. For this reason the study of the midlife period is a contemporary development. The number of individuals traversing this period could easily be pointed to as the raison d'être for interest. However, size of population is not the only reason for focusing on this group. Baby boomers, particularly those in the United States, represent the healthiest, best-educated, and most-affluent group of individuals to pass through this period. Their presence will influence how we will come to think about the transition from early adulthood to late adulthood. Their impact will continue to be felt as their later years unfold. How late adulthood will be perceived and enacted will be markedly different from what has been seen and experienced by others before. The preferences, expectations, and voices of the boomer generation will be heard and will result in new conceptualizations of the life span.

PUBLICLY AND PRIVATELY HELD MYTHS OF MIDLIFE

How does the average American feel about midlife? Some individuals do not feel positive about that part of the life span. Being referred to as a midlife adult is not generally regarded as a compliment. One reason for this reaction has to do with the plethora of negative connotations placed on this period of life. These images abound in the popular written media, television, and movies, and they find their way into day-to-day conversations, despite attempts to celebrate its arrival via the American Association of Retired People's (AARP) magazine, *My Generation*. The 2-year-old may tell you that he or she wants to be 5 years old. There is clearly something of a distinction in the preschool set about the age of five. The 13-year-old wants to be 16, so he or she can drive. The 18-year-old wants to be 21. After 21, however, the designation of age goals begins to break down . Few 20-year-olds, if any, will tell you that they wish that they were 35, and it is the rare person in his or her 30s who reports that being 45 is their goal. Instead, individuals may begin to report their age incorrectly in everyday conversation, covertly shaving a few years off. There's a popular conception that saying that you are 35 is better than *admitting* that you are 40.

Notice the negative connotation associated with the term **admitting.**

Myths pervade this period of midlife. Some individuals believe that it is the beginning of the end, the beginning of encroaching mental incompetence, the end of sex, the end of love, and the end of life worth living. They believe that the potential for contribution, to say nothing of growth, is minimal. They are becoming less strong, less attractive, and generally useless.

Do you hold any of these beliefs?

What I have presented is a Western view, or more specifically, a view held by many U.S. North Americans. In many other cultures, becoming an "elder" is a goal to which to aspire. In previous historical eras, even residents of the United States fashioned their clothing and hair styles to portray themselves as older, more mature, and wiser. Then, in the latter half of the twentieth century there was a movement that came to idealize youth and all its connotations. There was an emphasis on acting young, dressing young, and being young! Much of this emphasis on youth came from the numbers of baby boomers moving into their late teens and early twenties. This group was active, vocal, and omnipresent due to advances in mass media, most notably the growth of television, the chief source of information. People of all ages, nationally and internationally, joined in this celebration of youth to varying degrees. Later, the baby boomers moved into their thirties with little fanfare. Many of their youthful ways in their twenties could be maintained in their thirties. The one clear difference between then and the thirties had to do with the increasing number of roles and responsibilities that they were accepting. However, you could still act young, dress young, and be young.

But inevitably, this generation of individuals moved into a relatively unpublicized, little understood, and somewhat feared period of life.

Why do you think midlife is feared?

They began turning forty. For many of them they knew only that they were not going to "do midlife" as their parents had done it. Even for those who had not rebelled against their parents during the late sixties, this generation had not done anything like their parents did. But, how do you do 45, 50, or 55? (Greer, 1991) There were no models for this group. Because of their number and the changes brought about through technological innovations, this generation has been thrust to the forefront to define how this period of life can be experienced. How this will be enacted, we have yet to see. However, we may see many myths of midlife cast aside for a more realistic and constructive view. One of the purposes of this text is to provide evidence from a variety of domains and cultures to replace the many myths with information that reflects the many possibilities that accompany midlife.

Meanwhile, outside the borders of the United States, life has been going on. Nations of individuals have traversed young adulthood and have experienced midlife. Have trauma, crisis, and a devaluation become the hallmark of the midlife experiences for these individuals? Or, are there things to be learned from these cultures as we consider the growing up of the boomers? Can this healthy, most-affluent, and best-educated generation now step forward to be models, not for the older generation as to how to be young, but as models for the younger generation as to how to be old? The lessons learned at midlife, if one is successful, can only serve to pave the way to a better older adulthood and a better transition for future generations.

What will you expect for your midlife transitions if the baby boomers fail as models?

OVERVIEW AND STRUCTURE OF THE TEXT

This book is divided into 15 chapters. Chapter 1 is an introduction to the concept of midlife as a definable area of lifespan developmental investigation. The focus of Section I concerns itself with basic ecological and non-ecological theoretical approaches to this part of the lifespan, empirical treatments of data and design, as well as addressing culture and context as it applies to midlife. Section II provides information regarding the perception and understanding of men and women at midlife, physiological and health-related issues relevant to midlife, fertility, cognitive processing abilities, along with the psychological issues of identity, self-esteem, and personal meaning to life. The final section, Section III, allows for an examination of the social persona of the midlife adult. The variety of contexts of social life includes the myriad of midlife relationships, their roles in the workplace, educational settings, and in the community in terms of volunteerism. Chapter 15 provides a series of integrative and summary statements regarding the impact of gender, culture, and history on the life of the maturing adult.

Throughout the text, theoretical statements and empirical findings will be presented separately for women and men. This intentional division of the sexes is being used to highlight the fact that although all of the above mentioned issues are experienced by both men and women, women and men experience these differently. These differences should be clearly noted and understood, not merely relegated to a footnote.

Preface to Section I

This section represents the foundation of the text. Without the background material in theory, method, and culture, the student would have little basis for understanding the content of the chapters that follow, as well as little basis for understanding the broader theme of lifespan development. Midlife merely represents a period, although a long period, in the life of the human. The thoughtful student should be able to extrapolate from the information in these chapters to the broader picture of human development.

The primary purpose of this section is to introduce the student to the relevant theoretical positions that relate to the midlife process. Theories with broad overarching implications to this lifespan period are introduced. In addition, individual theories that have addressed particular aspects of the midlife experience are included in a separate chapter.

To accompany these theoretical views, the student will find the most frequently employed experimental designs found in the literature. Advantages and disadvantages of these methods will be highlighted. Reference to the most profitable approaches in the understanding of midlife behavior will also be described and endorsed.

Finally, the issue of culture will be introduced. The impact of culture, as related to human behavior, plays a major role in every chapter of this book. Culture is introduced in the last chapter of this section. The goal is to not only highlight culture as an independent construct but also to demonstrate the way culture weaves its way into our lives. The implications of the subtle impact of culture will be shown throughout this text. Chapter 6 merely highlights the importance of acknowledging its present and long-range impact on our lives.

CHAPTER 2

Ecological Views of Development

"Midway this way of life we're bound upon, I woke to find myself in a dark wood, Where the right road was wholly lost & gone"

—DANTE

Perspectives on Midlife

—*young adult*—*"I don't think much about being middle age, there's just too much to do now at 18. My mom's kinda weird now." (high school student)*

—*middle aged adult*—*"Whoa, I am so confused about what's going on! Is this how it's supposed to be?" (44-year-old veterinarian)*

—*late middle aged adult*—*"I'm keeping midlife a secret. I don't want anyone to know how great it is. Let them be surprised." (55-year-old reporter)*

THEORETICAL ORIENTATION OF THE BOOK

I know that you're thinking "Oh no!! Not the boring part!!" But this is really a good part. It should get you thinking about life around you.

In 1992, Ford and Learner introduced the developmental systems theory as a new way to conceptualize human development. They put forth the proposition that people are "fused" with their contexts across life. This is shown in Figure 2.1

How would you draw your current life-context figure? Highlight those elements most critical at this time.

Do you see any additional levels being added later in your life? How might the highlighting change?

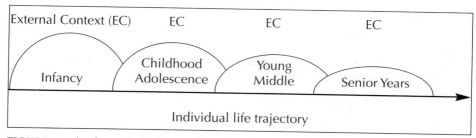

FIGURE 2.1. A schematic diagram of the developmental systems view of Ford and Learner. This represents the fusion of the individual context.

This view, however, does not represent a fatalistic view of development such that the individual is fated by birth to a particular course of development. Rather, it presents a more dynamic picture of human development. Ford and Lerner refer to the thoughts of Brim and Kagan (1980) in quoting There are important growth changes across the lifespan from birth to death. Many individuals maintain a great capacity for change and the consequences of the events of early childhood are continually transformed by later experiences, making the course of human development more open than many have believed.

Fundamental to this view is that of developmental **contextualism,** which describes the influences between an individual and his or her environment as a two-way street. In short, a variety of contexts influence the individual, and the individual influences the context(s) through his or her actions. This potential for change within the individual and between individuals/contexts is the hallmark of developmental systems theory. The structure and function of variables from any one level influence, and are in turn influenced by, the structure and function of variables from the other levels. It is Ford and Learner's contention that looking at development in this way is positive and optimistic. It differs from other theories in that it posits the potential for a dynamic exchange between levels that can significantly alter the internal (biological/psychological) and/or external (the broader context) life of the individual. These theorists caution, however, that a complete alteration of the person-context system is not possible. There are constraints impinging from within and without that limit a complete metamorphosis.

In 1999, Brandtstadter and Learner further developed the idea of developmental systems into one that incorporated action as part of intentional self-development. From this view, the individual should be considered the product and active producer of his or her development. "It follows that we cannot adequately understand human development over the lifespan without considering the ways in which individuals in action, cognition, and social interaction construe their development," and correspondingly, how their development is construed by others. The insightful writings of these authors have led to a new conceptualization of the process of development. Rather than adopting the traditional models of development that conceive of developmental change as an outcome of the developmental process, they consider human development as a self-referential process that creates and is formed by intentionality and action. The process of development is viewed as a result of goal-related activity (Brandtstadter, 1984; Lerner, 1982). However, self-directedness and intentionality do not mean that humans are the sole producers of their development. Like any other human activity, intentional self-development is structured by the interaction of biological, social, and cultural forces. Human life histories are always a mixture of controllable and uncontrollable elements. Over the course of one's life, some desired goals and developmental outcomes are accomplished while others remain unachieved or drift outside the individual's span of control, which is subject to developmental change and modifications across the life cycle. (See any of the "Voices of Our Parents" sections.) Notions of self-regulation and personal control over development must always include an emphasis on the impact of contextual embeddedness, sociohistorical specificity, and sociocultural forces.

> *What aspects of you and your context have the potential for change and which do not?*

Action and intentionality are embedded in the sociocultural forces that structure human activity. As Boesch (1991) has said, cultures "develop, change and remain constant as a result of individual actions and interactions." This holds even if the results are not desired or anticipated.

> *The implication of this may not be as apparent in your life now. As years pass, decisions made and actions taken may lead to situations not previously anticipated.*

Cultural systems maintain, reproduce, and reform themselves across historical times. For this reason, the midlife experiences of one generation may not match that of another. If the cultural system changes so dramatically that a cultural revolution has been said to occur, the individuals experiencing this change directly should, hypothetically, be markedly changed physically, psychologically, and/or culturally. As an example, we will examine the transition of the baby boomer generation and examine the commonalities and differences compared to other generations throughout this text.

Bioecological Theory as a Roadmap to Human Development

Over the latter half of the twentieth century, with its breakthroughs in genetics and neuroscience, there was a tendency to downplay or even neglect the role of social, cultural, or historic factors as being critical in human development. A notable exception was the bioecological framework put forth by Bronfenbrenner in his 1979 book, *Ecology of Human Development: Experiments by*

Nature and Design. Bronfenbrenner built his framework from the pioneering theoretical work of Kurt Lewin (1931, 1935). Lewin postulated that behavior was a joint function of the person and environment (B = f(PE)). Bronfenbrenner's major modification to Lewin's theory was to substitute a D for B, thereby positing that development was a joint function of the person and environment (D = f(PE)). Development, for Bronfenbrenner, was defined as a lasting change in the way in which an individual perceives and deals with the environment.

Bronfenbrenner's Conceptual Framework of Development

Bronfenbrenner's framework can be conceptualized as a multi-layered sphere with each layer nested within the next higher level. Bronfenbrenner proposed a five-layered environmental system that impacts the course of development, see Figure 2.2. At the core of this sphere resides the individual. The structure and processes in the immediate setting containing the developing individual are labeled the microsystem. The microsystem contains the setting for activities, the activities themselves, the participants, and their roles in those settings.

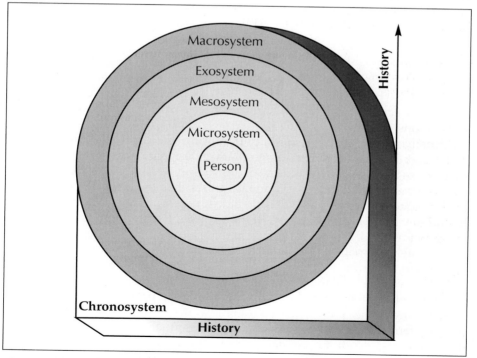

FIGURE 2.2. The five levels representing Bronfenbrenner's ecological model, with the element of history.

Describe a microsystem of two middle-aged adults in and out of the presence of their adolescent children.

The next contextual level is referred to as the mesosystem. The mesosystem moves beyond single immediate settings to include the connections and processes occurring between two or more immediate settings in which the individual is present. The mesosystem represents a network of microsystems.

The third level of this sphere is called the exosystem. As we move farther from the individual at the core, it becomes clear that one's development can be significantly impacted by elements of the environment in which the individual is not directly involved. For example, think about how an upper middle-class American middle-aged couple's plans for a winter holiday in Jamaica might be impacted by a tuition raise at their son's or daughter's college?

As one proceeds to the most global level, the macrosystem, it becomes evident that the previous layers are a part of a culture or sub-culture. The macrosystem consists not only of physical settings, but also is composed of the values and beliefs held in a particular culture.

Imagine traveling to another country where your access is denied to a tourist attraction because you are not wearing long sleeves, long pants, and a hat. How might the typical American react?

In addition, it represents the overlap of cultures and can be used to examine the occurrence of "culture clashes." However, clashes of culture do not only arise between nations of the world. The most savage cultural clashes are between cultural groups within nations. They can also occur between generations.

Finally, and probably most importantly for the conceptualization of the midlife adult, is Bronfenbrenner's final level designated as the chronosystem. This refers to the stability and change in the individual's environment over time. History serves as the coating to this sphere. Historical events affect resources, coping strategies, cultural values and norms, and societal demands. It represents the passage of time as it filters through each layer, thereby impacting the individual. Of the many factors that shape human behavior and experience, interpersonal relationships across time are among the most powerful and important forces in connecting people to the larger environment (Peterson, 1992). As we seek to understand various levels of the environment that affect lives, we must understand the relationship between people and groups within these settings.

Bronfenbrenner calls his most recent conceptualization of the previously described framework the person-process-context-time (PPCT) approach. The final addition of time to his framework emphasizes that processes, people, and contexts are dynamic, not static. They constantly impact each other in various ways at various levels over various periods. This final component to the model emphasizes the importance of history in the lives of people. It is one thing to read about and understand an historic event and a different thing to have experienced it (i.e., the Great Depression). The passage of time provides all generations with a framework for comparing then and now.

When Bronfenbrenner initially introduced his framework of development, its most unusual feature was its conceptualization of development. Its emphasis was not on traditional psychological processes such as perception, learning, and cognition. Instead it was on the content of these processes; that is, on what was perceived, feared, thought about, or learned as a result of environmental interaction. Development was redefined as the individual's evolving conception of and relation to the ecological environment and the individual's growing capacity to discover, sustain, or alter its properties. This definition incorporates Bronfenbrenner's emphases on reciprocal activity and interaction between the individual and the environment and on ecological transitions in which the individual experiences a shift in settings, a change in roles along with a shift in settings, or a change in behavior within an existing setting (Moen, Elder, and Luscher, 1995).

MAGNUSSON'S DEVELOPMENTAL FRAMEWORK

Consistent with Bronfenbrenner's framework, Magnusson (1995) elaborated on the dynamic nature of development by introducing the concept of dynamic interaction. Dynamic interaction is postulated to be based on several inter-related principles. These include the principles of (a) *multidetermination,* in that one must consider all levels of the system and the ways in which development is determined by those levels; (b) *interdependence,* in that factors in the system may be mutually dependent on each other without having reciprocal relations; (c) *reciprocity,* in that some factors will influence each other reciprocally; (d) *temporality,* in that development is an ongoing, temporal process, and time must lie at the heart of any model of development; (e) *nonlinearity,* in that neither the relationships between factors nor the functional form of development need be linear; and (f) *integration,* in that operating factors at all levels of the system must be coordinated to maximize its functioning. (See a special "Voices of Our Parents" section at the end of this chapter to illustrate these elements at work.)

Given the emphasis on the dynamic and interactional nature of development, I hope that it is apparent that the old saying "You can't tell a book by its cover" is true. Taking a systems approach reflects an acknowledgement of the true complexities of human behavior. It takes time to understand another individual. However, the greater the overlap of micro-, meso-, exo-, and macrosystem experiences you and another individual share, the easier it will be to understand where "he or she is coming from." However, as diversity of experience increases, the less common ground is shared and as a result, less immediate understanding exists. Therefore, it becomes necessary to get some perspective on the course that life has taken for this person.

List a few experiences that you share with your parents and a few that you don't. Share the list with them and note their responses. Then ask them to do the same exercise as they consider their experiences and that of their parents.

When considering the importance of shared experiences and history, it is true that you travel your life with the generation in which you were born. Today, a large generation is making its way through midlife. Although today's young adults will never experience life as it was experienced by the midlifers, there will be common experiences that will be shared with them and that the midlifers will have shared with their parents (e.g., emancipation, marriage, children, acquiring a first occupation, the death of a loved one, greater overall responsibilities). However, given the historical statistics presented in the introduction, not many generations prior to those born in the late 1920s, the World War II generation, rarely lived to or beyond midlife. For this reason it has been said that the belief that midlife comprises a separate and distinct stage of life is a construction of the 20th century (Skolnick, 1991). This may be true but, nonetheless, a valid construction for study by researchers in psychology and sociology, in particular. However, as our species continues to approach the upper limits of our projected life span (ninety–ninety-five years as projected from the Human Genome Project, 2000), it is not to be unexpected that further segmentation of the life span into more distinct periods will emerge.

Given its recent recognition in the developmental literature, it must be asked if midlife issues are only a North American or Western construction and thus are of limited value or interest to the other two thirds of human population. Is there such a thing as a "midlife crisis" or an "empty nest," or is midlife just a "woman's thing"? Is midlife nothing more than a staging area in anticipation of death? We hope these questions will be answered as we adopt a life course analysis of the individuals facing and experiencing midlife and the contexts in which they are experienced.

THE LIFE COURSE ANALYSIS OF DEVELOPMENT

One of the first questions encountered when the topic of midlife is introduced has to do with chronologically-based estimates of middle age—when does midlife begin and end? There are two ways to approach this question. First, one can designate thirty five years as the lower limit and sixty five years as the uppermost limit. Immediately, someone will say "I'm X years old, and I don't consider myself middle aged"; or "I'm only Y years old, and I feel like I'm middle aged."

You might be asking, "Isn't there something hormonal to do with the differences in these statements?"

For this reason, a second way to define middle age, a life events approach, is not by specifying an age. It is best to consider middle age as the period in one's life during which the greatest number of responsibilities are taken on, a significant number of experiences have been experienced, and one has the perspective to look back and review the many paths taken that have led them to the current point in their lives. Taking this view, it would be difficult to imagine a future point where more responsibilities exist—the number of "firsts" yet to be considered outweigh the already existing number, yet the awareness that many paths still beckon along with the full and complete understanding of one's ultimate mortality.

Taking a Life Course Systems Approach

A systems approach to the study of midlife allows for examination of the commonalities and differences experienced by the individuals in this and other groups. Using Bronfenbrenner's ethological framework of the entire life course, you can see that "multiple meanings of age" (Moen and Wethington, 1999) can be identified and examined in comparison to other age groups, genders, and cultures, and across history and generations. The following elements and exemplars serve to further explicate the systems approach.

Themes or Aspects of Potential Relevance to Individuals in Midlife

Social change can best be interpreted via the recognition of the interplay of macrosystem changes as they impact and channel through all the lower layers until life changes are experienced at the microlevel or that of the individual. Therefore, the midlife experience of the baby boomer generation is, or at least could be anticipated to be, markedly different from midlifers experiencing this stage of life after World War II. Not only is lifestyle impacted but the experiences encountered by the individual are unique unto himself/herself and will not be experienced in the same way by other generations.

Exemplar elements of and in social change. The relevance of this first dynamic component of behavior highlights that individuals are embedded in a changing social, cultural, and economic environment. The implication of this for individuals during the midlife transition is that the greatest impact comes from around them in the social and cultural structures as opposed to changes occurring within themselves (Riley, 1987). This social/generational/cohort effect results in differentially experienced and interpreted events. For example, in cultures where gender expectations are clearly defined and share little overlap, individuals will demonstrate different motivations, take different advantage of opportunities, and have a different set of opportunities made available to them when compared to societies that attempt to provide greater access and balance of opportunities to both genders. Consider, for example, the differential expectations for men and women in Amish communities compared to the expectations held for men and women in more secular communities. For this reason, the social changes that have occurred with regard to educational and employment opportunities for men and women in the West impacts not only how we are viewed by the rest of the world and how *we* view the rest of the world, but also, how we view ourselves at different points in our lives. As "progress" continues, socially, technologically, and medically, the experience of midlife today is markedly different from midlifers in the past generations and that of the midlifers of future generations.

In addition to changes in technology and employment opportunities, midlife individuals today face greater diversity in roles of individuals who are the same age but are at markedly different places in their lives. For example, consider the way the individual views his or her life and how society views him or her as a new grandparent at age 43, a first-time parent at age 43, or as a single mother at age 43. The implications of these events are not static but rather have the potential to send shock waves through the phenomena represented in Bronfenbrenner's ecological system.

Roles and relationships. During the course of one's life, there is a constant shifting of roles taken on by an individual and the implicit responsibilities demanded by these roles (e.g., an adolescent, new employee, new spouse, parent, widower, or divorcee). Along with these roles, relationships, and responsibilities, come expectations for the enactment of these roles. These expectations may be dictated by the person, family, society, and/or culture. Violations of these expectations, at any and all levels mentioned, lead to repercussions that the individual will need to address. As a result of these expectations, a third theme plays a critical element in the life of the middle ager.

Exemplar elements of and in roles and relationships. Usually, one of the first relationships that people think of is the relationship that they have with family members. These are usually the first and most long-lasting relationships. Whether good, bad, or strained, these relationships are the first we come to know and understand. The relationships can involve as few members as the individual and his or her parents or the individual and his or her extended family and their families. Either way, these relationships exist, and across development, these relationships change or are elaborated upon as children mature and parents and grandparents age. Cousins may move in and out of lives depending on the family and their needs at specific points in their lives.

Who comprise the major relationships in your life?

Are extended family members important in your life?

All relationships are bidirectional and interdependent. The demands and responses to these demands change at different points in development. Being a mother or father to a six-year-old yields different demands and rewards than does being a parent of a sixteen-year-old. One typically finds that the roles of the woman, particularly at midlife, are more closely linked to the needs of her family and other individuals in her circle than is the role of the man. Men typically define their role in the family much more linearly, as bread-winner and family provider and protector. Universally, women are often seen as the primary caretakers and caregivers who have the responsibility for assuming many different roles specific to their cultures, a much more circular trajectory of life. They move in and out of these roles as needs change and family members mature and age (Moen, 1992). The complexities in the roles of the midlife man are typically outward focused toward the roles and relationships created in his job or sphere of activity. These interrelationships change as the man matures and he assumes new roles outside the home. In the home his role is changing, too. However the man may not be as aware of the new and revised perceptions that others have of him and may not easily respond to the new demands placed on him as a result of these new perceptions.

As one breaks down the traditional sex-role definitions of behavior, gender lines become fuzzy as work outside the home no longer serves as a good definer of gender identity and role. This example is a reflection of the societal changes and movements in which today's midlifers were engaged in as young adults. The "radical supporter of movements" as well as the "side-line observer" during the late 1960s and early 1970s were forever changed as a result of encountering the ideas that have had a major impact on general American society. Many young adults today have come to experience these changes and now see them as "givens" in terms of goals and expectations. Many midlifers, however, know this has not always been the case.

Another context for involvement and the development of relationships outside the home or workplace, occurs in the form of volunteerism. The professional volunteer, or the part-time volunteer, encounters new roles and establishes new relationships that may be markedly different from those encountered on a daily basis. For example, the senior male account executive who volunteers one day a week at the local hospital to rock babies in the special care nursery or the homemaker with two adolescents and two preteens, who spends one weekend a month building houses with Habitat for Humanity, develops alliances and relationships with individuals out of their usual sphere. These volunteer activities further define who the individual is and how broadly they define themselves.

The roles and relationships in and out of the home may be different but are nonetheless dynamic as the individual matures. At midlife, however, one tends to encounter the greatest number of changes in roles than at any other point in life.

Subjective definitions of self. The way in which individuals define and enact their lives is subjective. The designing and redesigning of the professional self, external self, and internal self, are a personal action that will either resonate with the meso-, ecto-, macro-, and chronosystems or may, depending on the degree of change, set up shock waves that will impact all aspects of the individual's life at all levels and across all time spans. For example, choosing to change one's conservative wardrobe for a much more stylish and "freer" collection can usually be considered a relatively minor, yet still noticeable, change.

To make the decision to change one's career from a respected college professor to the owner and operator of a bait and tackle store is not unthinkable but would be considered dramatic. An even more dramatic example would be the decision to change one's sex.

Draw a Bronfenbrenner-like diagram for each of the changes mentioned to show the impact on all levels.

The majority of individuals conform nicely to society's expectations for them. However, individuals may appear to present themselves one way while they perceive themselves much differently. How can this be conceptualized? There may be the TRUCK DRIVING—poet, the WAITRESS—historian, or the HISTORIAN—motorhead. At midlife, the individual seems to be able, and perhaps more willing, to make major or minor modifications to himself or herself as the subjective evaluations of one's place in life becomes more important.

Exemplar elements of and in subjective definitions of the self. The experiences encountered up to midlife may significantly alter what we want and expect out of life, things that perhaps may have not been considered during one's young adulthood. New insights into one's self, important others in one's life, and situations that are encountered may lead to a redirection, change, or improvement of one's life. Midlife marks the important point in the course of development during which the potential for these changes are the greatest. Researchers and theorists (Brandtstadter and Lerner 1999; Bronfenbrenner, 1979; Ford and Lerner, 1992; Magnusson, 1995) who have adopted a dynamic view of development refer to the potential implications for interactions between roles, relationships, life situations, and psychological changes during midlife. These interactions result from expected and unexpected accumulation and loss of roles that can impact the ability of the midlife adult to make successful (or unsuccessful) adjustments and develop (or fail to develop) coping strategies that would be helpful in navigating theses changes and moving the person forward. The lack of these successful adjustments have been linked to psychological distress (Moen, 1997) and poor coping strategies and ineffective defense mechanisms (Labouvie-Vief, Hakim-Larson, and Hobart, 1987) and have been found to be associated with a lack of a consistent and well-defined identity during this time (Donahue, 1993). These changes reflect personal growth and involve ways of thinking, reasoning, and self-perception that may not be easily seen by the casual observer. Major changes in one's identity may only be considered as a "blip" in behavior with no understanding of the extent or depth of the personal self-examination and redefinition required to elicit that blip.

Have you noted any subtle changes in a midlife adult?
Most of the changes are subtle, although some individuals may experience and exhibit drastic changes. Discuss why this happens.

Context. One's context or culture frequently determines the acceptability of particular behaviors for members of its society at particular times. For example, Western women of all ages are free to converse at every point of their lives with men of all ages. In contrast, some Muslim women are permitted to "shed their veil" and to "sit in their courtyard and converse with any man passing by" only at midlife (Mernissi, 1987). The younger women, however, are kept hidden indoors and are expected to be covered from head-to-foot when outdoors. Additionally, while certain castes in India respect and vie for a man's right to care for his infants, the "Mr. Mom" of Western culture is viewed as an anomaly (Langer, 1997).

Exemplar elements of context. All aspects of the previously mentioned factors, social change, roles and relationships, and subjective definitions, are embedded in a sociohistorical framework. The context further aids in the understanding of the midlife individual across cultures. One factor that has an impact is the social class of the individual. Individuals who at midlife have prestige, privilege, access, and security defined by high socioeconomic status benefit on all fronts. Individuals of higher class status have always had the opportunities associated with better education, better health, better living conditions. Better educated individuals, in addition to having careers that may be healthier and safer, show fewer psychological and cognitive impairments at midlife and beyond. Access to health care impacts the individual at midlife when physiological changes may require closer monitoring, care, and perhaps medication (e.g., blood pressure, cholesterol level, potentially cancerous cellular changes).

Two other factors of the context of life are gender and race. While the greatest amount of attention has been given to women's advancements in the workforce, the home, and the community, both men and women have benefited from these advancements. Men now have the opportunity to adopt a nontraditional role as their first or second career choice (e.g., the older, retired man who becomes one of the most sought after nannies in the community) as do women supposedly have to adopt nontraditional career paths, with several noticeable exceptions (e.g., captain a submarine, break through the managerial glass-ceiling). When the discussion comes to the impact of race at midlife, one finds a surprising lack of information (Ramseur, 1989). The ability to say anything of substance regarding the nature of the African American, Hispanic American, or Asian American midlife transition is nonexistent. All one can reasonably say is that the midlife transition has been different for individuals from these cultures, not better or worse. Perhaps it will be found that racially different groups have surprisingly similar life experiences of midlife and the result will be a greater coming together of people of all walks of life during this period.

Summary and Comments

The systems view or ecological perspective provides the researcher or general observer with a unique window by which to examine and understand human behavior. This dynamic view allows for the broader understanding of developmental transitions across the life span. The individual in this perspective is seen as moving in and out of roles, relationships, self-evaluations, and contexts in response to social, economic, and infrastructure changes.

Depicting the individual as an active and reactive agent in his or her environment challenges past research portrayals of the individual at a "frozen" moment in time. One-time assessments rarely consider, or even more rarely specifically incorporate, dynamic factors into their explanations of research findings. The systematic study of human behavior demands clear and unambiguous relationships between variables considered to be of value. However, relying on the stripped down views of human behavior explains everything and nothing at the same time. (Issues of experimental design and interpretation will be discussed in a later chapter.) Physiological, psychological, social, and cultural impacts at different points in the life of the developing individual produce a different variety of interlocking pathways that may result in similar behaviors with different initial causes. Midlife is that one time when the majority of potential influences converge, thereby resulting in major or minor periods of defining, redefining, or restructuring one's identity, life course, and life decisions. For example, the midlife couple that takes custody of their five-year-old grandchild face many decisions as a result of this new commitment.

What additional factors need to be considered in the development of a successful resolution for this decision? What changes might be expected at all levels in the Bronfenbrennerian system?

It is important to employ the multilevel perspective in understanding the individual at all stages in life and at midlife, in particular. No individual's life or behavior can be adequately understood from a snapshot approach to human development. We need to remember this as we continue to explore the midlife adult during what may be the period of greatest consolidation of identity and related domains than at any other point of life.

VOICES OF OUR PARENTS

I am a forty-eight-year-old, white female. Born the oldest of three children to an uneducated mother and a father with a high school diploma.

Shortly after the birth of my brother, the third child, my father left my mother. Never to be heard from again until his death some thirty years later. Having no education to stand on, my mother was forced to live with her parents and work wherever she could find work, life began for us. Still, being a young woman and not wanting the responsibilities of children, she left us with our grandparents to pursue her own life. So my grandparents raised us the best they could.

My mother went on to marry a man with two children and they shortly began their family by having a child. My mother gave birth to a daughter,

Interdependence { now making three siblings. Life for her was complete. Meanwhile, someone else was ??? children.

Reciprocity { *At the death of my grandmother, my sister and I were removed from the home of grandfather. Society did not think it was proper for an old man to have two young girls living with him, and we were placed in the foster care system.* We stayed in foster care until I was thirteen and my sister was twelve when my mother's family made the choice to add us to her family.

Temporality { *My stepfather was an angry, abusive, drunk who beat his kids and my mother. After living like that for three years, I left home.* Had it not been for the kindness of a classmate's family, I do not know what I would have done. I only knew that I could not live like that anymore. I finished high school, graduated ??? out of my class. This is something I know I would not have done had I stayed at home. I would have ended up like each of my sisters, married and pregnant by the age of fifteen.

Nonlinearity and Integration { *After graduating, I married my high school sweetheart. We soon were faced with the possibility of my husband being sent to the war in Vietnam and decided to start our family. My first child was born in 1971 when I was 18 years old.*

That marriage lasted 10 years and we divorced. I met a wonderful man and we were married in 1980 and our first child was born the next year. We are still married and our daughter is graduating from college this year.

What I have learned . . . Life is what you make it. You can take a situation given to you and turn it around to be successful or you can accept it as it is. A successful choice is always better. Had I accepted what I was given as a choice in life, I probably would have followed in my mother's footsteps and been in an abusive marriage and been miserable, as she is today. I chose not to accept that.

What would I have changed? Education . . . I would have loved to have been able to go to college. But life has been a good educator for me.

By the way, I have one very large, loving cat.

MULTI-DETERMINATION

CHAPTER 3

Nonecological Theories of Development Applicable to Midlife-Related Issues

As we proceed with the theoretical underpinnings of the study of midlife, it is important to recognize components of more finely focused theories that may shed additional light on the conceptualization of this life period. The work of neo-Freudians Levinson, Gould, Valliant, Havighurst, Neugarten, Jung, Maslow, and Erikson will be highlighted in this chapter. As you recall, Bronfenbrenner put forth an elaborate framework to explicate the varied influences that interact with the whole of development and one's progress through the life span.

The authors highlighted in this chapter have preferred to focus on one particular aspect of development. While they do not provide a life span perspective and do not specifically address the possible impact of culture, context, or history, they do generally address the midlife experience.

THE SEASONS OF A MAN'S LIFE— FUNDAMENTALS OF LEVINSON'S THEORY

Daniel Levinson is usually one of the first contemporary theorists named when the period of midlife is mentioned. Like Bronfenbrenner, Levinson's theory holds that any social system, from a family group to a large corporation, exists only through intentional human activity and that the influences of the context and the individual are reciprocal and bi-directional. Context influences the individual and the individual influences one's context (Levinson et al., 1978; Scarr and McCartney, 1983).

Two different views have been put forth to explain some of the changes noticed at midlife. On the one hand, it has been suggested that the perception of "time left to live" over the life course might be expected to have an impact on the types of goals selected in mid- and later-life (Brim, 1992; Carsten, 1993; Levinson, 1978; Tomae, 1989). This mortality view of life stands in contrast to Levinson and others who have highlighted that psychological processes in midlife such as changes in identity, ways of thinking and reasoning, and self-concept may be brought on by normative life transitions and unexpected life events rather than the expectation of death (Levinson et al., 1978; McCrae and Costa, 1990).

The writings of Levinson (1978), Gould, (1978), and Vaillant (1977) are based on fundamental ideas derived from Erikson's theory (discussed later in this chapter) that changing circumstances, personally and professionally, and resolution of feelings about aging and mortality increase in importance as one ages. As a result, the person continues to develop in terms of a better articulated identity and sense of self throughout the life span.

Levinson (1978) held that individuals form a **dream** (usually about career success) in young adulthood that serves as a guide for the better part of their adulthood. Then during midlife this dream is likely to be reevaluated and revised if it has not been fulfilled.

> *But if one has achieved his or her dream, is there no reevaluation, no new dream set into place?*

This reevaluation and revision constituted a form of **life review**. The purpose of this revision is to evaluate the impact of one's accrued life and work context on the individual's development at a given time (Levinson and Gooden, 1985). The goal of Levinson's research was to obtain answers to two general questions: 1. "What does it mean to be an adult?" and 2. "Is there an underlying order in the progression of our lives over the adult years?" (Levinson, 1978). Setterstein (2000), in particular, feels that life review helps the individual to understand and to bridge the various segments of the life span. While life review can occur at any point in the life span, it has particular salience during midlife. The review activity provides a sense of integrity in life, organization and unification of one's identity, personality, and behavior.

Levinson's method involved the extensive biographical interviewing of forty men representing four occupational subgroups: blue-collar workers, white-collar workers, university faculty in the biological sciences, and creative writers.

His results detailed a structural view of development in adulthood that comprise a nonhierarchical universal sequence of eras and periods. From his perspective, these periods follow one another and are interrelated but one is not of greater value than another, nor does one period represent a more advanced level than another see figure 3.1.

In his conceptualization of a man's life cycle, Levinson described each developmental era as lasting about twenty-five years and possessing unique biological, social, and psychological challenges. His cross-era transitions are said to last about five years and represent critical turning points at those stages in one's life. These transition periods can serve as a bridge between major developmental periods and may show themselves to be major life disorganizers.

This theory is not necessarily a dynamic theory as previously described. It reflects a static place and time, presenting the current view of the individual's

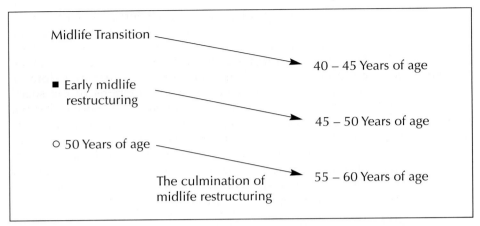

FIGURE 3.1. The midlife transitions and phases of life leading to the late–life period.

thinking regarding and maintaning the status quo. However, a frequent criticism of this theory is that it reflects the perceptions of life from a primarily male perspective (despite the after-thought piece, *Seasons of a Woman's Life*, written and published after Levinson's death).

In response to this latter criticism, research involving women (Mercer, Nichols, and Doyle, 1989), found that women had more complex and problematic lives than was reported by the men in Levinson's study. Women tended to experience Levinson's developmental periods at later points in time, to follow a more irregular pattern, and to focus on different aspects of the life structure than were reported by the men. These researchers concluded that women's lives, as that of men, are embedded in a particular sociohistorical context along with a set of cultural expectations; hence, the differences noted in the priorities given to particular life events.

HAVIGHURST'S DEVELOPMENTAL TASKS AND NEUGARTEN'S SOCIAL AGE CLOCK

An alternative stage model proposed by Havighurst (1953), has as its focus the major accomplishments required of an individual at a particular time. From his theory, it is suggested that successful completion of the variety of developmental tasks throughout the life span are related to satisfaction and success. Between thirty-five to sixty years of age was designated as middle age. Seven tasks were considered to be critical to this particular period. They include: 1. achieving adult, civic, and social responsibility; 2. establishing and maintaining an economic standard of living; 3. assisting teenage children in becoming responsible and happy adults; 4. developing adult leisure time activities; 5. relating to one's spouse as a person; 6. learning to accept and adjust to the physiological changes of middle age; and 7. adjusting to aging parents.

Similarly, Neugarten (1968) suggested the use of the term **social age clock,** learned from society, which tells us about the "shoulds" in our lives. One may also think of this as age-appropriate behavior in terms of life goals (i.e., when to complete education, acquire first job, marry, have children). The notion of the social age clock is dictated by the social environment of a culture. Therefore, as the sociocultural context changes, so will timing expectations of the social clock. For example, until nearly the 1930s, most parents died shortly after the last child left home. (Glick, 1977). Today, many parents will not only live beyond their last child's departure, but will also experience the return of their adult children and live longer thereafter, hence the term **sandwich generation.** The changes that we have been observing in Western society have been toward later marriages, later childbearing, having fewer children, being the gray-haired parent of a kindergartener, earlier retirement, and so on. These dramatic changes call for the resetting of the social clock of expectations.

What this means to individuals in our society is that there is a blurring between the boundaries of once chronologically and biologically-dictated life events. As we live longer and healthier, consensus on how age-appropriate behavior is to be defined has grown increasingly vague. According to Neugarten and colleagues, we may be moving toward an age-irrelevant society (Neugarten and Hagestad, 1976). Imagine the potential!

THE THEORIES OF CARL JUNG AND ABRAHAM MASLOW

While Jung (1875–1961) is often credited with extending stage theory of development beyond that of childhood, his contribution to the understanding of the life span is rarely cited or footnoted. After breaking away from the Freudian perspective and its primary reliance on the import of infancy and childhood, Jung focused on the second half of the life cycle. It was his firm belief that midlife was the point in the life cycle that was dominated by a drive toward illumination of the self. He characterized the 40s as the **"noon of life,"** the beginning of the process of **individuation.** During this time, the individual shows an increase in introspection and self-reflection and a period of coming to grips with inner conflicts revolving around polar opposites. These opposites include resolution between masculinity-femininity, creation-destruction, youth-age, and separation-attachment, to name a few (Jung, 1933) see figure 3.2 here. From this view, midlife can be considered a time when persons are going through a fundamental shift in their alignment with life and the world. This realignment involves not only social dimensions, but also psychological and spiritual dimensions. Jung would argue that this is a time when new aspects of the self come to the forefront (Stein, 1994). During this period, one's identity is hung in suspension awaiting changes. Stein describes these as a series of micro- and macrochanges. Despite his theory's lack of recognition in standard life span texts, Levinson (1978) considered Jung to be the "father of the modern study of development."

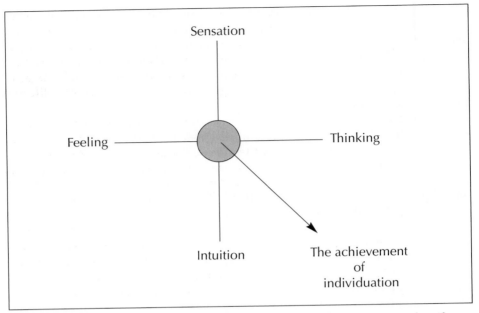

FIGURE 3.2. The balancing of the four aspects of life. Individuation occurs when the individual has command of these four elements.

Along the same lines, the theory of Abraham Maslow as it relates to the concept of **self-actualization** has not been commonly cited as relevant to midlife. Maslow's theory emphasized the importance of the development of the autonomous, independent individual. Like Jung, Maslow portrayed the second half of life as providing the opportunity to work toward individuation and self-actualization, a deeper understanding of oneself and one's place in and relationship with the world and others.

THE THEORY OF ERIK ERIKSON

Finally, and perhaps most closely related to the ecological theory of Bronfren-brenner, are Erikson's eight stages of psychosocial development. Erikson's (1950, 1968) theory can be considered to be contextual in its emphasis on the interaction between the individual and society. Erikson's initial theory (1968), as presented in most texts, consists of a linear succession of eight psychosocial crises. These crises or developmental issues represent differing demands on the individual in order to meet personal needs, deal with social demands, and increase personal competence and satisfaction (Shibley, 2000). Erikson's theory includes the description of eight distinct stages, during which period unique problems may preoccupy one's view of life and level of involvement with others. Erikson's periods or stages have been termed as crises and represent the crossing or intersection of an individual's abilities and needs with that of the expectations of one's culture. As these crises are resolved in a positive way, the individual becomes increasingly competent and satisfied. According to Erikson, the successful resolution of these crises across the life span, promotes the growth and development of ego strengths delineated as hope, will, purpose, competence, and fidelity. These ego strengths are critical at any point in life and especially during the midlife transition.

In his initial conceptualization of his theory, Erikson proposed that the convergence of biological, social, and psychological factors drive the unfolding of each to these unique crises. However, the aspect of Erikson's theory given little note is his view of the concept of **revisitation.** He suggested that the crises are interrelated in that earlier crises are continually revisited throughout the life span, invoking more refined and sophisticated interpretations and responses to the previously experienced crises. It has been posited by some that through revisitation an earlier developmental task can be approached with newer skills and attributes than was previously possible (Antonucci and Mikus, 1988; Benedek, 1959; Clarke, 1978; Clark and Dawson, 1998; Elson, 1984). Figure 3.3 represents a pictorial schematic of the more cyclical nature of revisitation across the life span. A thorough review of this position can be found in Shibley (2000).

The Eriksonian crisis most relevant to the midlife adult has been termed as the crisis of **generativity versus stagnation** (self-absorption). During this crisis, those who succeed in the resolution show greater concern about future generations and

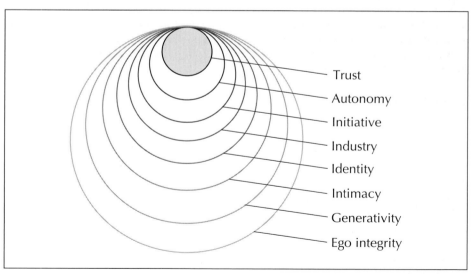

- Trust
- Autonomy
- Initiative
- Industry
- Identity
- Intimacy
- Generativity
- Ego integrity

FIGURE 3.3. A representation of the concept of revisitation as described in Erikson's theory for the various parts of the life span.

Infancy	Toddlerhood	Early childhood	Late childhood
Adolescence	Young adulthood	Middle adulthood	Older adulthood

the legacy that one will leave behind. Those who fail at this task remain focused on their own needs and wants.

In their 1980 investigation of the variety of Eriksonion stages, Vaillant and Milofsky reported that only 30–40 percent of their two samples reached the age-appropriate stage of generativity by age 47, and 1 out of 6 men were still challenged by adolescent issues of Identity and Role Confusion at age 47.

> *Considering the concept of Revisitation, this should not be so surprising, should it?*

These researchers went on to state that failure to master the crisis during adolescence predicted lack of generativity in adult men, and maturity was predicted by the positive resolutions of childhood crises including trust, autonomy, and initiative, and particularly that of the industry crisis. Similar patterns of relationships held for fertile but not infertile men (Snarey et al., 1987).

This view of revisitation is consistent with the ecological framework of Bronfenbrenner and will be integrated as we progress through future chapters.

Summary and Comments

The previously outlined theories represent the coming together of different lines of thought that have the potential to be particularly relevant to the understanding of midlife. They all have the potential to be considered culture neutral and therefore, if applied in a thoughtful and appropriate way, universal. For example, manifestations of Erikson's theory-specific concepts can be found in most cultures. However, most of these crises, while not openly stated, are operationalized in many cultures by way of ceremonies and rites of passage rituals. What tend to be missing in many Western cultures are the ceremonies and rituals. How all of this may impact the midlife transition will be further examined.

CHAPTER 4

Experimental Investigation into the Life Span Process

Fundamental to the study of human behavior is a clear specification of the phenomena of interest, a proposed methodology to provide a guide to experimental manipulation, and hypotheses regarding expected findings along with the appropriate analytical tools to evaluate the soundness of the hypotheses. This chapter will review a number of experimental and nonexperimental research designs employed in the study of human development.

When it comes to evaluating the results of research studies, it is important to determine **the research design** employed and to evaluate its appropriateness. Regardless of your level of sophistication or expertise, you should be able to comment upon their strengths and weaknesses.

All of the studies cited in the earlier sections that will be referred to later in the textbook have employed a variety of designs and measures to validate the theories to which they subscribed. Theories are fundamental to the guidance of and construction of meaningful research questions. For this reason, the foundation of all aspects of this text is theory-based.

Students frequently make the mistake of dismissing a theory because it does not, on the surface, appeal to them. Or, they will repeatedly say that they have "a theory" regarding a behavior X, Y, or Z. That proposition is highly unlikely given the level of general observation and logical postulation that must be developed and articulated for a theory to be submitted and examined (see Pepper, 1942, for review). A theory can neither be proven nor disproved. It can only be said to be more or less useful in explaining the research findings and observations of human behavior. Theories deemed less successful in explaining particular behaviors under consideration or the **constructs** being examined are discarded by the field and other more potentially fruitful theories gain acceptance. The discarded theory may continue to be potentially viable, merely awaiting new ways of conceptualizing and testing empirical questions. Alternatively, the theory may be regarded as fundamentally flawed and thus not resurrected in any form.

The purpose of this chapter is to provide the student with some tried and true basic designs employed in developmental research and to provide some food for thought as issues of cohort, history, and time are included as dimensions in the research concerning the midlife adult. These latter three issues are of particular concern to researchers adopting the 'bioecological' framework of Bronfenbrenner. These researchers have found the traditional methods that are typically taught, and reviewed here, to be unsatisfactory in explaining lives from different times and places. This chapter will end by posing questions currently being asked and examined by individuals who take the interaction of generation, cohort, and place as relevant factors in understanding the midlife adult, in addition to understanding development in general.

FUNDAMENTALS OF RESEARCH DESIGN

A research design can be considered to be the basic blueprint followed to examine some behavioral phenomena under investigation. This is the blueprint that includes the who, what, why, how, when, and where of the design.

The *who* component is a statement of the participants in the research study. It should include the gender, ages, sample size, and other characteristics relevant to the questions being addressed. The *what* is a statement of the issue under consideration. *What* is the behavior being examined? *Why* is this particular behavior or construct of interest to the field of study? *How* will this issue of interest be investigated? The *how* explicates the methodology including methods of measurement to be employed in the investigation. The *what* and *why* serve as the core to the design proper. *What* and *Why* serve as the foundation to supplying the purpose or rationale to the conduct of the study. The *when* can be conceptualized in two ways. First, it may be used to designate times of multiple or repeated measurements. Second, it can serve as an index to the point on the more general historical timeline, reflecting time of measurement. The *where* of the research investigation is a statement of culture and cultural influence and the potential for cultural comparisons.

These aspects of a research investigation should be kept in mind and identified as one considers and evaluates the work. The reader should identify the experiences of the participants, any manipulations or treatments, and the stimuli being used. They should also be aware of the schedule of the time of measurement and any concurrent factors that may influence the performance of the individual and the conclusions. Many events can occur in the time between testing. Initially comparable samples may be markedly different at later testing times. Should the investigator not obtain these potentially influencing factors, the generalizability or even general understandability of the findings may be far from possible.

BASIC DEVELOPMENTAL DESIGNS

The frustrating aspect of this section is the realization that although the experimental designs to be described will differ in their complexity, efficiency, and ability to answer a variety of questions, they leave some questions unanswered. No single design or form of measurement and analysis can answer the whole question. Questions arise from the answers found. That is the nature of empirical investigation.

Methods of Collecting Data

Why collect **data**? We are natural observers and frequently ask questions about some behavior. Who does what, how, when, where, and why? We watch the *whos* in our lives doing *whatever* they do, *how, when, where,* and *why* they do it. We are natural born observers, asking questions and making hypotheses about human behavior all the time. The focus of this part of the chapter rests on basic designs of developmental research. The designs described are the most commonly employed in the study of midlife behavior. There are a variety of design methods. One can, for example, choose to begin theory construction by way of **naturalistic observation, self-report surveys, interviews, case studies,** or **correlational studies.** These approaches have the potential to play a role in the study of human behavior. They have their advantages and disadvantages (see Rosenthal and Rosnow, 1991, for a review).

For the purposes of this review, the classic designs that have been employed will be presented and discussed in light of their treatment of cohort and generation. Until recently there has been little study of midlife. Individuals in their middle years have appeared in some recent work to avoid the research being criticized as an **extreme groups design** (Hertzog, 1989) and therefore the lack of midlife research be seen as a weakness of the investigation. However, research that has midlife as its central focus is scarce. With that said, this discussion moves forward to the description of the most common designs used by developmental researchers: **cross-sectional studies, longitudinal studies, time-lag studies,** and **sequential designs.**

Cross-Sectional Studies

A review of the literature will show that cross-sectional designs have been the most commonly used approach in developmental research designs. This design compares participants from different age groups at one time. The question has to do with how two or more groups of individuals change over time. With cross-sectional designs, the researcher has the potential to estimate differences in behavior at different ages. The results of this work are descriptions of age differences. For example, one may be interested in the decision making abilities of young adults and late middle-aged adults. The researcher would recruit individuals between the ages of 18 and 21 for the young group and 55 and 65 for the late middle-age group. Conclusions are then made regarding the decision-making abilities of individuals between the ages of 18 and 65 see Figure 4.1.

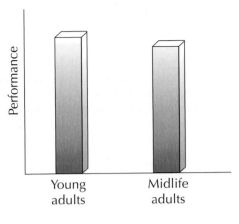

FIGURE 4.1. Graphic representation of a cross-sectional research design. Different individuals are tested at the same time.

You can see the problem inherent in this type of design.

Cross-sectional designs are useful in finding age norms for specific behaviors. Additionally, they are more time efficient and less costly in personnel, subject attrition, practice effects, and finances. However, cross-sectional designs are not without their disadvantages. The primary drawback of this design is the confounding of age and cohort differences. When one finds differences between two or more groups, it is unclear whether the differences are due to the participants' sociohistorical experiences or the developmental process. For this reason, researchers are only able to make statements regarding **age differences** between groups. These are referred to as **between subject differences.** When differences are found between a group of 18-year-olds and a group of 48-year-olds, the researcher is unable to make a statement of causality relating to the differences observed. The researcher cannot say with assurance that the 48-year-olds performed at the same level of today's 18-year-olds when they were 18, or that today's 18-year-olds will behave the way the current 48-year-olds behave when they are 48.

A related disadvantage of this type of design is that it does not provide a picture of how individuals develop over time. This is particularly meaningful as we consider the behavioral work to be done at midlife. It will be shown that so many of the changes observed during midlife can be termed internal, therefore the confounding of age, cohort, time of measurement, and the occurrence of life turning points obtained in cross-sectional studies will provide little insight regarding this period of the life span.

What underlies the overwhelming reliance on cross-sectional designs?

Longitudinal Studies

Longitudinal data are collected from one group of participants over repeated times of measurement. For this reason, results stemming from this type of design provide insight into **age-related changes** in the selected behavior. These have been termed **within individual changes** as can be see in Figure 4.2.

Why isn't everyone using longitudinal designs?

As with cross-sectional designs, longitudinal designs also have their advantages and limitations. The major advantage of the longitudinal study is that it provides a good picture of individual changes over time and developmental differences among individuals. Baltes and Nesselroade (1970) state that longitudinal designs allow for the evaluation of long-term life events, the making of predictions and observing outcomes, and the implementation of retrospective analyses allowing for patterns of causation to emerge. For these reasons, longitudinal studies are preferable to cross-sectional designs.

There are several practical and pragmatic limitations associated with longitudinal studies. The first practical limitation is that longitudinal research is time consuming (e.g., attempting to investigate a particular behavioral phenomena over 10, 20, or 30+ years). Second, it is expensive to

FIGURE 4.2. Graphic representation of a longitudinal research design. The same people are tested at different times.

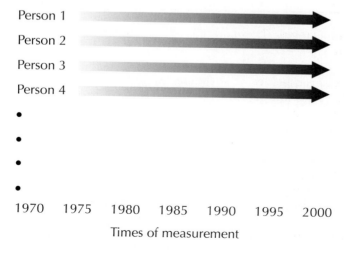

maintain, financially and with personnel. Third, there is a greater tendency toward increased participant attrition over the years. While not insurmountable, the pragmatic limitations prohibit frequent design and implementation of longitudinal designs. Specifically, research awards are frequently given for periods of three–five years, during which significant progress must be demonstrated for future funding opportunities and career promotion (Hayflick, 1996).

Time Lag Studies

In time-lag studies, the same age groups are evaluated at different times. In this design, age is held constant while cohort and time of measurement vary. For instance the type of attachment patterns found in forty-year-olds in 1950, could be compared to the patterns found in 1970 and 1990. The primary benefit is the ability to pinpoint the impact of cultural change on the behavior of interest. What time-lag designs provide as shown in Figure 4.3 is a measurement of how the same age group behaves in different historical periods or contexts.

Unfortunately, cohort and time of measurement influences are confounded. Therefore, it is not possible to discern if the differences were due to being born at a particular historical point or a result of the general sociohistorical setting at the time of measurement. This design is also expensive and time consuming. More important, however, is that only one age group is studied during the specified time.

Sequential Designs

Sequential designs represent various combinations of the three previously mentioned designs, cross-sectional, longitudinal, and time lag. These designs,

FIGURE 4.3. A representation of a time-lag study. Cross-sectional information and inferences regarding longitudinal features and historical components are possible.

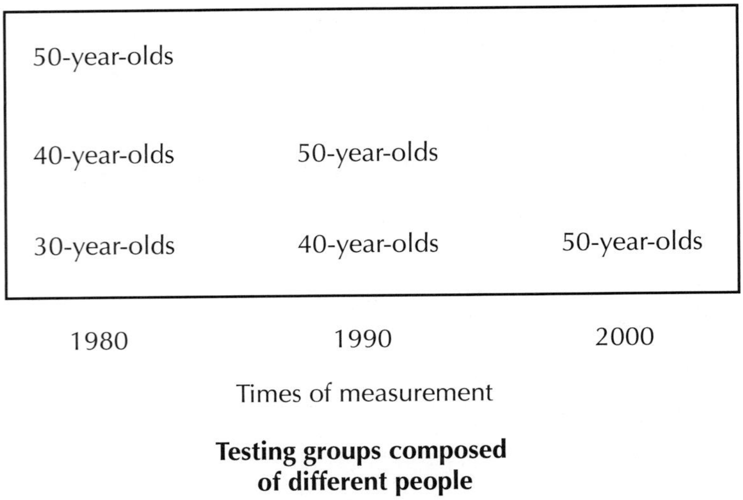

50-year-olds		
40-year-olds	50-year-olds	
30-year-olds	40-year-olds	50-year-olds
1980	1990	2000

Times of measurement

**Testing groups composed
of different people**

proposed by Schaie (1965/1979), were meant to provide alternative forms of measurement to the most traditionally employed methods. Two subcategories of sequential designs exist. In the first, **cohort-sequential designs** follow two or more cohorts over a period and second, **cross-sequential designs** in which comparable cross-sectional studies are performed at different historical times. While sequential designs aid in disentangling the confounding effects found in other designs, the major disadvantage is their complexity. See Figure 4.4. (See Setterstein, 1999, for a thorough and thoughtful review of the process of developmental research.)

Summary and Comments

As Caspi (1998) suggests, a limitation of much developmental research is that of historical specificity. Most of the research today is cross-sectional. In addition, even the longitudinal findings are often limited to a single birth cohort. Therefore little is known about the extent to which developmental knowledge is historically specific. Yet, researchers tend to discuss findings as if they are generalizable across historical periods. The problem is that historical specificity has been generally dismissed by researchers and has, as a result, limited our understanding of basic development and the extent to which historical events play out in the lives of humans.

For this reason, consumers of research need to arm themselves with valid questions regarding the design and deductions derived from the literature. Be mindful of alternative designs and how those alternatives may have provided different information, interpretations, and generalizations. Defaulting to the researcher's interpretation is too easy. None of the methods discussed is perfect. Combinations of designs can be employed to achieve more sophisticated and informative results. No single study is sufficient to warrant its findings to be fact (Botwinick, 1984). A series of well-planned

FIGURE 4.4. A representation of a cross-sequential design. This combines longitudinal features with cross-sectional information and historical components.

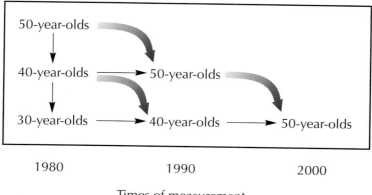

50-year-olds

40-year-olds   →   50-year-olds

30-year-olds   →   40-year-olds   →   50-year-olds

1980   1990   2000

Times of measurement

**Testing groups composed
of the same people**

experiments are required to provide converging evidence regarding the phenomena of interest. Rather than jump into the fray, the thoughtful researcher must decide exactly what the question of interest is and the impact of the individual x context x culture interaction on the potential findings. This approach will provide better information and a better understanding of the developmental process.

As you proceed through this text, remember that the data being reviewed have been subject to their own type of historical and political pressures. Therefore, the conclusions are limited. See if you will be able to improve on the methodology, choice of design, and even the question. Being an active consumer of data will not only lead to the next generation of better questions but will make the learning more meaningful and the material easier to understand.

CHAPTER 5

Culture, Context, or Place: Important Distinctions in Understanding the Life Span

"My mom says, 'What's the big deal? Get on with it.'"

(STUDENT—CHINESE NATIONAL FROM SINGAPORE)

In the Native American culture, in recognition of a woman's transition to midlife, she is given rolled and tied sticks of sage. She is to burn these in her home so that anyone entering will know that a Wise Woman is present.

(AN EXAMPLE OF RITUALS MARKING LIFE TRANSITIONS)

"When the Internet goes down, I'll ask my dad the question. He's been around."

(AN EXAMPLE OF THE CONTEXT IN WHICH THE MIDLIFER
IS LOOKED UPON AS A SOURCE OF INFORMATION)

Implicit in the Ecological Model of Urie Bronfenbrenner discussed in chapter 2 is the relative importance and subtle impact of culture on the individual. Culture, or the macrosystem in Bronfenbrenner's model, has the potential to impact all lower systems as the lower systems have the ability to impact the social, psychological, and biological aspects of a culture. Further, his model holds that the passing of time influences the nature and institutions of a culture as well as all other systems in the model.

This chapter takes on the broad task of attempting to understand what we mean when we speak of culture, how time can affect culture, and how culture influences human development in general and the midlife experience in particular.

WHAT IS CULTURE?

Stop for a moment and ask yourself, What does culture mean? The term is used in many ways. It is commonly paired with "diversity" as in "celebrating cultural diversity." But does anyone know what that means beyond introducing "mainstream" individuals to traditions, people, or food from different countries—a kind of "culture zoo"?

CULTURE AND PSYCHOLOGICAL RESEARCH

The term culture is used so frequently that it is on the verge of losing its meaning and value. In much of psychological research, culture has been dismissed as a source of noise that only clouds the research picture, and any behavioral phenomenon that does not match the European or North American norm is treated as an aberration or "cultural difference" in behavior. For example, you may want to understand the engineering aptitude of an international group of young girls touring the United States. Let us say that the findings indicate that the young girls from Asia score highest on your test, with German girls ranking second, and U.S. girls ranking last out of the fifteen countries on this fictitious tour. You may conclude that the findings reflect cultural differences and expectations regarding engineering aptitude among girls.

This explanation is insufficient. Why? If all human behavior is declared to be cultural, which it is, then a general reference to culture is of no scientific value as an explanation of specific behaviors. In this example, there was no attempt to understand the nature of cultural expectations about the engineering aptitude of young girls; therefore, ascribing the differences to culture is of no use. Dannfer (1984) wrote:

> To state that the environment/culture is important, to mention it often, and to include it in definitional statements does not together mean that research will be designed, nor findings interpreted, in a way that apprehends social structure, and that views the social environment or culture as more than a setting that facilitates maturational unfolding. pp. 847–850.

Instead, we need to explore the interactive and dynamic components of cultures that influence the development of individuals.

You can see the problems inherent in this approach.
Go to the library and select three psychological journals off the shelf. See if any random article contains reference to culture or the possible implications of culture in it's findings.

Most psychologists have dealt with culture in four ways that make it functionally unimportant and analytically trivial:

1. Culture is *generally dismissed* as not warranting further investigation. Investigators who take this approach, work to obtain homogenous groups to remove the impact of culture on their findings. This approach leads to the lack of generalizability beyond the specified sample, usually, Caucasian college students between the ages of eighteen and twenty-two.

2. Culture is treated as *powerful but unorganized*. It is treated as a phenomenon that relates to the behavior being studied that could play an important role, but that is too unspecified and amorphous to incorporate into the research question or explanations.
3. Culture is considered to be *organized but passive*. This perspective suggests that culture can be studied and follows observable rules, but that a cultural contribution is of no relevance to the behavior under investigation.
4. Culture is *seen as interactive and consisting of set relationships and processes* (largely independent of human volition). This view ignores or dismisses the powerful impact that a person can have on culture (Dannfer and Perlmutter, 1990).

> *What is an example of a behavior of interest to social scientists that might not have a cultural impact?*

Researchers who adopt this last perspective suffer three shortcomings:

1. They *lose sight* of the way individuals develop in the process of adapting to changing social contexts. One need only look to nations that have undergone political or cultural revolutions to see the impact on the well-being—economically, psychologically, or medically—of the individuals experiencing these changes. Take for example the changes in the political, economic, and medical arenas that the citizens of the former Soviet Union had to encounter.
2. They *downplay* the interactive role of people and events in shaping and initiating change in these contexts. Individuals within a culture are vehicles for change, and the changes they initiate are felt by many not directly involved in the movement. For example, the "in-group" determines who will be educated, how worship will or will not be conducted, and who will be involved in decision making, among other things. The "out-group" will either accept the dictates of the in-group and change their lifestyles or may respond with a backlash and initiate their own change. Consider these points within the context of apartheid in South Africa and the all-race elections that followed.
3. They *underestimate* the degree to which contexts respond to the individual. In this case, one need only track the impact of the World Wide Web on individuals' expectations regarding information and product access. If you don't have a website, or at least an e-mail address, you are out of the loop. There are fast-paced individuals whose lives are impacted by access to the Internet and e-mail on their cell phones. This can be contrasted to the pace and needs of the individuals in the Amish culture. Their needs are markedly different, and we would say that they are in a different kind of loop. These two lifestyles can coexist in near proximity to each other while still maintaining a distinct cultural identity.

A SIMPLE DEMONSTRATION

Walk up to individuals on your campus that represent different ages, genders, races, and height, and ask them if they have an e-mail address. What generalizations can you make? How comfortable are you with these generalizations?

HOW THE TERM CULTURE IS COMMONLY USED AND HOW IT SHOULD BE USED

The term culture has most commonly been used in two ways. First, it has been used to designate a group of people who belong together by way of shared geography. Most often this approach uses a name of a country to designate a culture thereby creating an illusion that, for example, all Italians are the same by virtue of being born in Italy or all Americans are the same because they are from the United States. It has been suggested that the best terms for a group of this type are society, ethnic group, or tribe (Valsiner, 2000).

Delineate why you may find this definition to be a bogus definition.

Second, culture has been defined as a **semiotic (sign) mediation** that is part of the system of organized psychological functions. This form of cultural communication and representation can be intrapersonal (feeling, thinking, memorizing, forgetting, or planning) or interpersonal (chatting, fighting, persuading, or avoiding others). Semiotic function can be seen as a tool for goal-oriented actions by social institutions. Most transitions in the life course are organized by social institutions to assist the persons involved in that culture. The social institutions engender the rules and laws of the culture, its dominant religious beliefs, political leanings, and role expectations (see Van der Veer and Valsiner, 1991, for review).

Use both definitions of culture to provide a personal profile of yourself. Which is richer and more reflective of who you are?

When we speak of a culture in this way, to what are we referring? The most fundamental cultural unit is the family. Now, traverse the other Bronfenbrennerian levels. Add to the family unit the neighborhood; family church; political views; explicit successes or tragedies that impact the family; other demographics such as age, gender, and geographic region of the country—all the way to the national level and its guiding principles. These are part of the culture. To understand the "ecology of human development" (Bronfenbrenner, 1979), we need to incorporate these factors into our understanding of particular behaviors, such as

gender differences in map-reading ability. There needs to be careful consideration of all the dimensions, components, and levels of the environment that may
influence a phenomenon. These will vary with the target behavior under consideration. There will be different cultural influences on one's ability to interpret
symbolism in a film and one's ability to articulate one's sense of self-esteem.
However, the burden still rests on the researcher and the interpreter of findings
to articulate and defend the exclusion or inclusion of particular levels of analysis. This requirement will raise awareness of the importance of culture as an
ever-present factor and will move the science toward explanatory models of
context rather than descriptive models or models of context rather than descriptive models or models of passive exposure (Wohlwill, 1991).

This will require researchers to broaden their knowledge to include understanding the variety of cultures represented in the population being studied
and to design their work to acknowledge this potential impact. The issue is the
generalizability of findings. As we move away from sterile, esoteric, and mech-
anistic views of human behavior, it will be the responsibility of researchers to
broaden their cultural horizons.

In short,

> In the end, we cannot deal with context by simply dismissing it as error vari-
> ance nor can we control for it with distal background variables. We fail to
> take context seriously if it affects neither the framing of our questions nor the
> expectations of interpretations of our findings. pp. 73–100 (Modell, 1996).

Human lives must be understood in light of the many social spaces and
interrelated systems in which they unfold (Bronfenbrenner, 1979). Single social
contexts must not be studied as entities unto themselves but must be studied
as interdependent and interactive entities. To make it more complex, contexts,
like individuals, are changing, multidimensional, interactive, and interdependent. However, the social world cannot determine how individual development takes place, it can only guide its direction. The course of personal
development is constructed by the person in relation to that cultural guidance.
In this sense, human psychological development is jointly constructed by persons in their social worlds, or co-constructed by the two. This **co-construction**
represents the personal development of psychological functions of the individual directed by the social world, which sets up directions for the personal
construction of psychological functions.

*Given this view of individual development, how is it possible for a person to
construct adaptive psychological stability on the basis of never-recurring life
experiences?*

*Also, given such potential for diverse interpretations and constructions,
why is it that people share a common understanding and interpretation of the
world and their respective cultures?*

THE CONSTRUCTION OF SELF

The interaction between the individual and his or her culture is critical at all stages of life, particularly during the transitions to midlife. Life transitions call for a reformulation and a new understanding of what personality psychologists have called the self. Two theorists have played critical roles in contributing to the understanding of the relationship between the individual and the culture. George Simmel, in sociology, and George Herbert Mead, in philosophy, provided the initial conceptualizations regarding the way that a person changes the environment and the way that feedback from this process leads to the reconstruction of the self. These theorists postulated that roles are constantly being constructed, defined by the respective culture, and assumed by the person. It is through the movement into, through, and out of the roles of other selves that the construction of inner autonomy becomes possible. It is at the turning points of development that the individual is actively or passively involved in the construction/reconstruction of the self. For example, after his father's death the oldest son in the family often becomes the family patriarch to whom other family members turn for advice.

In midlife, the assumption of nearly every role one will assume peaks. Because of the number of roles, and corresponding number of selves, the midlife adult can be viewed as psychologically fragile. Cultural, familial, and personal expectations for one's self may clash, resulting in a time of confusion, discontent, and personal disorganization.

> *Can you develop a scenario in which this may occur?*
> *Does the idea of burnout fit? How?*

Claussen (1995) suggests that one may participate in only so many roles without damaging major responsibilities. Conflict that arises from lack of support or an overextension of assumed roles may lead to the attenuation of one's self-identity.

> *What are some of the cultural messages of which you are aware?*

In each culture there is always a transfer of information about the current status of the culture, how life was before the current time, and how it should be moving into the future. The older generation, family, peers, and the media assemble messages as to how life should be enacted at all ages. Midlife adults actively analyze cultural messages about their roles and reassemble them in novel forms.

What are some of the cultural messages of which you are aware?

Take for example the considerable number of U.S. midlife women who "know" that they must ask their spouse for approval regarding any activity they wish to become involved in . . . a church sewing group, a writing class, a martial arts class. The midlife man may feel that his current path no longer suits him. However, he is faced with the message from the older generation that a career choice is one to which you commit for life. The idea of having multiple career positions across one's life is a foreign concept to that generation.

At midlife, the interpretation and evaluation of cultural messages result in a personal transformation that shapes the person's choices of which roles to maintain and to assume. Figure 5.1 presents an analysis of the communication of cultural messages. The message never exists in standard form because it is reconstructed by the communicator, who may start with a goal in mind, and by the listener, who may already have a set of expectations. The listener then synthesizes and internalizes the message. What happens when there are conflicting messages or at the extreme, no messages?

Describe an event in which you and another person heard the same message and constructed a different interpretation of what was said.

Or, try to think of a statement that when spoken by two different persons might convey a different meaning. Give one such example.

FIGURE 5.1. A model of information transfer reflecting cultural expectations and individual interpretation of the message.

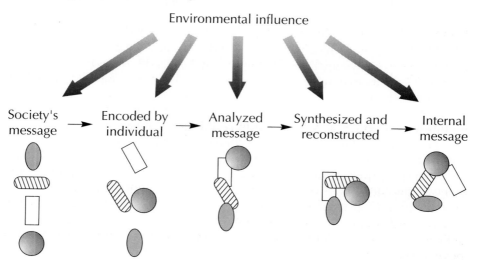

Environmental influence

Society's message → Encoded by individual → Analyzed message → Synthesized and reconstructed → Internal message

THE MANY FACES OF MIDLIFE

Many of the changes that occur during midlife are silent changes in the sense that they are changes of the self. A number of events occur across cultures. Most midlife adults, across cultures, have raised or are nearly finished raising a family; have established a means of supporting the family; are responding to the needs of aging parents; have their own health concerns; and have dealt with death in their families, in their circle of friends, and in the community. Each of these events has the potential to enhance the depth of the individual, add to his or her understanding of the complexities of life, and provide an opportunity to guide others through various life transitions. In the United States however, the potential benefits of midlife may be difficult to realize. U.S. midlifers are likely to find that being involved in a celebration of their children's achievements seems to require an apology ("I'm sorry that I can't make the meeting, but my child's receiving an award at school and I guess I should be there."). Any pride taken in the achievement of the child must be submerged. A 40th birthday is frequently met with black crepe paper, black balloons, and an "Over the Hill" banner. The good-natured implication is that life is essentially over and there is nothing to look forward to. The 40-year-old who is told that he or she doesn't look 40 but 30, takes that as a compliment. The not-so-subtle message is that there is something wrong with being 40 or older. One must continue to look, act, and be young. Furthermore, criticism faces the midlifer if the loss of a parent, friend, or child produces a long period of mourning ("Why doesn't she/he get over it?"). Middle-aged U.S. adults it seems, are supposed to mute their pride in their children, minimize all that has led up to their 40th birthday, and show minimal signs of the impact that a loss has had upon them.

The difficult times that Americans have with this period of life is also evident in how they talk about it. For example, the thirty-five-year-old person who turns in the family van for a hot, new convertible; divorces after twenty-five years of marriage; leaves a productive career to go back to school or start a new career; or who takes up rollerblading is frequently referred to as going through a midlife crisis. The term is not positive and is usually meant to describe aberrant behaviors or dysfunctional thoughts. But these individuals have no guides to midlife and are making it up as they go along. They may not know why they are exhibiting these behaviors, silently experiencing confusion, and feeling adrift. But these are not universal feelings. Why is midlife difficult for the U.S. midlife adults, and how can one's culture aid in the passage through midlife?

It has been said that the "greatest change occurs when there is no information as to how to behave adaptively" (Caspi and Moffitt, 1993) pp. 247–271. People need models. Children, for example, tend to look to their parents and other adults for models of adult behavior and sometimes they look to older peers as guides. Transitions through life are also eased by consensus about appropriate tasks for that stage of life and by rites of passage. These rites help individuals find consistency in their lives during times of change. The birth of a child, a marriage, the taking on of new responsibility in the community, and the transition from childhood to adulthood are more or less universally celebrated.

During the 20s and early 30s, for example, young adults see a series of "musts" as markers for their transition to adulthood. Many consider the completion of high school as a minimum requirement and the completion of college or graduate school a maximum achievement for an educated adult. The next goal is to establish a career to be considered a contributing member of the community. Then, at some point in one's 20s, establishing a long-term permanent relationship with another individual is usually another outward sign of commitment and responsibility. Individuals begin to consider the possibility of adding children to the core family unit. The events could occur in any order; but they are typically considered to be the task of young adults even though the events themselves are not age restricted. Furthermore, the family and community typically meet these events with some form of recognition. Similarly, in some cultures, special recognition is given to the individual moving into midlife. For example, in the Native American culture, there is a recognition of the mature woman becoming a "wise woman." A ceremony acknowledges the woman's rising status. She serves as a model for the younger generation. The older man is also revered in a number of cultures. The 60-year-old man in Japan is recognized by family and community in a celebration to note his designation as an elder.

Not all life transitions are *equally recognized* by family and community. Confusion comes with a lack of recognition of a particular life period, and there is a paucity of models to serve in the transition. The greatest disruption in midlife occurs when (1) there is no guidance, support, or clear demonstration as to how to enact the roles of this period, and (2) one lives in a society that venerates youth. As one approaches and enters midlife, marked differences between young and midlife adults become evident. It is apparent to midlifers that aspects of their lives are changing on a variety of fronts. How to enact these roles with grace and maturity serves as the point of greatest confusion. In her book, *The Change*, Germaine Greer (1991) emphasizes the lack of models and ceremony for the midlife adult. She states that the individual (woman) is left on her own because of the silence surrounding that period. This sentiment may be even more true for the Western midlife man, frequently discouraged from expressing confusion of a personal nature or even in addressing any questions or concerns regarding this period of life.

Summary and Comments

The role of culture is critical in the development of the individual. It is said to permeate every aspect of development—from prenatal existence through old age. This chapter emphasized the importance of culture in the areas of social and personal development. Beyond this, one's culture has the potential to impact both proximal and distal processes in development. Specifically, one's cognitive ability, how one thinks about, interprets, and acts on information (proximal processes), is often culturally based. The neurological development that occurs pre- and postnatally (distal processes) can directly influence the way behavior is enacted (proximal processes). One clear and striking example relates to the effects of alcohol consumption during pregnancy, its impact on brain development, and subsequent behavioral disruptions. Cultures that promote this damaging behavior or cultures that have little access to healthy nutrition and prenatal care, or that pay little attention to or derogate the benefit of low-fat, high-fiber diet, impact both proximal and distal processes of the individual.

Examining the social function of culture, one finds that different cultures have different expectations for individuals of different ages and differentially recognize the relative importance of these individuals. The purpose of this chapter was to highlight the importance of culture throughout the course of development. Much of the midlife transition is a personal one of reorganization and self-discovery. This transition goes relatively unnoticed by most individuals in Western societies unless the family and possibly community notice what might be termed aberrant behavior. In other, non-Western societies, greater recognition is given to the full extent of the life course. Having models, recognition, and celebration for each age transition is an integral part of the fabric of their lives.

Gaining a better understanding of cultures and incorporating the varying aspects of the culture of the participants in our empirical studies will lead to a richer understanding of human behavior.

Preface to Section II

In this section, the student is introduced to the international face of midlife adults. Census data from around the world show that, with few exceptions, midlife individuals represent an increasing proportion of most nations' populations. This statistic, along with predictions of longer life spans for individuals of this age bracket, suggests a continued impact of this group on society.

General health, fertility, and cognitive process represent the bulk of this section. Findings regarding these topics are presented separately for men and women. While women and men both experience similar changes with regard to these general domains, particular differences exist and are noted in detail. Lifestyle factors that can have a positive and negative impact on midlife adults' general health and cognitive functioning are articulated for the reader.

The cognitive changes in midlife are subtle at best. Emphasis is placed on the broader issues of the changes in the way intelligence, memory, and wisdom are viewed. Overall, the picture of cognitive processing in midlife is positive.

Throughout all of the chapters, comparisons are drawn between Western and non-Western cultures. Note the differences in health patterns and cognitive performance of individuals from different cultures. The reader will find that certain non-Western cultural practices prove to be more beneficial to the whole adult, particularly benefiting the midlife adult. Students should note the practices and cultures from which they originate, then refer back to Table 6.1 and examine the population projections for those groups.

A clear understanding of the issues in this section will help the student accurately evaluate the validity of many of the stereotypes surrounding midlife. This understanding should also facilitate the reader's progress through his/her midlife.

CHAPTER 6

Those Were the Times,
Those Were The People

The socio-cultural milieu during my young childhood was still much in the harsh stages of racism. The schools were still segregated. Busing had not begun. Black people were still known as colored with colored water fountains and bathrooms. At 15 I was pregnant, still in school and working for the white lady my great grandmother worked for, and I was being paid $5 a week. I would have lasted longer if she had not loaned me to her neighbor.

51-YEAR-OLD SECRETARY AND ASPIRING WRITER

To me, this was a more simple time—mainly because I had so few responsibilities. Oh, there were responsibilities, but not like today. You were allowed to make mistakes back then, because, at 18, you were expected to—and be forgiven. Today (teens) don't have that luxury, you are paid to perform and you must—or no longer be paid.

49-YEAR-OLD COMPUTER SOFTWARE DEVELOPER

I went away to a hospital-based nursing school that was SO last century. We had to wear a uniform that was almost down to your ankles. You were expelled if you got engaged. They weighed us every month, and if you gained weight, they asked if you were pregnant.

51-YEAR-OLD CRITICAL CARE NURSE

One very strong memory was of being in a group of thousands of students, marching against the Vietnam war, and being surrounded by National Guardsmen with fixed bayonets. Some idiot student, surely trying to provoke a Kent State incident, set off a string of firecrackers. We all hit the ground. I realized later that the Guardsmen were also kids and I realized how scared they must have been, being outnumbered 100 to 1 by screaming student protesters.

52-YEAR-OLD COLLEGE PROFESSOR

THE INTERNATIONAL PROFILE
OF MIDLIFE ADULTS

We have been covering the more traditional theoretical/conceptual understand-ing of this portion of the life span. We have addressed the following points:

1. The importance of an ecological/contextual approach;
2. the variety of theories that focus on this particular period of the life span; and
3. Methods for the scientific study of this particular point in the life span.

While much has been said about the American baby boom generation, born between 1946 and 1964, an increase in births at this time in history was a world-wide phenomenon. An examination of Table 6.1 indicates that:

1. A majority of industrialized nations underwent a parallel population boom soon after the end of World War II.
2. This significant population increase currently represents 1/4 to 1/3 of their respective nations' populations.
3. If we accept taking a broader definition of middle-age (35–64 years), midlife individuals predominate the worldwide population.
4. These midlifers are projected to live longer and healthier than did previous generations.
5. These individuals not only have the economic, social, and political power to influence their current midlife experience, they also have the power to alter their experience of aging and lay the foundation for the midlife expe-rience of the next generation (today's 18–34-year-olds).
6. Sub-Saharan Africa is the one exception to this international phenomenon of having a heavy representation of midlife adults in their society, reflect-ing instead the traditional demographic population pyramid; the pyramid shows that the largest group includes individuals from birth to adoles-cence, with an ever-decreasing number of individuals in the subsequent age brackets. This is the current status of sub-Saharan Africa and it is not predicted to change through the year 2025.

The sub-Saharan pattern exists in sharp contrast to the rectangular popula-tions of the other nations.

Why do you think that the population pyramid is the model of sub-Saharan Africa demographics?

What is the inherent problem with a rectangular-shaped population distribution?

It is apparent, given the population distribution on the one hand and the concentration of economic wealth and political and military power on the other hand, that the industrialized nations will continue to have a pervasive

TABLE 6.1. Percentages of the Midlife Population Currently Exceeding 1/4 to 1/3 of the Nation's Population. Source: Taken from the US Bureau of Census— International Database, (5-10-2000)

Nations	Year: 2000 ↔↔↔↔↔ % Population Age 35–54 Years (Baby Boomers)	↔↔↔↔↔ % Population Age 35–64 Years	Year: 2025 ↔↔↔↔↔ % Baby Boomers Projected to Reach 60–74 Years	Future ↔↔↔↔↔ Projected % Population 35–54 Yrs	Midlifers ↔↔↔↔↔ Projected % Population 35–64 Yrs
United States	30	39	83	24	36
Canada	31	40	89	26	39
United Kingdom	28	39	83	25	40
Australia	20	38	86	26	39
Mexico	19	24	77	27	37
Norway	28	38	84	25	38
Finland	31	41	81	24	37
Sweden	28	39	85	25	39
Peru	20	26	77	26	35
Argentina	23	30	79	27	36
Chili	26	33	81	27	39
Brazil	23	29	71	28	39
Bolivia	19	23	67	26	33
India	21	27	68	27	36
Russia	30	40	70	31	44
Japan	28	41	84	27	40
Singapore	34	40	94	34	46
China	26	33	77	28	42
Hong Kong	34	42	89	27	44
Korea, South	20	37	79	28	42
Korea, North	24	33	74	27	41
Germany	29	41	85	25	41
France	29	40	89	25	38
Saudi Arabia	21	26	75	16	21
Egypt	20	25	67	26	36
South Africa	21	27	43	20	27
Uganda	12	18	51	13	16
Rwanda	15	18	39	20	24
Nigeria	15	20	52	17	21
Kenya	13	17	50	22	27
Congo (Kinshasa)	13	17	54	15	18
Congo (Brazzaville)	15	19	53	18	22
Central African Republic	15	19	47	17	21

impact on life on this planet. This midlife group has the potential to wield enormous power given their current standing in their respective nations. They hold the power and purse strings in all walks of life. They are influencing local, national, and international decisions that have broad impact now and in the future.

THE USE OF GENERATION AND COHORT

Understanding Generation and Cohort

Before beginning a discussion of today's midlife individuals, a better understanding of what people mean when they say generation or cohort is required. You have probably already noticed in some of your developmental psychology texts that the author(s) may use the terms generation and cohort interchangeably. You may even wonder if there is a difference between the two terms. A look at the way generation and cohort have been evaluated and defined by scholars over the decades illustrates the confusion that has reigned.

Common Uses of Generation

First, the term has been used to designate kinship relations and structure, such as the first generation of Whipples in Massachusetts or the second generation of Whipples in Massachusetts. This definition represents a more biological view of the successive generations of genetic strands passed down over the years (in the case of humans), litters (in the case of dogs), or varieties (in the case of corn). Many scholars feel that this contained and restricted use of the word generation should be the sole use (O'Rand & Krecker, 1990). Other individuals take a broader view such that it has been used to designate a stage in the life course such as the current college generation as opposed to the former college generation, the current generation of new fathers as opposed to the former generation of new fathers. In this second use, it is relatively clear to whom one is referring in the former (current new fathers) but not the latter case (could include any male, living or dead, that has fathered a child in the past). Third, the most common, yet inconsistent, use of generation is to designate or refer to a group of people alive in the same historical period; for example, those born before the Vietnam War and those born after the Vietnam War. People who fall into this category can range in age from newborn to over 100 years of age. The fourth use refers to a particular age group in history, who during that time became aware of their uniqueness compared to other members of society, the Hippie Generation, the Yuppie Generation or Generation X. The fifth and final way generation has been used has been in reference to a particular age group in a population whose primary membership is designated by the date of their birth. For example, you may currently be a member of the 20-year-old generation, but after your next birthday you won't be a member. Or, in the context of midlife, you can be a member of the middle age generation from the ages of

35 to 65. You can be middle-aged for 30 years; but in the end, it only takes 1 day to move you out of that generation.

> *How would you designate your generational status according to these five definitions?*

Common Uses of Cohort

What is a cohort? According to Mannheim (1928/1952), two elements are critical in the construction of a cohort. They focus on the impact of (1) social and (2) cultural change on the individuals at a particular time. The most important feature of both of these types of change has to do with the **pace** of social and cultural change. When the pace of social change is rapid, many of the traditional ways of expressing and understanding the culture may not be possible. As a result, new modes of expression and understanding will develop and, perhaps, be in sharp contrast to the former ways of knowing. The information and knowledge of heritage gained from the earlier or older generations may no longer be of relevance. Take, for example, the once universal view that women should not appear in public without their bustle or hat. That view changed during what was called the Roaring Twenties with the advent of the flapper. In more recent times, the furry caterpillar has been replaced as a forecaster of weather by sophisticated weather satellites. You may ask if this last example is a reflection of societal or cultural change. In this case the impact of technology has had an amazing impact on the pace of living of technologically advanced societies. A recent presentation at the meeting of the American Psychological Society is a clear example of what the implications are (APS Observer, 2000). This presentation concluded that because of the rapid advancements in technology alone, today's world does not closely match the world of a short fifteen years ago.

> *How do you see the pace of life impacting you now? Can you imagine it moving faster, and how will you respond?*

Just as a fast pace of societal and cultural change impacts the younger generation's way of living, a slow pace of change will not show the dramatic differences in behavior and thought from that of preceding generations. However, in some societies the rate is so gradual that the change may not even be observable, such that individuals may live out their entire life span without seeing any difference in current and former lifestyle. But a historical review may show how a culture may have changed, not over decades but over centuries.

In addition to Mannheim's early thoughts on the issue of cohort development, Ryder takes a broad conceptualization of a cohort beyond that of mere birth year, by defining cohorts as a group of individuals within a population who experience the same event within the same time interval. To the baby boom generation, what tied them as an age cohort to some older and some younger individuals, was the assassination of President John F. Kennedy in 1963. While this incident is often thought of as an event in American history (something for the history books), for many individuals around the world, this assassination reflects a living part of their history and collective social memory. It is this memory and shared experience that brings these many-aged individuals together as a cohort.

Other elements that serve to define a cohort (defined by age alone) have to do with (1) relative size and (2) the rate of appearance of new, future cohorts. The larger the size of the specified cohort, the greater will be its potential for societal impact. Their mere presence will have a marked influence on social institutions, for example, education, health care, and recreation. As this large group moves through the life span, it will increase in power and influence. Any drop in that culture's **fertility rate,** will afford greater influence of the older and larger cohort.

In summary, if one assumes a general biological definition of the term generation, one should see that an individual can belong to only one generation while having multiple chances to be a member of multiple cohorts. The term cohort then may be considered to be composed of individuals of potentially many different generations. Cohort is more flexible with regard to membership, while individuals representing the fourth generation in a family can neither move up nor down. A graphic simplification of this few as seen in Figure 6.1 may be helpful.

FIGURE 6.1. A schematic diagram of the potential generation and cohort overlap.

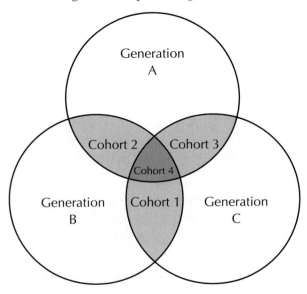

ABOUT THIS CHAPTER

The composition of this chapter is guaranteed to change with each succeeding generation of midlife adults. None of the chapters that precede this chapter nor any of those that follow will undergo as dramatic a change as will this one over the years. The next generation of midlifers will be both similar and dissimilar to the boomers that preceded them. They will comprise a generation unto themselves with a unique identity developed over time and experience.

What are the major characteristics of your generation?
How will we come to understand you?

As mentioned previously, those individuals falling within certain age parameters represent a generation, as commonly conceived. Whatever the designated age brackets, we travel through life with those of our generation, and like it or not, they are our fellow travelers. To understand the American boomers and the individuals at the upper and lower end of the midlife bracket (thirty-five to sixty-five years of age), you should consider the culture in which these individuals spent their young adult years.

CROSS-CULTURAL CONVERSATIONS

What follows reflects a composite commentary derived from a number of individual interviews with European-American, Native Chinese, European, and South American midlife adults. The primary focus of the conversations was on the individuals' childhoods and young adulthoods.

The European-American (U.S.) Community

Many of those considered as part of the boomer generation were born in the middle of the twentieth century. For those coming of age in the United States, broad and sweeping changes were on the verge of happening. Their parents, who had just endured the perils and uncertainty of a world war, were intent on providing a better life for their children. The term frequently used to describe the parental generation was innocent—an innocence born out of hard times and hope. The Cold War that followed WWII probably shaped the American collective psyche in terms of the children of the time. The children of these individuals were given more materially than their parents were, given a better life, and sheltered from life's harshness. Was this all it took to create the generation now termed as baby boomers?

An unprecedented birth rate during the years 1946–1964 was not the only contributor to the changes that followed. An interaction of societal factors contributed to the mentality that blossomed in these individuals. It has been said that "continuous wire-service transmission, an insatiable appetite for repetitive images of local events, a peace-time return to *managed* news events, and the triumph of the consumer culture with its relentless photo-advertising" epitomized the postwar culture (Lacayo and Russell, 1995). One might consider this to have been the dawning of the Information Age. The radio and telephone were already present in many households, and with the addition of the television, no event was so distant that a visual image was not soon available. Access to and awareness of events at home and in other nations provided moderately sanitized and censored food for thought. Other images brought into our homes challenged the censors (e.g., *Laugh In, The Smothers Brothers Show*) and the traditional conservative, middle-class, white portrayal of life in the United States (e.g., *Donna Reed Show, Father Knows Best*).

Another series of emerging realities penetrated the national consciousness. The first had to deal with the plight of Black America, in the form of the Civil Rights movement and its impact on the entire nation. Second, the slowly increasing but steady U.S. involvement in the civil war in Vietnam brought international events and national responses directly into the home. Third, the population had to make sense of the challenge leveled by the women's movement to the traditional roles of American women and men. No matter where you stood, there was no lack of opinions. Families, friends, coworkers, neighbors, religious leaders, and fellow worshipers were all drawn into the discussion. At times it felt that there was no escaping any of the hot topics of the time. Emotions ran high. Opinions ranged from the extremely conservative to the extremely liberal and to everything in between. Again, television held up a mirror to society through its programming (eg., *All In the Family, Maude*). Television was the tool of information as well as critical comment.

Also during this time, the greater mobility available to individuals in all walks of life made the nation more accessible and seem smaller than before. There were greater geographic access to the country, greater access to a myriad of ideas, and greater availability of education. A president was assassinated; a Civil Rights leader murdered, and thousands of young men were brought home in body bags. Idealism gave way to cynicism for many of the youth. Trust was questioned at all levels.

Despite this, children still went to school, teachers still taught, farmers still farmed, mill workers worked their shifts, and fishermen still tended their nets. Life went on in this nation as it had done for nearly two centuries; but no one was the same, no one went untouched.

Terms from the Times

Peace and Love

Flower Power

The
Boardroom not
the Bedroom

Equal Rights

Midis
Minis
Maxis

Draft Cards

The Lottery
(it was a life
and death issue)

Tune In, Turn On, Drop out

Malcolm X
Martin Luther King
Selma, Alabama
Skokie, Ill.

Drugs,
Sex, and
Rock 'N Roll

Finding Yourself

Getting Your Head
Together

Free Love
Free Sex

Make Love not War

Question
Authority

Motown
Rock
Psychedelic Sounds

Hot Pants

Trippin'
Tokin'

The Right To Vote

The Right To Drink

The Right To Die

Burning Bras

Burning Draft Cards

Burning Flags

Understanding Today's Midlife Adult

- All born post-World War II
- Korean War did not penetrate their consciousness
- Had a stand on the Vietnam War
- Knows what a turntable, a stylus, and a record are
- Cars were made in the U.S.A.
- Food was cooked in aluminum or cast iron pots and pans
- Gasoline cost less than 20 cents a gallon
- Most TVs were black and white and had three channels (on a good day)
- Could remember the first color TV
- Knew Carlos Santanna when he was young
- Typewriters and carbon paper were how to copy material
- Cancer was rarely spoken of
- Nearly everyone smoked cigarettes
- Clear and distinct roles for men and women
- Space race, satellites, first man on the moon
- Segregation, Civil Rights, women's rights, antiwar protests, availability of illegal substances
- Kent State massacre
- Very much aware of the Cold War
  - Bomb shelters
  - The possibility for the total "destruction of the human race"

Terms That Once Had No Meaning to Today's Midlife Adult

- In Vitro
- Freeze dried
- Cable TV
- Teflon
- Cell phones
- Wireless
- Microfiber
- Cyberspace
- Super Bowl
- Fiber optics
- MTV
- Microwave ovens
- Duh

Were other nations experiencing national upheavals and a generational schism such as appeared to be happening within the United States?

The Native Chinese Community

Life was much different growing up in China. The cultural revolution had taken its toll on families and the nation. Sure, young people had their adolescent thing, but freedom and mobility were lacking. We couldn't just take off in your car. We didn't have access to one.

Another big difference compared to Western young adults had to do with the understood responsibility toward one's family. The notion of **filial responsibility** was strong. Your behavior reflected on the honor of the family. We were responsible to the family and had a duty to respect and serve the elders of your family and community. There was not the level of disrespect for the elders as we were told was happening in the United States.

One proceeded through youth and into midlife, now, with a sense of family, honor, and responsibility. There continues the expectation that one remains responsible to the elders. Even those who may be twenty to twenty-five year residents in the United States often make regular trips back to their ancestral home. These visits reflect a sense of enduring duty.

The European Community

The postwar years were a period of rebuilding in Europe. It was a time of hard work even for the children. So many people had been touched by the tragedy of the war that it was hard to get away from it. They were aware of the national strife in the United States and of the societal changes occurring. Many of the young people took up the trends in dress, music, and personal freedom. It, however, seemed that there was still a balance between what existed currently in the European culture and what the youth were becoming. There wasn't the pervasive "us and them" mentality as seen in the U.S. we had access to so many different national views that never created a singular cultural identity. We sampled bits of other cultures and bits of other kinds of freedoms. We could be separate but still very much a member of our immediate and extended families. No matter what our appearance, there was a strong sense of belonging within our families and for the most part, in our communities.

The South American Community

South America is a class-oriented society. There are the very poor and the very rich. Growing up in what would be called the middle to lower middle-class was hard (in retrospect). Children had their freedom and their responsibilities to the family. The fathers were the power in the families. Mothers and elders were respected. Fathers were feared and respected. Expectations regarding sex roles and proper behavior were clear. There was not a lot of rebellion during the teen years and young adulthood. We did have our ideas and dreams. We adopted new ideas but were clear as to our status in society and were well aware of the sacrifices of our elders. We grew up looking forward to, someday, getting the respect we showed to others.

Again, these community views reflect a compilation of conversations with a number of foreign nationals and do not reflect the sole perspective of one individual.

Summary and Comments

An analysis of the actions of the young people in the United States between the years 1959–1976 is more the purview of historians and sociologists. The prevailing psyche of the nation was reflected in the unbridled freedom made available during a time of increasing prosperity. This sense of unlimited freedom, imagination, and opportunity served as the foundation for many of the social and scientifical achievements of that time and the time that followed. Today's midlifers, who were the American young during that period of turbulence, carry some measure of that time with them, which continues to be reflected in the lives they have chosen to live.

Midlifers, internationally, have been exposed to varying degrees to the events of the '60s and '70s. Today, their expectation for their lives continues to mirror what they came to know, hear about, or live during that period.

Identify cultures that have been little impacted by what we know as fast-paced change.

In 1984, I was 18 years old. It was the year I happily transitioned from high school to college. High school did not appeal to me; I could not relate to my peers. I failed to see any reason to "belonging" in that subculture. In college I found other young people cut from the same fabric as I. I grew up/came of age in the 1980s. This was an era of punk, new romanticism, Madonna, Janet Jackson, and the birth of the music video. I did not subscribe to the irreverence of the punk movement, although I appreciated the rage that drove them. Rather, I did not have the courage it took to be a rebel—even a trend rebel. But music provided the escape needed to survive high school. I am white, middle class, an apparent girl-next-door. I always attended public schools in south central Los Angeles. Gangs, drugs, fights, weapons, fear . . . all integral to how my character developed. I was part of the "Crypt" part of town. This is opposed to the "Bloods" (red bandannas). I observed. I escaped without fighting, except one afternoon I nearly had my first fist fight with Cricket, a girl at my high school. A senior I think. She already had one baby. She had gang ties with the Bloods. I, true to form at that age, backed down. I had no pride, just fear.

Seeing my future from the 18-year-old vantage was always grandiose. I was going to be a psychiatrist, single, beautiful, thin, with my own apartment in West L. A. and a convertible Mercedes Benz. I was going to eat out every night, drink the best wines, and see theater every week. I would be strong, respected, and envied. Then I went to college, majored in biochemistry. Became a socialist and a poet, then a psychology major. I rowed crew, stayed up talking all night with my best friend, Janine, about art, music, and drama. We would break into a theater on campus in the middle of the night. Turn the stage lights on. She sang, I danced. She had one of the most emotive, fullest voices I have ever heard. From these nights, I

(continued)

VOICES OF OUR PARENTS 6.1

flirted with rebellion. Not only "breaking in" forbidden places, but I'd often skip calculus the following morning.

After two years, I dropped out of school. Only then did I begin my self-discovery. For the first time I actually found bits of who I actually was . . . already—not who I needed to become, but the pre-existing self. There was the confidence. Identity, however, is best developed without certainties. People raised in social environments can't know their own true identity easily. It is a concept that can undermine the survival of the "group." Because of the shadowed parts of our true selves, being/feigning certainty about your identity is deceptive, misleading. I am confident that I am who I appear to be; I cannot be certain that I am who I truly am however. Oh well.

PERSONAL PROFILE

Age:	36
Region raised in:	Southern California
Military service:	no
College:	yes Major: Psychology
First Career:	Statistical consulting
Current Career:	University Professor
Changes in Career:	Now have a PhD; had a Masters for consulting work
Marital History:	Single
Children:	no, not human
Pets:	currently: 3 cats, 1 rabbit, 5 guinea pigs, 1 hamster

VOICES OF OUR PARENTS 6.1

CHAPTER 7

General Health in Midlife

I don't smoke, I don't drink, I don't exercise, although I know I should.

—50-YEAR-OLD MALE

My body has stretched past its boundaries twice in five years. Gravity has not been that kind, either. I'm entering midlife at high speed. Help!

—35-YEAR-OLD FEMALE

I want my heart to be healthy. I worry more about heart attacks and more and more about things like cholesterol and blood pressure (thanks to the kids).

—58-YEAR-OLD MALE

"One glass of red wine 3x a week and Vitamin E daily."

—NEUROLOGIST TO 43-YEAR-OLD STROKE SURVIVOR

While this is a stand-alone chapter, it reflects the basic tenets of the ecological model in that one's health is a reflection of culture, lifestyle, family history, and time in history. As you proceed through the chapter, take figure 2.2 and map the potential influences of health factors as they relate to the different levels in the model. Try to do this for each of the following chapters. In this way, you will see the interconnectedness of all aspects of the life course.

OVERVIEW

We live in a health-conscious society. Sometimes the motto appears to be "Be healthy, live healthy, look healthy." This is a good approach to life. However, we as a society must look deeper into our values and views of growing older before we can evaluate whether this motto is a positive approach to life or a weak and fearful approach to aging. With regard to health issues during midlife, it can be said that we have a lot of statistics, we have a lot of demographics, we have a lot of information *but* we have little insight into the implications of these findings for the midlife adult.

Mention has already been made elsewhere that midlife as a new and definable point of the life span is only a recent phenomenon attributable to a huge increase in the midlife population. This increase is due to advancements in medical knowledge; availability of the most modern medicines; better hygiene, resulting in cleaner living conditions and minimizing the transmission of infectious diseases; and a lower mortality rate for children and women (in particular).

If midlife is a new area of study, one must ask why this is so. There have always been old adults, so why not midlife adults? It could have been that the midlife adults were considered the older adults. Therefore, one went right from being young to being old and nothing in between—hmmm.

A number of physiological changes occur during midlife. There are a considerable number of changes that can be said to be universal, others that can be found primarily in Western industrialized men and women, and others still that are specific either to women or men. However, two things need to be remembered:

1. change is always occurring from the time of birth onward and
2. the rate of pathology in general is rather low in the population, despite the frequency of cautionary comments regarding cancer and cardiovascular accidents.

Life span developmentalists have long been stating that aging is not pathology. Being old is not a disease. You cannot catch it. Being in midlife is no more a pathology than being ninety years old. A distinction must be drawn between the potential for contracting or developing conditions congenial to disease on the one hand and the normal process of developing on the other hand. There is an increasing likelihood for the appearance of disease or medical disorder with increasing age beginning in midlife, but it is not guaranteed. In fact, it is not a common occurrence.

As you read through the various sections of this chapter, a number of questions need to be kept in mind and regularly reviewed. They are:

1. How are we to interpret the physiological changes that occur? Is young adulthood the appropriate yardstick for comparison?
2. Should we be making negative attributions to the changes that occur?
3. Are we overrating being young?
4. Is it all negative from thirty-five onward? Can we put a positive spin on it or do we need to spin at all?
5. What are the assumptions that young adults and midlifers are making to this period of life and the path beyond?
6. Do we as a society need to grow up and stop being afraid of growing older?

Erik Erikson has been quoted as saying "Children will not fear life, if the adults have the integrity not to fear death." (Erikson, 1950/1963). The definition of trust (Erikson's first stage of psychosocial development) has been defined as the "assured reliance on another's integrity." Are we, as a society, a little low on trust and therefore full of fear (of moving on)?

Remember, the jury is still out as to how to interpret the facts that follow.

HOW DO WE COME TO KNOW AGE?

Satchel Page once asked, "How old would you be if you didn't know how old you was?" In a survey of Finnish elderly adults, their response to a comparable question was "50 years old." Elaboration of their modal response suggested that fifty reflected the peak of their lives, with respect to every domain of their lives, health, activity, and opportunities (Alban, 2001). A similar attitude can be attributed to European colonists in colonial America. A look at the dress and styles of the early colonial residents in America and in those individuals living in Great Britain were styles that reflected the older adult in their community. The wearing of a gray wig, styling hair by both older men and women, the wearing of a bustle by women to emulate a wider hip and overall girth, were by no means accidents. They were chosen specifically to enhance one's status in the community by looking older. This look afforded greater respect, signaled wisdom, and exuded authority. This look was the look of the older adult, the midlife adult if you will, not young adult nor aging/old adult. Again, the unspoken choice in preference for this unarticulated age was comparable to the Finns—"a mature adult," neither the inexperience of the young nor the diminished energy of the old.

Health-related data point to the middle years as a time of exceedingly good health and productive activity (Avis, 1999). The changes, both physical and mental, this time are gradual. *Physical changes* and *current life situations*, frequently used in the absence of chronological indices, provide clues to the age of the individual. However, while useful, these markers are not as informative as one might like.

> *How old is an individual who has no children, no gray hair, and lives in an apartment? How old is the person who has only one child and is a grandparent? How old is the individual who owns his/her home, has a steady job, both parents are living, and has no children?*

The previous box reflects examples known to the author. These examples were chosen so that all the responses to the question described twenty-eight-year-olds and fifty-year-olds and older in the community. One's place in life is often indicated in the state of one's body, family and career situations, and expectations for one's self.

Consider an example in which you are presented with an individual suffering from total amnesia. There is no recollection as to who the person is, how the person came to be this way, no record of identity. How would you evaluate this individual? What steps would you initiate to determine a life-frame for this individual? Many of you would probably take the path of the archaeologist or forensic pathologist. You could probably start by brief visual examination to determine gender, race, age bracket (child or adult), height, weight, and then you're pretty much on your own. Where do you go from here? What do you know? You must also realize that even this visual inspection may not be accurate.

What factors might cause your observations to be in error?

As a result, you may feel that other information is required such as:

1. the individual's lifestyle in childhood because it will have an influence on one's youth and through young adulthood, midlife, and old age;
2. the individual's genetic makeup given the potential for genetics to determine general aging pattern and whether a chronic disease will emerge at some point (e.g., the 95-year-old, 3 pack-a-day smoker since he was 12 years old with no impaired lung functioning or signs of heart disease or cancer); and
3. the recognition that the observed changes vary greatly between and within individuals.

There is also the view that midlife is one of the healthiest times in an individual's life (Avis, 1999). Although changes are newly occurring or have been proceeding for a brief period, the midlife individual is encountering one of the healthiest periods in his or her life. You might want to counter with statements like "It was during midlife that my mom found out she had X or my dad found out that he had Y." That medical detection has arrived at the point of early diagnosis for many individuals does not negate that these individuals probably would have proceeded through midlife with little awareness of the disease. It would have had no impact on their lives. The disease may have, by old age, progressed to the point where medical intervention would have had limited impact. This is probably much of the case in the past. This individual would probably die in early old age. That does not negate that the midlife experience of this person would have been a relatively healthy experience, only impacted by high demands on time and energy at this point in life.

General Physical Changes Not Specific to One or the Other Gender

- decline in systemic functioning
- decrease in bone mineral density
- presbyopia
- skin changes: wrinkles and sagging
- age spots

- hair thinning and graying
- decrease in sweat glands
- finger and toenails grow thicker, more brittle, and develop ridges
- loss in height
- gain in weight
- decrease in muscle strength
- decrease in muscle size
- joint stiffness
- decreasing ease of movement
- decreased efficiency of O_2 consumption
- heart rate slower and more irregular
- arterial walls more rigid and thicker
- increase in aortic stiffness
- loss of heart-related aerobic power
- decrease in heat production
- decrease in number and size of **nephrons** in the kidneys
- immune response becomes weaker
- gradual hearing loss
- 1/3 of the midlifers are **myopic**
- problematic sleep
- chronic illness, persistent symptoms, and disability begin to rise
- decrease in accident frequency
- less susceptible to colds and allergies
- decrease in energy, decrease in pain
- increase in tiredness and fatigue
- most problems are musculoskeletal

The most common midlife conditions are not fatal. See Table 7.1 for their listing.

So, thus is the profile of the healthiest, most productive, and most influential point in one's life.

Elaboration of the Constituent Changes

Despite what you may be thinking about the number of changes listed, they are relatively minimal compared to the the dramatic changes that occur in childhood and youth, from infancy to adolescence.

Midlife changes fall into five categories. First, are the *systemic functioning changes*. These changes are reflected in the changing metabolic rate. The ability to increase body heat production and reduce it when required shows a change that continues to lose efficiency with increasing decades (Smith, 1992). The middle-aged adult may begin to report increasing difficulties with sleep. Wakeful periods become more frequent, and a progressive decrease in stage 4—deep sleep results in feeling less rested in the morning (Dement, Miles, and Bliwise 1982; Katchadourian, 1987; Webb, 1982). These sleep disturbances are the cause of the increasing reports of tiredness and fatigue at this time of life. Also, the

TABLE 7.1. Most Common Nonfatal Health Conditions in Midlife

Condition	Men*	Women*
Arthritis	193 [2]**	285 [1]**
Hypertension	242 [1]	245 [2]
Chronic Sinusitis	148 [6]	193 [3]
Deformities	160 [4]	150 [4]
Hearing Problems	179 [3]	107 [7]
Heart Disease	153 [5]	117 [5]
Allergies	98 [7]	115 [6]
Hemorrhoids	72 [8]	65 [11]
Diabetes	58 [10]	57 [12]
Varicose Veins	26	89 [8]

*Number of conditions per 1000

**Superscript represents relative ranking by gender

Taken from Adams and Benson (1992)

increased number of roles adopted at this time and the demands resulting from these roles interact with the sleep loss to provide an even more extreme assessment of tiredness and fatigue.

There is also a decrease in general thermal regulation that may start as early as age forty. Increasing bodily temperature when necessary and decreasing it accordingly becomes a problem and continues to increase as such through old age. Changes in the functioning of the **hypothalamus** are posited to underly this regulatory problem (Miller, 1990). There is also a decreasing tendency to sweat due to the decreasing number of sweat glands.

One finds that individuals continue to gain weight throughout their young and middle adulthood (Katchadourian, 1987). It becomes increasingly difficult to lose weight during the middle to late years. The change is manifested in terms of a decrease in lean muscle mass and bone mineral and increasing fatty tissue to approximately 20 percent of body mass, compared to the adolescent level of 10 percent of body mass.

Second, marked changes in the *musculoskeletal system* have been noted. One of the first changes is in bone mineral density. There is a thinning of intervertebral disks in the spinal column. As a result, adults lose about 1/2 inch per decade beginning in their 40s. Bone density is maximally achieved by mid- to late-thirties. The progressive loss from this point is due to the increased tearing down of bone and a decrease in the building of new bone (Memmler and Wood, 1987; Whitbourne, 1985). Bone loss increases into the fifties but can be somewhat delayed through weight-bearing and aerobic exercise.

Similar to the kidney, muscles show a decrease in cell number and cell size. The impact is a loss of strength most apparent in the back and legs. At the level of the joint, it is found that the **collagen;** tendons; ligaments; and **synovial fluid,** which serves as the cushion for movement of bones, become less efficient resulting in joint stiffness and decreased ease of movement. In addition, decreased muscle strength, first noticed in declining **grip strength** at about age twenty-nine, appears most noticeably by age forty-five (Merrill and Verbrugge, 1999).

Third, the *sensory* changes to vision and hearing are among the first age-related changes noticed by the individual. With regard to vision, many individuals experience **presbyopia.** This change, reflected in the inability to focus on near objects, is the result of a failure in the accommodative ability of the lens of the eye. This stiffening of the lens is due to the drying of the nourishing **vitreous humor** behind the lens of the eye. This change in the eye is gradual.

It is common for younger adults to read the small print on medication bottles for their parents and perhaps to be asked to help in threading a needle.

Visual performance peaks by age 8 and thereafter decreases in performance by 50 percent by age 35 (Horvath and Davis, 1990; Whitbourne, 1985). Corrective lenses to aid in seeing near objects and print will be required by most individuals between 45–55 years of age. While being unable to focus on near objects is nearly universal, almost 1/3 of midlife adults, age 36–45, are **myopic,** manifesting an inability to focus on far objects with near vision relatively unimpared. This particular sensory change continues to increase throughout midlife (Grosvenor, 1987; Horvath and Davis, 1990).

Have you ever noticed an individual taking off his or her glasses to look at a menu? This is myopia.

The hearing loss that begins in the thirties is referred to as **presbycusis.** The loss is not an across the board decrement; rather, the loss is associated with the higher frequencies, first and most severely at around the 2,000 Hz area (within the range of adult human speech, particularly a woman). Loss of sensitivity to high frequency sound is the hallmark of the midlife adult.

The relationship between smell and taste have been well documented in the physiological literature (Carlson, 1991). With midlife, approximately in the forties, the number of olfactory cells decrease significantly. Loss in the number of taste buds also begins to increase. In addition to the loss normally brought about with aging, certain lifestyle factors (the regular consumption of spicy foods and the eating of foods of extreme hot temperatures) contribute to greater taste bud loss. Fewer olfactory cells and taste buds are often associated with dietary problems. For example, adding excessive amounts of salt or sugar to enhance flavor of foods may result in health problems for the potential diabetic or hypertensive individual.

Fourth, changes in the appearance of the *skin, hair, and nails* become increasingly observable during midlife. The skin begins to wrinkle and sag. These changes can be attributed to a loss of fat and collagen in the underlying tissue. Areas of the skin, specifically the hands and face, will begin to show **age spots.** These spots first show up in areas that have been chronically exposed to the sun. Hair becomes thinner and grayer due to a decline in the replacement rate of hairs and a decrease in **melanin** production, respectively. Fingernails and toenails develop ridges and become thicker and more brittle (Memmler and Wood, 1987; Whitbourne, 1985).

Cardiovascular changes, the fifth midlife change, can best be seen when observing oxygen consumption, **vital capacity,** function of the heart, and integrity of arterial walls.

Around age forty, the midlife individual may begin to notice a decrease in endurance due to the body's decreasing ability to consume oxygen efficiently. Related to this is the finding that the vital capacity of the lungs begins to decline about this time.

The heart muscle does not show significant changes, especially if the individual has been physically active. Yet, by the mid-fifties the heart rate is detected to be slower and more irregular (Katchadourian, 1987). As a result of the change of O_2 consumption and heart rate, the heart becomes a poorer pump. The arterial walls become more rigid and thicker with a resulting response in aortic stiffness (Lakatta, 1990) and an increase in arterial **lipids.** The interaction of these changes leads to increases in the potential for an increasing rate of cardiovascular disease.

LIFESTYLE FACTORS INFLUENCING ADULT HEALTH

Much of the way we live has the greatest influence on the degree to which these normal changes occurring with maturation are exacerbated to the point of pathology. While there is nothing that you can do to impact your genetic heritage, you do have control of **lifestyle** behavior that may exacerbate a genetic weakness or genetic predisposition toward a particular pathology.

You are a mirror of your maternal grandmother's health at the time she was pregnant with your mother. Think about the implications.

Modifiable Factors

1. *Cigarette smoking* has been shown to have a direct relationship to the occurrence of lung cancer, heart disease, and stroke. Smoking while taking birth control pills further increases the risk of these diseases in women. Findings indicate that stopping smoking has an almost immediate influence on lessening the chance of developing lung cancer, heart disease, and stroke. Stopping, no matter when, will always show a benefit.

The relation to lung cancer is readily apparent, but what is the relation to heart disease?

2. *Alcohol use/abuse* is associated with impaired judgment, impaired coordination, and increased accident risk. Chronic and sustained use permanently damages the brain (i.e., Korsakoff's Syndrome).
3. *Dietary influences* include diets high in fat, low in fiber, and low in potassium. All are strongly associated with coronary heart disease.
4. *Physical activity* promotes the functioning of a better immune system and lowers the risk of premature death. Weight-bearing and aerobic activity can be a positive influence on the health of the midlife bone.

Develop a daily living program that would be appealing and healthy and not carry the stigma of sacrificing.

5. *Toxins* at work or at home are related to increased rates of cancer and lung disease (e.g., household cleansers, asbestos).
6. *Sunbathing,* of fair-skinned people in particular, leads to a higher risk of developing melanoma or other skin cancers.
7. *Excessive weight gain* alone contributes to heart disease, hypertension, diabetes, and a multitude of other pathologies when combined with smoking, lack of physical activity, and illicit drug use. Recent findings point to a significant increase in young adults' cardiac arrest rates (The State Newspaper, 2 March 2001). The rate dramatically increased for young women in particular.
8. *Illicit drug use* is the use and misuse of prescription drugs and the use of illegal drugs.

All of these lifestyle choices will have a direct impact on the quality and healthiness of young, middle, and older adulthood. They reflect aspects of one's life over which one has direct control. The earlier a healthful lifestyle is enacted, the healthier and more fit will be the body accompanying the adult into the middle years.

THE MIDLIFE WOMAN: HEALTH FACTORS SPECIFIC TO WOMEN

Leading Killers of Women

Cancer

Cancer is one of the leading killers of midlife women, second only to heart disease. Fifty percent of the midlife women today are more likely to develop some form of cancer than their ancestors. A significant rise in the cancer rate, 50 percent for all cancers and 30 percent in smoking-related cancer, compared to previous generations of women has been exhibited in baby-boom women. In addition to lifestyle issues, environmental carcinogens contribute significantly to the cancer rate.

Breast cancer. One in eight women in the United States will develop breast cancer in her lifetime. In the years between 1940 to 1987, the statistics went from 1 in 20 to 1 in 10. One woman dies of breast cancer every 12 minutes, second only to the number dying from lung cancer. Despite the early detection and aggressive forms of treatment employed today, the mental, physical, and economic costs are severe for the possibility of five additional years of life after treatment. While there exists little scientific research as to the cause of breast cancer, specifically, it is strongly hinted that lifestyle factors play a significant role in its development. Asian women show relatively no rate of breast cancer. What protects them in their culture, that becomes ineffective when these women emigrate to the United States and adopt an American lifestyle? After emigration these women manifest the same rate as those of American women (Osteen, et al., 1990).

Speculate as to what societal factors may contribute to this rise in breast cancer rate.

Factors associated with prevalence of breast cancer.

1. *Family history* is the major risk factor for developing breast cancer. There is a 90 percent increased rate for a woman whose mother had breast cancer and a 200 percent greater risk if she has a sister with the disease.
2. *Vitamins* are needed daily. The majority of women diagnosed with breast cancer did not take daily doses of vitamins. Vitamins A, E, and C and selenium have been found to protect against cancer.
3. *Alcohol* consumption, of any amount, was associated with an overall increased risk of up to 50 percent. Breast cancer was more likely to show up in 59 percent of the women who consume alcohol and was dose-related such that those women who drank 5 grams of alcohol per day showed an increase rate of 30 percent–60 percent compared to those who drank little to no alcohol.

> *Remember, this is correlational. What else goes on during alcohol consumption?*

4. *Dietary* considerations are important. Being overweight is related to breast cancer. It is suggested that limiting fat intake to 20 percent of the diet is a protective factor.
5. *Pregnancy* does not reduce the risk of breast cancer (contrary to common belief).
6. *Age of first menarche* has no association to the breast cancer rate.
7. *Oral contraceptives* have been found to have some association to hormonal level and breast cancer; an early teenage history of oral contraceptive use has yielded itself to be a high-risk factor.
8. *Benign breast disease* has no clear association to increased rate.
9. *Hormone replacement therapy (HRT)* is associated with a greater risk of breast cancer, as well as other cancers, particularly, uterine cancer. In 2001, estrogen was placed on the national listing of cancer-causing agents.
10. *Early detection* is important. The incidence of breast cancer was found to be higher in women who failed to practice self-examination (also reflective of cultural beliefs regarding touching oneself) and yearly checkups (also culturally related to being touched by others, in addition to the societal issues of access to medical care and financial ability to absorb the costs associated with early detection technology).

Cardiovascular Disease

Approximately, 485,000 women die each year from all heart and blood vessel diseases combined. One in 9 women, 45–64 years of age, has experienced some form of cardiovascular disease (i.e., stroke, hypertension, rheumatic heart disease, heart disease, in general). Approximately 6,000 heart attacks will be had by women each year, with 25 percent of the women being under the age of 45. Black women are 1.4 times more likely to suffer deadly heart attack rates than are white women. Smoking is related to a 2–4 times greater risk of a heart attack, and smoking, combined with oral contraceptive use, increases the risk by a factor of 22. Risk of heart disease increases in the menopausal and post-menopausal woman. This increase is associated with a drop in estrogen-related cardiovascular protective factors.

Treatment problems. The techniques employed for the cardiovascular treatment of women are inadequate or ineffective for women. The most common procedures have been predicated on male physiology (bigger veins, bigger arteries). As a result, angioplasty procedures and bypass surgeries show poorer results and are less effective, respectively, for women (Avis, 1999).

Also, the lack of knowledge regarding women and heart disease is overwhelming. Typically, one finds that women are more likely to manifest a primary diagnosis of unstable angina with a secondary diagnosis of congestive heart failure and diabetes mellitus, rather than myocardial infarcts or chronic ischemic heart disease.

Unstable angina and congestive heart failure are more nebulous assignments leading to less effective treatments than are the more specific heart attack and heart disease diagnoses. Until there is better understanding of women's cardiovascular health and functioning, women can improve the quality of their cardiovascular health via healthier diets, smoking cessation, and exercise.

Other Health Issues for Women

Hysterectomies, Plastic Surgeries, Pregnancies

1. The hysterectomy is the second most frequently performed surgery in the United States. It is the opinion of Doress and Siegel (1994) that women may be submitting themselves to this surgery unnecessarily. This surgery is usually elective and involves the removal of healthy ovaries. Only 8–12 percent of hysterectomies are performed because of uterine or ovarian cancers. The rest are usually performed before menopause for conditions that would have corrected anyway. It is projected that 50 percent of all women will undergo hysterectomies.

   Hysterectomy is a regional idiosyncrasy, with higher rates noted in certain cities, hospitals, and states.
   What might be contributing factors?

Hysterectomies should only be performed in the presence of :
   a. cancer
   b. severe hemorrhaging
   c. large fibroids
   d. advanced pelvic inflammatory disease
   e. severe uterine prolapse
   f. untreatable endometriosis
   g. catastrophic conditions occurring during childbirth
The woman must become the knowledgable consumer of her health care services. Doress and Siegel's (1994) volume is an essential resource for women considering hysterectomies.

2. Millions of women have chosen elective plastic surgery to improve their looks for a variety of reasons, such as a genetic disposition to a particular appearance; a disfiguring bone structure; a response to disease, accident, or surgery; and vanity. Face lifts, tummy tucks, liposuction, and breast enhancement are among the most common forms of elective surgeries. The problems associated with silicone implants, most commonly used for breast enhancement, are known to include the potential for a variety of diseases and immune system impairments. For these reasons, silicone is rarely

used as an implant in this type of surgery. However, the woman choosing plastic surgery today needs to be aware that low-bleed saline implants also allow *in* bodily fluids. Peanut oil implants, if broken, would flood the system and be a considerable danger to women allergic to peanut products, and the breakage rate needs to be studied before investing in the procedure. Similarly, the safety of collagen injections, liposuction, and other plastic surgeries requires thorough understanding. Again, the woman will need to do her homework.

3. Postmenopausal pregnancies are currently a hot topic in the media and private discussions. The question has been raised as to whether the woman is putting herself at risk with a late-life pregnancy. There are more questions than answers regarding this topic. However, for the near future this topic will be of considerable public and private interest. (See chapter 8 for more detail on fertility and these choices.)

THE MIDLIFE MAN: HEALTH FACTORS SPECIFIC TO MEN

Men are commonly seen as defining themselves through force and power. The man's power lies in his physical abilities and financial standing. So, in midlife, when you feel the physical power slipping away, what do you do and what can you do (Diamond, 1997)? It can be said with equal certainty that a comparable lack of knowledge exists with regard to the health of the midlife male. Given that the majority of the changes that occur in midlife are gradual, most men handle the changes without many problems. The popular literature and discussion of the man's transition through this period of the lifespan either trivialize it as a midlife crisis or do not acknowledge it. Much of the research into health issues for the man focuses on the study of male sexual functioning during this period, despite more important issues confronting the health of the man over age forty (Diamond 1997).

Universal Physical Changes at Midlife

1. *Weight gain* is continual and occurs throughout adulthood for the man resulting in an increase in abdominal girth of 6–16 percent. The weight gain for men appears to be most predominant above the belt.
2. *Bone mass loss.* Normal aging produces a loss of bone tissue in everybody, with significant differences between individuals. Bone loss begins in the 50s, with the greatest loss appearing for 10–15 years thereafter (Diamond, 1997). Men losing approximately 17 percent of the bone mass that they had as young men.
3. *Hearing loss.* About age 40, men begin to experience greater hearing loss than do women. The hearing loss begins usually at frequencies greater than 2000 Hz and by the end of midlife, there is greater difficulty in hearing frequencies of 2,000 Hz (the average range for the female voice) (Whitbourne, 1985).

4. *Recovery time.* In general, it takes more time to recover from illness and injury beginning to midlife. Exercise tolerance and performance begin to decrease around age 30 to the point where muscle strength decreases 30–40 percent by late life (Hayflick, 1994), as does overall endurance.
5. *Organ changes.* Internal organs such as the brain and the kidneys decrease in size beginning in midlife. However, the heart, lungs, and prostate all increase in size. Skin folds increase and muscle mass decreases.
6. *Fatal diseases.* Men tend to have a higher prevalence of fatal diseases, for example, heart disease, cancers, stroke, and so an (Kandrack, Grant, and Segall, 1991; Verbrugge, 1988). See Table 7.2.

TABLE 7.2. Prevalence of Midlife Diseases

Condition	Men	Women
Coronary Heart Disease[1]	*9.1*	*4.1*
Breast Cancer[2]		9.6
Lung Cancer[2]	1.7	1.3
Prostate Cancer[2]	2.9	
Colon, Rectal, Stomach Cancer[2]	2.4	1.7
Skin Cancer[2]	20.4	10.5
Stroke[3]	1.4	1.1
Osteoarthritis[4]	3.7	8.7
Depression[5]	11.8	21.8
Dementia[6]	7.8	0.0
Alzheimer's[6]	0	0
Heart Failure[7]	2.0	1.0
Non-Insulin-Dependent Diabetes[8]	*11.1*	*20.6*

Numbers in bold, italic, and highlighted represent the percent of population rate. Remaining data represents #/1,000 persons.

[1]National Heart Blood and Lung Institute, 1992

[2]Collins, 1993

[3]Wolf, et al., 1992

[4]Lawrence, et al., 1989

[5]Kessler, 1993

[6]Bachman, 1992

[7]Kannel and Belanger, 1991

[8]Cowie et al., 1993

Examination of Table 7.2 indicates that 3 of the top 10 are fatal (heart disease, particular cancers, diabetes). Rates of psychiatric disorders are also greater for men. The incidence rate for selected diseases facing the midlife man is presented in Table 7.3.

7. *Nonfatal chronicities.* Men are more likely to be limited in a major activity defined as one's job, housekeeping activities, or pursuing an education. This restriction may be due to many of the lifestyle issues mentioned in the next section.

8. *Prostate problems.* The prostate gland is the most frequently diseased organ of the body with 100 percent of men encountering a prostate-related disease in their life. The three major diseases of the prostate are:

   a. Prostatitis, reflected in pain in the urogenital area, urinary flow dysfunction, and sexual dysfunction;

   b. Benign prostatic hyperplasia (BPH) also known as enlarged prostate due to benign cell growth causing more frequent urination

   c. Prostate cancer

Prostate problems are currently being studied. The hypothesis being evaluated is the tie between prostate problems and an undiagnosed viral or bacterial infection. It is believed that BPH may result from a chronic untreated infection and that prostate cancer may be connected to an unhealed prostatitis.

TABLE 7.3. Incidence Rate of Diseases for Men and Women At Midlife

	Men	Women
Disease Category		
Heart Disease[1,2]	6.7	2.6
Stroke[3,4]	5.5	3.9
Cancer: (per 1,000)[5]		
Breast	1.0	208.2
Lung	32.3	22.8
Prostate	22.5	
Colorectal	42.9	35
Diabetes[6]	61.9	41.3

[1] Kannel and Belanger, 1991

[2] Havas, 1992

[3] Wolf et al., 1992

[4] National Cancer Institute, 1993

[5] National Institute of Arthritis, Diabetes, and Digestive and Kidney Diseases, 1985

Lifestyle and Risk Factors Related to Disease

What kind of lifestyle is appropriate for men and women who live twice the lifespan of their grandparents? Despite enjoying one of the highest standards of living, North American men rank only fifteenth in the world regarding longevity. What kind of lifestyle is the U.S. male living such that he is relegated to such a status? The disease rate is relatively low. For most conditions and diseases, the way we live our lives has the greatest influence on delaying and/or preventing physiologic disease and decline. Those who engage in occupations, chores, or hobbies that may be considered dangerous (e.g., construction, household cleaning activities and agents, white-water rafting), are more likely to be injured in those activities. There are also certain occupations that contribute to the development of diseases (e.g., asbestos worker, nuclear power plant worker). Statistics still indicate that men predominate in these occupations.

Men tend to drink more alcohol and smoke more, which particularly results in higher rates of lung cancer (90 percent) and increased risk of heart disease (American Heart Association, 1994).

What are the implications for the widow who is typically younger at the time of marriage?

American men tend to die approximately seven years younger than a female peer. Factors that contribute to men's loss of health include:

1. *Men have far fewer checkups than women.* Regular checkups can influence health and longevity because the majority of diseases, particularly cancers, are curable if detected early.
2. *Men are less likely to practice self-care.* Self-screening is but one example of behavior that can positively influence the health of men. Another includes the importance of sleep in the individual's life. Men, in general, sleep fewer hours, thereby contributing to increased accident rate and decrease in immune system functioning.
3. *Men have poor diets.* There is a tendency to consume more dietary saturated fat and cholesterol obtained through red meats. Men are also less likely to limit sugar, sweets, and coffee and eat too few fruits and vegetables.
4. *Men tend toward being overweight.* Men with 40-inch or more waists are nearly three times more likely to develop heart disease (Andres, Muller, and Sorkin, 1993).
5. *Men are less physically active*—especially between the ages of thirty-five and fifty-four years of age. The weekend warrior mentality tends to lead to increased musculoskeletal straining and injury, which leads to the aforementioned limitations on major activities.
6. *Men drink more and use drugs more.* Men who engage in these types of behavior are likely to experience heart-related damage, immune system damage, and accident-related injury, to name a few.

7. *Men engage in more risk taking.* Vehicle-related death and injury, sports-related injury, and engaging in high-risk sexual behavior are the major contributors to health problems for men.
8. *Men engage in more violence.* Homicide-related death is four times greater for men, and firearm-related injuries are seven times greater in men. Men tend to willingly engage in more overall physical aggression that contributes to health risks.
9. *Men have riskier jobs and suffer more when they lose them.* Unemployment tends to be linked with a variety of negative health factors (to be discussed in a future chapter).
10. *Men have fewer social supports.* It has been shown consistently that a lack of social relations constitutes a risk factor for mortality (Berkman, 1984). Antonucci and Akiyama (1991) have gone so far as to conclude that most men have no close friends.

Leading Killers of Men

As noted earlier and seen in Tables 7.1 and 7.2, men show greater vulnerability to the major killers of midlife individuals—coronary heart disease, cancer, and stroke. Cancer in men and cardiovascular involvement in midlife deaths will be discussed in the following sections.

Cancer

Prostate cancer is a major killer of men over forty, despite the high survival rate with early detection. The average patient with symptoms of prostate problems is near the age of forty. The American Cancer Society projects an estimated 317,000 men will be diagnosed with prostate cancer, with African American men suffering the highest incidence rate.

What might account for this high rate in African American men?

Keeping the prostate gland healthy.

Lifestyle approach.

1. Increase the amount of zinc intake via supplements and diet,
2. drink a lot of water,
3. eat plenty of soy products,
4. reduce the amount of saturated fat in the diet, and
5. eat meals rich in tomatoes.

Other cancers.
a. Lung—cigarette smoking accounts for 90 percent of the disease incidence (American Cancer Society, 1994)
b. Skin—excessive exposure to ultraviolet radiation on the job or during recreation can cause skin cancer

c. Breast—although low in incidence, men are also vulnerable to the development of breast cancer

Cardiovascular

While the picture of coronary heart disease is changing—becoming more of an older man's disease—more midlife men die from cardiovascular-related accidents (see Table 7.2) than from other causes. In addition to the obvious lifestyle factors that contribute to heart disease, smoking and diet, the University of North Carolina Alumni Heart Study suggests that men tend to handle stress by engaging in risky behaviors such as eating more, sleeping less, drinking more caffeine and alcohol, smoking more, and using drugs more. Individuals who rated themselves high in neuroticism were more likely to be practicing risky health-damaging behavior along with the behavioral tendency toward hostility. It is estimated that 86 per 1,000 men will suffer from cardiovascular disease with the total population rate being 3 per 1,000 men.

> *Remember, the sample in the UNC study does not provide a view of the broader population profile of chronic heart disease.*

Other Health Issues for Men

1. HIV and other sexually transmitted diseases are more prevalent for men.
2. Just as women are cautioned with regard to the implantation of silicone for breast enhancement and reconstruction, men should equally be cautioned for the use of silicone packets to enhance their calves and pecs, to reconstruct chins and noses, or for use as penile implants, to name a few. Leaking silicone can have the same negative health effects for men.
3. Liposuction is second only to hair transplant as an elective form of surgery. Liposuction is increasing in popularity for men as they "hope to reshape, restructure, and recapture the bodies of their youth" (Calandra, 2001). Like any form of surgery, this decision must be made with consultation and study of the procedure and expected outcome before committing to it.

This last pattern in men's behavior speaks loudly to pursuing the societal view that young and youthful is the only way to age.

Summary and Comments

The purpose of this chapter was to provide the reader with health factors that become increasingly important to the midlife woman and man. Highlighted were the commonly shared changes that both sexes experience. Later, health factors specific to gender were accounted for. Emphasized was the importance of lifestyle on many of the changes that occur. It was stated that where one was not in control of genetic predispositions, the lifestyle that one adopts can very well impact the quality of the middle and later years. Additional coverage was given to address an increasing predominance of cosmetic surgery being sought by many midlifers today.

With regard to the issue of cosmetic choices being made the midlife individual must ask her-and himself to what degrees she or he is willing to put themselves at a health risk by pursuing the ever-illusive goal of eternal youth. Midlife individuals subject themselves to surgical procedures and to taking untested and tested medication in an attempt to slow the hands of time. At some point the individual reaches the limit on the amount of plastic surgery, collagen injections, and HRT that can be considered safe. Diamond (1997) has been quoted as saying, "the degree of pain [encountered during midlife] is proportional to the degree that we cling to the past and refuse to embrace the future." The medicalization of midlife is one such attempt to run from the inevitable.

How might these choices hurt the person and hurt the generations to come?

I was 18 years old in 1975 and I got married in November. I didn't really want to get married but my mother and my boyfriend both expected it of me. When I moved in with him in June, my mother asked if we were getting married and I told her "YES." He had proposed to me on our second date but I laughed at it. Looking back now, I realize that I only knew him about 6 months before I married him. I was young and stupid. I got pregnant almost immediately. He was thrilled, I was just sick all the time. When I was 5 months pregnant, my doctor finally believed me when I said the baby wasn't moving. In 1976, ultrasound wasn't readily available, so I had to ride 100 miles with a full bladder to Macon to be told the baby wasn't alive. I already knew that. They scheduled my D & C for the next morning, and my husband and I went fishing. Yes, fishing. Hi, my baby's dead, let's go fishing. I never forgave him for that. It still makes me mad today. I almost died in surgery. They had to stop, give me lots of blood, and sent me to ICU. I had repeat surgery 3 days later. For the next 18 months, I had to have blood work done to determine if I had uterine cancer. The condition that killed my baby often leads to cancer in the mother. I was lucky.

Where I grew up, what people expected of me, what I expected of myself—I was brought up to be a good little wife and mother. It was also expected of me that I would work. Women in my family have always worked outside of the home. Of course, they also were great wives and mothers. My mother was one of seven children; of course, I would have kids. When I was in my teens, I kept a book of things to share with my daughter when I had one. It just never occurred to me that I wouldn't have children. I was a disappointment to my father—still don't know what he expected of me, but whatever it was, I failed him. I was never good enough, and it was always clear to me. My Dad was in a secret part of the Air Force; he was gone a lot. Even when he was there, he wasn't there. I was the only girl and the oldest. I took care of my brothers, helped a lot with the house and yard. I taught my youngest brother how to read. I did

(continued)

VOICES OF OUR PARENTS 7.1

expect all this and more of myself. I wasn't a pretty child and I wasn't that popular. I felt like I'd failed in some way. When I was 16, my first serious boyfriend proposed to me and gave me a tiny diamond. Boy, did I rub some noses in that at school!

I was date raped when I was 15. My boyfriend and his friend raped me. I never told my mother. I was terrified that I would get pregnant. Didn't help my psyche, either. My friends were into more drugs than I ever was. I smoked pot 3–4 times, but it made me really paranoid. I always felt like an alarm was going off at the police station. My Mother worked for the police department. I was always afraid of drugs. I was a pretty uptight kid. This was in Georgia, where ladies were still expected to be ladies. I was real vulnerable, so I tried to stay away from people who could hurt me. When I was 16, I ran away from home to Virginia with my boyfriend. He hit me a lot, so eventually I came back. I had a roommate for a while who was high all the time. She'd have over all these guys she didn't even know and they would all climb into bed together. I just wasn't into that scene. But I was really screwed up sexually. I was equating sex with love. Did that a long time, thought that sex and love were the same thing.

Boys were . . . it depended. Some of them were really cool and I could talk to them. Some were abusive like my father.

Girls were . . . expected to do everything they were told and to keep quiet about it.

How my life was supposed to be. I was supposed to be happily married with my little family around me. My job would be great, my husband would worship me, and my kids would be perfect.

Identity—It's taken me a lot of years to figure out my identity. The outward me changed a lot, but the inward me didn't. I was still deep down a scared little girl, who needed a man to make her whole. Some days I still do. But, over the years, I've come to realize that June Cleaver wasn't all that happy. Life didn't turn out the way I planned it, but it's a fairly decent life anyway. There are things I'd like to change and that I would have done differently. But this is the only life I have, so I might as well make the most of it.

Back then, I knew I wasn't going to marry a man like my father. So, I married one who was pretty opposite. Didn't work. I had issues with my father to work out. I've worked them out—without my father. He isn't interested—what a surprise! I was going to save the world. Well, I haven't saved the whole thing but I have saved a few people. That'll have to do.

Confidence and certainty—Didn't have either one of those when I was young. They come more with experience, I think. Confidence, anyway. I'm not sure I've ever experienced certainty.

What I now know, for sure. Life is hard. It doesn't necessarily get easier, but you learn better ways to cope. Marriage and children aren't for everyone. We all get lonely, but we have to learn to be with ourselves. Loving yourself is the best thing you will ever do. Live your life fully. Play as hard as you work.

VOICES OF OUR PARENTS 7.1

PERSONAL PROFILE

Age :   44

Region raised in: I was raised everywhere. My father was in
                          the Air Force. My parents both came from
                          New England.

Military service: none
Any college: BSN in Nursing   Major-Nursing
First career opportunity: I worked in a fast food restaurant in
                               Charlottesville, VA.

Current career: Critical care nurse. Currently trying to decide
                          what I want to be when I grow up.

Changes in career in between then and now: I have done many
things for a living over the years. I was a military wife and we took what
jobs were available. I have inspected food and coke bottles, spray painted
car parts, cashiered, been a nurse's aid, a crossing guard, a receptionist, a
military interpreter. I've taught first aid to military trainees. Lots more.
For the last 15 years, I've been a nurse. I'm burnt out, I need a change.

Marital history: Married for 18 years, divorced at 36 years old. Half
of my life with one man. Now divorced for almost 8 years. One long-
term significant relationship since then, that really screwed my head up.
Went into therapy while I was dating him, and on antidepressants. Still
on/off in my life, mostly because I am truly addicted to this man. I want
him out completely but am still working on it.

Children: 5 pregnancies, no children. 4 miscarriages, one
                          molar pregnancy—an abnormal pregnancy in
                          which the fetus is destroyed by the placentas
                          overgrowth

Pets: 2 cats, one dog right now. My dog is 15 years old.

VOICES OF OUR PARENTS 7.1

CHAPTER 8

Fertility and Menopause

Sometimes I feel that this is my last chance at everything: life, love, success, children. Just all of it.

—56-YEAR-OLD MAN

I know what the statistics say. Maybe I've waited too long, but I think my eggs are still good. I can have a baby.

—42-YEAR-OLD WOMAN

There are numerous issues of a more immediate nature than menopause that affect women in their middle years.

—JACOBSON, 1995

In a society that places so much value on youth and beauty, it's not much fun to think about menopause. But when you get there, you find it really doesn't make that much difference; you concentrate on how you feel about yourself, not on how you think others see you.

—50-SOMETHING WOMAN
NIH PUBLICATION ON MENOPAUSE, 1992

OVERVIEW

In this chapter, **fertility** and **menopause** are placed in the context of normal changes that accompany increasing age for men and women. Factors such as health, sense of self, support from families and friends, and a sense of control will all impact the ease of traversing this period of life. Perhaps the most surprising section concerns **male menopause**. This relatively new phenomenon will be discussed and carried forward to other chapters.

THE MIDLIFE WOMAN:
MENOPAUSE AND FERTILITY

It may come as a surprise to some of you, but menopause is not the overriding issue in every discussion of the woman's midlife transition (Jacobson, 1995). Before discussing menopausal/fertility changes in midlife, it is important to point out that women need to be informed consumers regarding their physical and psychological health. Women need to take charge of their medical care and take the time to find a physician with whom they can talk openly and honestly and in whom they trust. They also should feel that they have the right to pursue a second opinion, not only in life-threatening situations but also in the less dramatic decisions concerning health care and maintenance. Underlying this emphasis on taking personal responsibility for one's medical health care is a severe lack of knowledge, both medically and scientifically, regarding women's health issues.

These statements are not meant to minimize the capabilities and potential contributions of the medical community to health in midlife. However, there has been a tradition in viewing midlife women as being considered ill and in need of treatment. From this perspective, the concomitant changes that accompany midlife are things to be "fixed" as if the midlife woman is "broken" (Greer, 1991). Many ageist physicians couch treatments in the context of "maintaining (the *illusion* of) youth" (Greer 1991). They appeal to the fears and vanities of women. Being an "older" woman in a culture obsessed with youth is daunting.

The medical community can offer assistance with the changes that do occur and that impact health and wellness. There are conditions accompanying midlife that are evident and can be treated—treated for increased comfort and improved quality of life *but* not to be young again. What needs to be changed is the view that there is something pathological about the midlife woman. There are gender-specific changes that occur in health, some pathological; many, however, are normal and should be treated as such. Recognition of normality must be made by women and the medical community in the United States. Not to do so will result in increased mental and emotional pain for the woman when she inevitably comes to the point when the reality of age presents itself.

BRIEF HISTORICAL AND CULTURAL
COMMENTS ON WOMEN'S HEALTH ISSUES
AND MIDLIFE IN WOMEN

At the turn of the twentieth century, there were few women that could be classified as midlife women. Yet, there were women who were not young and of childbearing age any longer, nor were they hump-backed "old crones" (Greer, 1991). They were in the middle, experiencing the change of life. If they complained or manifested any behavior thought to be unsuitable by their husband (or other man in their life), such women ran the risk of being institutionalized. Their treatment consisted of a variety of approaches to deal with the symptoms brought about by a problematic uterus. A review of the types of treatments, radiation and hydrotherapy to name two, can be found in Greer and Chesler (1972). Some of these women never left the asylum.

From the Victorian era to the present day, women have been silent with regard to the physical and psychological changes happening to them. This silence may reflect one or all of the following: (1) fear of being seen as old, (2) fear of being tagged a whiner or hypochondriac, and (3) ignorance resulting from a lack of a model to guide her. Gail Sheehy (1995a) speaks of this as the silent passage.

It has been posited that the reason Western women are experiencing such a range of emotions (usually negative) during this point in the life span is because this particular transition or turning point in life goes unmarked and unrecognized (Greer, 1991). It is argued (Bolen, 1994; Greer 1991) that this transition requires some form of rite of passage recognition as have other points of transition (e.g., births, weddings, academic graduations, etc.). Women birthing babies for the first time have the guidance and support of other individuals who have already experienced this; advice on marriage always has its share of commentators and opinions; and the graduate has watched others go before her, hearing their hopes dreams and fears about this time. The midlife woman is alone serving as her own counsel with no one to help her celebrate this transition.

Some societies reward women for their service when they reach the end of fertility. This is frequently marked by an increase in freedom and status that they lacked during their reproductive years. Women who live in such cultures suffer far less physically than other women, Western women in particular (Evans, 1988). As mentioned previously, some Native American cultures consider women of this age as sages, Muslim women in some societies are given more public freedom and the right to shed the veil, and Mayan women mark this time with new societal freedom (Berk, 2001). We need not leave our Western culture to see the changing and adoption of a new role for the midlife woman. An examination of the patterns of midlife African American females' status and behavior rarely reveals signs of depression during middle age. Often the "grannie" or "auntie" lives with the family and cares for the children while the children's parents work. The midlife woman attains new status in the family, has had models in the past, and finds this new role acceptable. Society's response to the European American Caucasian woman is best characterized in Leontief's poem "Painting in Pompeii":

> We shut the album on the mother
>
> who's always crying
>
> always wild
>
> with unrequited love

UNIVERSAL PHYSICAL CHANGES AT, DURING, OR AS A RESULT OF MENOPAUSE

1. *Bone loss.* Women experience two times the bone loss that men experience. As a result, the bones in the skeleton are less strong, more brittle, break more easily, and heal more slowly. The reasons underlying these changes, typically beginning at age fifty, were specified in chapter 7. The degree and speed of this bone loss are less for dark-haired, dark-eyed, and tall women. Existing data suggest that African American women are at less of a risk for hip and spinal fracture than are white women. The explanation for this is that more bone is laid down in their childhood and youth. Therefore, they have more bone to lose than does the fair, small-boned woman. One lifestyle factor cited as a way to strengthen bones in general is for the individual to engage in aerobic, weight-bearing exercise.
2. *Weight gain.* The general trend with regard to weight gain includes the increase in abdominal and hip width. The most marked growth is "below the belt," by approximately 23–35 percent of young adult dimensions.
3. *Nonfatal chronicities and immune system changes.* Table 7.2 shows the prevalence of the leading chronic conditions. Examination of this table shows that women have a higher prevalence of nonfatal chronicities such as arthritis, varicose veins, and bursitis. This table also indicates that the conditions experienced during midlife are nonfatal. It has also been pointed out that the woman's immune system is stronger and thus more resistant to diseases in general. In this sense, the woman is the more hearty of the sexes. Women show a significant advantage in mortality until about age fifty-four. They then become increasingly susceptible to coronary heart disease. This increase in risk is associated with the dropping estrogen levels at menopause. One can interpret these findings as suggesting that the older woman will live longer than the older man but will experience poorer health.
4. *Changes in fertility rate during menopause.* At birth, a girl's ovaries contain approximately 500,000 eggs.

Do you understand the generation effect? The quality of the egg from which you came was most directly impacted by the healthfulness of your maternal grandmother's pregnancy.

Over the course of her reproductive life, only 400 to 500 eggs will fully ripen and be released during menstruation. Between the ages of 25–37 the woman's ability to get pregnant is about the same. Then a drop occurs in ability to get pregnant, with a success rate of slightly better than 30 percent at age 38. Another drop occurs around age 40 to a 22 percent probability. Beyond age 43, there is only a 3–4 percent chance for a woman to get pregnant and have a healthy child (Sheehy, 1995b).

Underlying this more or less steady drop in fertility, are the increasing number of **anovulatory** cycles experienced by the woman. Beginning in her 30s, the number of **ovarian follicles** decline (Avis, 1999). This decrease continues until between ages 45 and 55, at which time the ovaries become chiefly scar tissue, that produce no ova and little estrogen (Memmler and Wood, 1987). **Estrogen** production does not stop. With the cessation of the ovaries' contribution to **estradiol** production, other forms of estrogen, such as **estrone,** are produced by the **adrenal gland,** and there is peripheral conversion of other circulating hormones such as **testosterone.**

The Medicalization of Menopause

Reducing menopause to medical conditions such as an estrogen deficiency disease makes it more understandable to many Western women. If it can be tagged as a disease, then it can be treated or controlled. Menopause is looked upon as an "it" rather than a "process." Many women find solace in having the words of menopause in their vocabulary. Terms such as **perimenopause, post-menopause, climacteric,** and **amenorrhea** roll off their tongues as easily as their names. As if knowing the words makes them different, more knowledgeable, more sophisticated, more worldly, but in reality the words make them no more in control than before. The better able you are to distance yourself with technical terms, the more distanced you are from the process. The individuals engaged in distancing will be fighting a very long battle—fifteen–twenty years. By virtue of distancing from this inevitable process, they will lose the opportunity for better personal examination and understanding of themselves. These women and men invest in the myths of menopause and communicate these myths to friends, fellow workers, and their children.

> *Sometimes, those so invested in the myths carry them out. Therefore, the myths become validated and are perpetuated.*

These myths (Avis, 2001; Banner, 1990; Doress and Siegal, 1994; Green and Cooke, 1976; Green and Cooke, 1980; Jacobson, 1995) include:

- all women in midlife become depressed and neurotic
- the change of life is an illness
- if a family member suffered from depression, you will inevitably experience depression
- you will become useless to society
- you will become sexually ugly and unappealing
- your bones will become brittle and dissolve
- memory loss is inevitable
- insomnia is to be expected

Is it possible that much of the discomfort, physical and psychological, expressed by Western women is a reflection of the degree of stress and frustration the women have in dealing with their society at this time?

The perpetuation of these stereotypical beliefs is often found to be a result of menopausal checklists filled out by women postmenopausally. Parlee (1974) argues that the stereotypical beliefs about menopause influence the accuracy of women's recall. The time lapse, between the beginning and end of menopause is anywhere from ten–twenty years. Often respondents to the survey default to what they believe was associated with a particular phase for the symptoms they had, but were unable to recall any specifics with accuracy. The majority of what we know about the effect of menopause on women's lives is a reflection of reports from clinical samples, in other words, women who have sought medical help. They do not reflect the average, nonclinical, sample of women in society. This is not meant to dismiss the importance of monitoring one's physical health or seeking medical help for actual problems. It is meant to highlight the naturalness of the physical process of maturing. It is time to move on to become what you are becoming and not invest yourself in recreating who you were.

Social Occurrences that May be Underlying Many Menopausal Complaints

- divorce
- biological illness (cancer, heart disease, osteoporosis, etc.)
- death of a spouse, a parent, or a child
- caring for aging, sick parents (a role expected to be enacted by the daughter or daughter-in-law)
- physical changes, including wrinkles, graying hair, weight gain, and so on
- alcoholism (self or family members)
- adolescent children and the ability to see them as individuals
- the balancing of work and home responsibilities
- lack of accurate information about the menopausal transition
- negative societal expectations and portrayals
- unaware and unsympathetic family members
- the empty-nest syndrome (the inability of some parents to refocus and redirect their lives after their children grow up and leave home)

Might not all of these myths of menopause be able to be explained by the overwhelming social changes listed here?

Take a minute, and match these to the behavioral outcomes that you find in the myths of menopause list.

The Physiology of Menopause

Menopause is most clearly seen as a change in the production of a variety of hormones. A decrease in ovarian hormones causes an increase in the secretion of **follicle-stimulating hormone** (FSH) and **leutinizing hormone** (LH). The levels of FSH can increase to thirteen times the normal level and LH to three times the normal level in an attempt to stimulate ovulation. During this period, the woman can be considered to be in a hyperestrogen level state. These levels reflect the state of hormones in the system within a year of menstrual cessation (Sloane, 1980). The changes observed in menopause are primarily hormonal, which result in the possibility of vasomotor instability yielding **vasomotor flushes** (presence, frequency, and intensity may be exacerbated by medications being taken such as antidepressants and antianxiety medications); **hot flashes; night sweats;** and the thinning of the vaginal lining, also called **atropic urogenital changes,** due to a lack of estrogen. These hormonal changes may impact as many as 75 percent of menopausal women. It has been found, however, that only 25 percent of menopausal women report them to physicians, with only half of these women (13.5 percent) having symptoms severe enough to be medicated.

Estrogen-related changes in bone mass, cardiovascular integrity, and cognitive functioning have been reported. Of these, estrogen-related bone mass has the strongest medical and empirical support. The other changes are still correlational and require further investigation to find a causal explanation.

SOCIETAL, INDIVIDUAL, AND CULTURAL VIEWS OF THE MENOPAUSAL WOMAN

The Society

The number of individuals traversing middle age (thirty-five–sixty-four years of age) is relatively new, a phenomenon of the mid-twentieth century. However, there have always been pockets of individuals living beyond their reproductive years into what could be called an older age. As statistics show, not many individuals were able to make it to that point. It was the lucky woman who did not succumb to the diseases of the time or die in childbirth. Mother and housewife were the two (and usually only) roles assigned to a woman. The negative views of menopause harbored by seventeenth and eighteenth century Western societies are still evident, to a lesser degree, in today's twenty-first century. Women were assigned the term "barren" should they be unable to bear children.

> *The man's contribution to fertility was never acknowledged. To some extent it is still the case.*

Menopause further stripped the woman of one of her acceptable roles, and as a result, negative attitudes began to emerge regarding menopause.

Menopause, at the turn of the century, was viewed as an illness, and according to some individuals (Tilt, 1857) was the cause of over 100 diseases, including tuberculosis and diabetes. By the end of the nineteenth century, the midlife woman was seen as suffering from a deficiency disease, and so began the slow but steady trek to the practice of hormone replacement therapy seen today. This approach continues to reflect the mindset of fixing a broken woman, rather than on responding to symptomatic problems associated with a normal process. It is hoped today's Western woman will begin to see menopause not as a negative commentary on her ability to continue her reproductive responsibilities, but to see this as a period of freedom from the responsibility of contraception and the annoyance of any symptoms associated with menstrual periods.

In 1960, the menopausal woman was referred to as a hump-backed individual, with a rigid, dry vaginal tube, hair growing from her face, and breasts covered with course skin and scales (Wilson, 1966).

While absurd, this message shows up in contemporary fiction. For example, "Petra was young and attractive, full of life and her interest in it . . . Elizabeth was menopausal and unattractive both to look at and to know. . ." (Starling, 2000, 218). Thirty-four years separate the writings, but the message is still there—there is something inherently wrong and unattractive with this normal part of life.

> *Look at the media, sources of fiction and nonfiction, and the film industry. Where do you see adherence to this view of the menopausal woman and where do you find exceptions? What do you think underlies the exceptions?*

The Individual

Consistent with the perspective of Costa and McCrae (1980), that personality remains relatively stable over the course of the life span, is the view that a woman's response to menopause is a function of the woman's premenopausal personality and similar to her initial reactions to puberty (Benedek, 1950; Deutsch, 1945). Similarly, Bart and Grossman (1978) stated that menopause does not turn a healthy functioning woman into an involutional psychotic. Several factors have been found to be related to a woman's view of menopause. They include:

1. the value she places on being young and attractive,
2. her views of women and roles in general,
3. how she views her family and career situation, and
4. other physiological changes.

The Young Woman Versus the Older Woman

Premenopausal and young women:

1. have adopted a negative view of menopause and
2. prefer to accept the medical view of menopause.

Menopausal and postmenopausal women:

1. have an ever-increasing positive view as they experience menopause,
2. express general feelings of relief, and
3. describe feelings of increased energy and postmenopausal zest.

Surgical menopause: An atypical group:

1. are more likely to hold negative attitudes.

The Culture

The culture in which the individual resides will also play a major role in this transition. The interaction of the biological, psychological, and sociological aspects of menopause are seen when one looks cross-culturally at the menopause experience. Examination of the data has established that menopause symptomology differs across cultures. The general findings include:

1. European Americans who could be described as highly-bred, civilized women; those with many troubles and ills are the primary sufferers of severe menopausal symptomology (Currier, 1897).
2. Different experiences were noted in Eskimos and Native Americans who reported few, if any, menopausal symptoms (Currier, 1897).
3. Hot flashes are uncommon in Mayan women (Beyene, 1986).
4. Fewer hot flashes are reported by Japanese and Indonesian women than are reported by Western women (Agoestina and van Keep, 1984; Lock, 1986).
5. There are lower levels of vasomotor and psychological complaints among menopausal Asian women in general (Payer, 1991).

Information such as this is plentiful. However, the important point is to recognize that how a society views menopause is a direct reflection of how it views aging women in general. Menopause is seen in a more positive light in cultures that impose strict behavioral prohibitions on menstruating women. In India the postmenopausal woman is given significantly more freedom in the public domain. In South Asia, the end of the childbearing years is positively greeted. In this Asian culture, social status is tied to motherhood and not to fertility (Avis, 1999; Vatuk, 1992). In Polynesian culture, menopause appears to be a nonissue to the extent that there is no word in the language for menopause. Similarly, the Japanese have no word for hot flashes.

In Western societies, where women are apparently valued for their sexual attractiveness and do not face the restrictions of other cultures, aging is not revered but viewed negatively. The negative view of menopause is found more in the society as a whole than among menopausal women. It is not surprising then to find the women in these societies in a fix-it mode.

A comparative analysis of Canadian women, Japanese women, and women of the United States was conducted by Avis (1999) and is one of the few cross-cultural investigations regarding menopausal meaning in the literature. The physiological and psychological aspects of menopause were investigated and reported by culture and point in time of menopause. The general conclusion suggested that although the cessation of reproductive capability is universally experienced by all women, the stereotypical psychological and physiological symptoms (i.e., depression or vasomotor instabilities) of menopause are not universally experienced.

> *What can Western women do to impact this culturally-held stereotype of menopausal women?*

Internationally, it appears that the majority of women have other events in their lives that they consider to be more important than the end of the menstrual cycle.

> *What is the possible interpretation of this final sentence?*

THE MIDLIFE MAN: MALE MENOPAUSE

Male menopause has also been termed **viropause** or **andropause** and has been defined as the hormonal, physiological, and chemical changes that occur in all men between the ages of 40 and 55 (range: 35–65 years of age). The changes that occur can affect all aspects of a man's life. The more precipitous the drop, the more dramatic the behavioral and psychological changes. Some of the changes that occur, that can serve as markers for male menopause, can include:

1. a loss of potency via premature ejaculation or inability to have an erection,
2. hot flashes,
3. a tendency to be nervous, indecisive in actions, confusion, and prone to angry outbursts, and
4. sleeplessness.

Lowered levels of certain neurochemicals are central to these and other changes encountered by the man. Those chemicals showing the greatest changes include:

1. **dopamine**—a neurotransmitter located in the arcuate nucleus of the brain, possessing many interesting qualities, one of which is motor movement
2. **oxytocin**—a peptide secreted from the posterior lobe of the pituitary gland, contributing to feelings of well-being and emotional bonding
3. **vasopressin**—also secreted from the same general area of the pituitary impacting the ability to focus attention; it is growth hormone, found in all neurons, with the ability to repair damaged neurons and thereby improve cognitive functioning
4. **melatonin**—produced in the pineal gland referred to as an antioxidant, and has most popularly become known as impacting the quality of sleep

5. **DHEA**—a steroid hormone, mainly produced in the adrenals, is the most abundant hormone in the body, and has been implicated in sexual functioning
6. **pregnenolone**—another steroid hormone that uses cholesterol for its manufacture and has been said to impact memory and cognitive functioning
7. **testosterone**—produced in the testes and is said to affect maturation of male genitalia and sperm production, among other things (Crenshaw, 1996).

The study of neurotransmitters and hormones and their impact on the human is still in the early stages of testing. The long-range impact of hormone replacement therapy for men is not known, and its prescription should be approached cautiously. The decline in the production of these hormones is a normal part of the maturing male's physiology. Given the existence for the potential abuse of such chemicals, the man needs to be an informed consumer taking personal responsibility for his health. One should be cautioned for looking at male menopause as one more example of a hormone deficiency disease, rather than one more example of a normal process.

What is the definition of a disease?

The physiological literature shows that not only is there a drop in the various hormone levels, a parallel drop is found in the receptor sites in the brain for these hormones. Therefore, flooding the system with hormones will not increase the number of receptor sites in the brain and has the potential to create negative side effects (Kelly, 2001).

Medical Response to Men Expressing Male Menopausal Symptoms

Since the physiology of the midlife man is as poorly understood as that of the midlife woman, the common medical response to expressed behavioral and emotional problems is the prescription of antidepressants or Viagra. The response of the medical community reflects the narrow and restricted view of men in Western society. Men in Western society are rarely given the opportunity to explore a diversity of emotions and behaviors beginning as early as infancy. Men's roles, responses, and responsibilities are tightly regulated, and men are given little permission to deviate from these assignments. Therefore there is a slow public and medical response to the psychological and physical needs of the maturing midlifer. Only recently has there been a public acknowledgment of erectile dysfunction and urinary functioning problems and incontinence in men.

Fertility

While there are still cases reported of men fathering children into their 70s and 80s, the quantity of viable sperm begins to decrease in the late 40s to 50s. This drop in sperm viability is tied to the normal drop in testosterone beginning in early adulthood and continuing through life. It has been reported that once a man turns 25, the older he is, the longer it takes for him to make his partner pregnant (Ford, 2001). As men get into their 30s, the quality of the man's sperm is also being considered as a cause of infertility.

Statistics have shown that as men age:

1. couples tend to have sex less often;
2. changes in their testes could impact the quality of the sperm;
3. as a result of long term exposure to environmental toxins and or disease, sperm can be damaged; and
4. miscarriages are more commonly linked to the age of the father, factoring out the age of the woman.

Just as with most thirty-something women, men have biological clocks ticking away. Research into their contribution to infertility is only now being investigated, and results are some years away.

Summary and Comments

Changing hormone status has been implicated throughout this chapter as a major factor in the physical and health changes beginning at midlife. Hormones are neither the only issue nor the only answer as one approaches and traverses this period. The medical community is still in the early stages of researching and understanding the implications of hormone use at any age, let alone at midlife. Men and women should not look to the hormone as a panacea to the process of growing older. It is not a magic bullet.

Adolescent Mama

The curved silhouette loomed back at me
A snapshot of my sin in shadow
a thin, frail standing child.
My imperfection well pronounced,
the extrusion of my body, proof of dark excursions

What is said of a woman in the flesh of a child?
Or the chicken before the proverbial egg
Too fast that girl, no good she'll be
Touché, the prophecy's fulfilled
Give the predictor a golden star
It came to life
This child within me grows

Fifteen in years
Still skipping rope
Not mama's plans, not for me
Too innocent, I cannot cope
Still wet behind naive ears
The future I cannot see
Budding hair still new to my frame
yet to reach maturity

My chest mounds
spoke a foreign tongue
Saying yes with its firmness, its scent
flirting unabashed
When he came around
Now nowhere to be found

Yesterday, only a game
I still had a doll baby to name
quickly taken away
now rock, rock
rock the cradle
the real thing

Thank God, Mama's here
To raise us both
Watch us grow
Send us to school
Little girl no more
my baby's cries for a lullaby
Just a mistake, my daddy says
no one has to die

I still wonder where the daddy is
When I hug and kiss my son

VOICES OF OUR PARENTS 8.1

PERSONAL PROFILE

Age:	50
Region raised in:	Upper South Carolina—City of Greenville, Greenville County
Military service:	None
Any college:	2 years—Major: Business
First career opportunity:	Criminal Justice—Legal Secretary, paralegal
Current career:	Secretary, Graphic Designer
Marital history:	1 failed, 1 current
Children:	1 son—35 years
Pets:	Just my husband

VOICES OF OUR PARENTS 8.1

NG is a 44 year old dentist. Like many women, I assumed that I could get pregnant any time before age 50. I got established in my career by the time I was 30. I looked for a partner, but was unable to find one. I decided then to go it alone as a mother. Starting at age 38, I tried artificial insemination from a sperm donor. After 5 years of trying, 3 miscarriages, and over $40,000, I realized that it wasn't going to happen.

Right now I'm looking into adoption.

PERSONAL PROFILE

Age:	44
Region raised in:	Northeast
Military service:	None
College:	BS, chemistry then a DDS
First career opportunity:	Dentist
Marital history:	Single
Children:	None

VOICES OF OUR PARENTS 8.2

CHAPTER 9

Cognitive Processes in Midlife

The chemo treatments really affected my memory. I couldn't keep two ideas in my head at a time. Everyone was really worried. I'm back to normal now.

—50-YEAR-OLD WOMAN

I sometimes think that young folks know a lot from books, but don't have much day-to-day sense. At least I got that.

—48-YEAR-OLD WOMAN

You've got to keep your brain active. I read 3 newspapers a day. I think that helps me stay sharp and current.

—50-YEAR-OLD MAN

I worry a lot about my memory failing. I have 4 kids, all going in different directions and I'm supposed to keep track of all of it.

—45-YEAR-OLD WOMAN

OVERVIEW

How one thinks about the world and how one processes the information one is given, in a general way, reflect the health of one's neurological and sensory systems and the way one was taught (explicitly or implicitly) to think about the world. These perceptions are influenced by one's personal history, cultural traditions and values, and the times in which one lives. Cognitive processing can be influenced by a myriad of factors reflective of health-related considerations, psychological well-being, family, work, or educational status, to name a few. One must also remember that cognitive processing is involved in every aspect of human behavior. We are always working with information. How we do it and why we do it the way we do are a complex and interactive process.

This chapter will be divided into the following sections: (1) a general review of memory functioning; (2) intelligence in adulthood, including every day problem solving and wisdom and psychometric measures of intelligence; and (3) cultural differences in memory and intellectual functioning.

A General Review of Memory Functioning

Memory involves the ability to detect relevant information; **encode** it into a useable form; and **retrieve** it when necessary to carry out a task, whether it be remembering a series of numbers for a long distance telephone call, remembering the name of a friend, or recalling items to purchase at the grocery. It is not uncommon to hear people of all ages complain about their memory functioning. However, midlifers tend to take memory failures a bit more seriously out of fear of impending **dementia** or worse, **Alzheimer's disease.** While there exist numerous models of and presentations of memory functioning, the most commonly presented view is that of a three-store model of memory (Atkinson and Shiffrin, 1971). These stores are:

1. Sensory—the first contact with information be it a sound, a smell, a sight, a taste, or a particular touch. The information being transferred from this store (i.e., **sensation**) is assigned meaning (i.e., **perception**) such as the voice of your professor, the smell of spring flowers, a beautiful piece of architecture, the taste of a cold beverage or the touch of cotton. Upon the assignment of meaning to the sensory information, the signal is then transferred to the short-term store.
2. Short-term—a brief holding system said to be the seat of conscious thought. The capacity of this store is relatively small, five–nine individual items, and the duration of information in this store is brief in duration, depending on the source. Information, when it is not being used in conscious activity or processed via some memory strategy, rehearsal for example, will be lost.
3. Long-term—considered to be relatively limitless in its capacity and storage time. Information is routinely accessed via retrieval processes, for example, recall or recognition, from the long-term store and used in the short-term store (conscious awareness). When the information is no longer required or of interest, it is encoded, in its new or original form, and returned to the long-term store.

Most researchers of memory and cognitive processing would assert that a critical element of memory functioning involves the process of attention. **Attention** (Cowan, 1982) is defined as the mechanism responsible for continued cognitive functioning. Attentional processes are limited, such that all stimuli are not available for processing simultaneously, and selective, in that effort may be directed toward focusing on particular information (Willingham and Goedert, 2001). Failures in attention due to distraction or fatigue will have a negative impact on information encoded or retrieved.

A memory failure can occur at any of the aforementioned processing stages, due to encoding or transfer problems brought about by any of the following factors:

1. attention failure or distractions
2. stress
3. anxiety
4. depression
5. loss and grief
6. lack of physical activity
7. certain physical illnesses
8. certain medications
9. alcohol use/misuse
10. poor nutrition

In addition to midlife being the prime of life, midlife adults may confront a variety of factors that may influence their cognitive well-being. Can you see how any or all of these factors influence the cognitive functioning of midlife adults in your life?

Many of these are discussed in the chapter on health-related factors in midlife (chapter 7). Factors such as depression, loss and grief, and psychological stress will be discussed in a later chapter addressing psychological well-being and identity in midlife (chapter 10).

Most of the research on human cognitive performance has been laboratory-based in an attempt to control for potentially confounding factors. The specific influences of culture and context are purposefully and selectively eliminated from most experimental designs. Much of the research reported here reflects this limited, nonecological approach to memory and intelligence research. This is an unfortunate limitation of the field. However, available ecologically based treatment of memory and intellectual functioning is provided whenever possible.

Memory research that includes the midlife adult in the sample is nearly nonexistent. The most common form of empirical investigation is what Hertzog (1985) refers to as an **extreme groups design** in that only young and old adults are compared. The impact of this type of research is that one is left to make assumptions regarding the course of cognitive change. Is there a steady decline from young adulthood, a plateau through adulthood, a continued increase followed by decline, a vacillation in performance across adulthood, and so on?

There is, however, limited research that has, as part of the research design, included midlife adults. A few information-processing studies of cross-sectional design have included age groups across the span of adulthood, and results from these studies provide a window on how mid-life individuals stack up against younger and older adults in the realm of cognitive processing. A study by Kirasic, et al. (1996) serves as an excellent example. Results showed that although accumulated ability, such as vocabulary, increased steadily into old age, information-processing capabilities, such as processing speed and **working memory** (i.e., retaining information temporarily while doing other mental tasks), showed a decline that is small into midlife but more substantial into later adulthood. Importantly, learning speed was found to decline after early adulthood, again minimally up to age fifty, and more noticeably thereafter. In short, these experimental results agree with those of psychometric studies; knowledge-based abilities are maintained or increase slightly, while cognitive speed and flexibility decrease slightly. As an information processor, the midlife adult is extremely competent. It could be said that a slight decline in speed of learning novel material (and speed of processing in general) is compensated for by increased knowledge and acquired expertise. Therein lies the bulk of planned, midlife inclusive, research on memory functioning.

INTELLIGENCE IN ADULTHOOD

What Is Intelligence?

Over the past decade it has become increasingly more difficult to make a clear and unchallenged statement regarding intellectual ability and **intelligence.** While there is limited agreement as to what intelligence *is,* there is greater agreement regarding what intelligence *does.* Most researchers of intelligence will agree that intelligent thought and behavior are a result of conscious and deliberate processes aimed at identifying and solving problems. There is nothing accidental about intelligent thought. Despite this limited agreement, consensus begins to dissolve at the intersection of cultures. Different cultures have different views of what is intelligent; therefore it again becomes difficult to frame a clear, uniform, and unshakable understanding of intelligent thought and behavior.

A review of the intelligence-testing domain inevitably leads at some point to the discussion of crystallized and fluid intelligence; a comment on different types of intelligence; and to perhaps, a brief mention of the most recent writings on mindlessness and sideways thinking. Issues of mature thought, day-to-day thinking and problem solving, and wisdom are given a token nod. The substance of any chapter section addressing this issue tends to fall into a lengthy discussion of the Seattle Longitudinal Study and the performance of the test population on the Wechsler Adult Intelligence Scale (WAIS).

While that approach has been the tried-and-true method of presenting adult intelligence, perhaps the best way to approach the findings regarding the midlife adult's intelligence is to present it in a less traveled format. It is highly likely that the individuals at the zenith of their careers, at the highest level of responsibility, in what has been called "the prime of life" (Neugarten, 1968) enjoy intelligence that does have at its foundation a rigid psychometric structure, but which manifests in a less laboratorylike and more real-world way. For this reason, we begin our discussion with crystallized and fluid intelligence, emphasizing the importance of different types of intelligence, and a thorough discussion of mindlessness and sideways thinking in addition to everyday problem solving and thinking with comment on the burgeoning of wisdom.

Additionally, differences found on traditional tests of intelligence that highlight gender differences will then be covered.

Crystallized and Fluid Intelligence

A line of research that has added greatly to the understanding of intelligence test performance has been the specification of two types of abilities, namely **crystallized intelligence** and **fluid intelligence.** Briefly, these two types of intelligence reflect a divergence between a type of intelligence that is relatively enduring and at times improving across the life span reflecting a form of intelligence largely affected by culture and a type of intelligence affected primarily by genetic and physiological factors (Cattell, 1965; Horn, 1967, 1968, 1970, 1982a, 1982b).

Crystallized intelligence is reflected in the ability to apply information acquired through formal learning and through life experience. The emphasis is on the influence of education and culture. Crystallized intelligence depends on well-learned, often automatic, processing in situations requiring skills grounded in what has been called **semantic memory.** Semantic memory is involved in situations that require language skills and mathematical skills, application of known facts and social customs, and is reflective of crystallized abilities. Typically, crystallized abilities are measured by tests that require vocabulary skill, general information, analogies, and knowledge of one's cultural functioning (traditions, values, customs, etc.).

Fluid intelligence is reflected in the ability to process novel information with which one has had little previous experience. This type of intelligence is based on the perception of complex relationships, implications, and inferences. The tasks chosen to measure fluid abilities are primarily speeded measures placing strong demands on the integrity of the nervous system. It is not surprising then, to learn that declines are observed in fluid abilities over the course of the life span as the transmission of neural signals have been shown to slow with age. Figure 9.1, page 100, graphically demonstrates the differences between the two.

Why might a slowing in response to stimuli be considered beneficial?

Impact on the Midlife Adult. How are these types of intelligence relevant to the midlife adult? Some midlife adults may report that they are unable to think as fast as they once did, that taking in new information takes longer. These types of personal reports can be said to reflect self-perceived, subtle changes in fluid abilities. These subjective reports may well reflect the changes that researchers observe in laboratory studies of fluid and crystallized abilities. It has been reported that fluid abilities begin to show a decline in young adulthood around age 25, while crystallized abilities begin to peak around this time and improve through midlife to approximately age seventy-two, and often

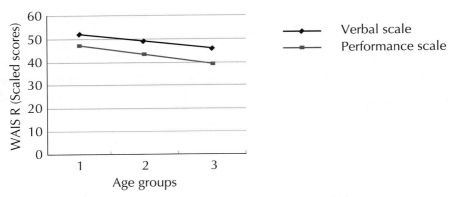

FIGURE 9.1. Pattern of verbal and performance measures at midlife.

GROUP 1—35–44 YEARS
GROUP 2—45–54 YEARS
GROUP 3—55–64 YEARS

Source: Botwinick 1984.

until near the end of life (Botwinick, 1978). Decline in these abilities is relatively insubstantial in healthy adults. Declines most noticeably occur in those individuals developing health problems that impact the flow of blood, oxygen, and nutrients to the brain such as cardiovascular disease, high blood pressure, and high cholesterol to name a few.

> *Where do you see crystallized abilities in action during midlife? Are these abilities evident in younger adults?*

Different Types of Intelligence

The difficulty in defining intelligence is only the tip of the iceberg in determining whether intelligence consists of a single ability or multiple abilities. This latter, multidimensional approach is more appealing to researchers and students of life span development as opposed to the former, unitary view.

Two psychologists in particular, Robert Sternberg and Howard Gardner, have introduced a broader way to conceptualize intelligence that allows for a more culture-congenial implementation and understanding of intelligent behavior.

Sternberg's Triarchic Theory of Intelligence. Robert Sternberg's theory (1985) consists of three fundamental elements useful in different life situations.

1. **Componential element** is reflected in how efficiently people process information. It is said to be fundamental in solving of problems, monitoring of solutions, and evaluating results.

2. **Experiential element** is seen in the different approaches taken to familiar or novel tasks. Critical to the experiential element is **insight** that allows the individual to compare new information with an existing knowledge base in an attempt to deal with a situation effectively.
3. **Contextual element** involves the recognition of the impact of the environment on a particular situation. This has been referred to as the practical side of intelligence that allows the individual to evaluate the situation, adapt to it, or change it as the situation demands.

How might midlife adults employ this type of intelligence in their daily lives? Select specific incidences.

Consider today's megacorporations who attempt to span the globe.
    Discuss how a singular approach to a market may fail while a multidimensional approach might better succeed.
    Provide specific examples.

Beyond these three fundamental elements to his theory, Sternberg and Wagner (1994) and Wagner and Sternberg (1986) indicated that a major component to successful intellectual functioning is **tacit knowledge.** This type of knowledge is not found on any educational curriculum. Rather, it reflects a certain sense or know-how regarding situations and circumstances, in other words how to best communicate information to different groups of people, how to work effectively in both positive and negative settings, how to 'read' the opposing defensive alignment in the NFL, or how to choose the correct lure to maximize one's catch for the morning. This sense frequently comes with experience or through observing others. It is an ability that appears to be acquired more easily by some than others and whether it can be taught in the academic/curricular sense is still in question. Interestingly, this type of know-how has been reported to be unrelated to IQ and academic performance. Instead, it reflects an everyday intelligence (Berg and Sternberg, 1992; Sternberg and Wagner, 1994).

Gardner's use of Multiple Intelligences. Howard Gardner's approach is similar to Sternberg's. Gardner, in his theorizing, moved away from the unitary view of intelligence to propose **multiple intelligences.** It is his contention that there are seven types of intelligence or "seven frames of mind" (Gardner, 1983). These multiple intelligences include **(1) logico-mathematical intelligence, (2) linguistic intelligence, (3) visual/spatial intelligence, (4) musical intelligence, (5) bodily/kinesthetic intelligence, (6) interpersonal intelligence, and (7) intrapersonal intelligence.** We, as a species, possess all of these intelligences to varying degrees. High levels of intelligence in one of these seven areas are not necessarily accompanied by high levels of intelligence in the others. Consistent with one of the themes of this text, Gardner emphasizes the importance of the environment in contributing to the development of specific competencies or intelligences. It is held that people develop the particular competencies that their family and culture value and encourage. Additionally, a developmental theme comes out of Gardner's belief that different intelligences develop and change throughout the life span, thus accounting for the variability and plasticity observed in individuals.

Relevance to the Midlife Adult. These two frameworks of everyday intelligence, its components and manifestations, speak strongly to the potential for change across the lifespan but particularly at midlife. It is not uncommon at this time of life for the adult to evaluate his or her strengths and competencies and decide to parlay or channel these efforts into a new professional effort. The midlife adults see the potential for change so that with considerable self-determination, family and cultural support, they are able to take an avocation or talent and develop it into a new manifestation of their abilities. Examples are the housewife/hobbyist painter who opens her own gallery and shows and sells many of her works or the twenty-year naval Non-Com who chooses archaeology as his next career after graduate school. Even more extreme life decisions are made on this potential for plasticity and growing expertise over the course of one's life to the middle years An example would be the individual who becomes fascinated with Eastern religions, gives up his/her current career, and moves to India to practice and study, perhaps never to return to the United States.

It can be said that the midlife adult, through either formal or informal education, has progressed to the point where life experiences may direct him or her to a new area of intellectual expertise or ability. Midlife is the time to enact these potentials and possibilities.

A STRAIGHT-ON AND MINDFUL LOOK AT SIDEWAYS THINKING AND MINDLESSNESS

The terms **mindfulness** and **sideways thinking** have recently been the focus of the research and writing of Ellen Langer (1997). Her theory is a work in progress and has considerable potential in explaining the thinking and learning processes of the adult over the life span.

Basic Principles of Langer's Theory

Langer takes a strikingly different view of memory and learning than do most traditional theorists. She bases much of her conceptualizations around four myths that *undermine* learning, run counter to the idea of mindfulness, and promote the idea of **mindlessness.**

1. Paying attention means staying focused on one thing at a time—distractions may be useful in order to break rigid forms of thinking.

2. Forgetting is a problem—rather, Langer states that forgetting allows us the pleasure of re-experiencing an event.
3. There are right and wrong answers—what is correct or incorrect depends on the context.
4. Intelligence is knowing what's out there—this presupposes the idea that there is only one way to conceptualize reality.

Employing a mindful approach to one's thinking and learning allows for

1. the continuous creation of new categories,
2. openness to new information, and
3. a pleasant awareness of more than one perspective.

Correspondingly, *Sideways Learning* (Langer, 1997) is a version of mindfulness. It is reflected in the type of awareness termed by some as **being present** in the situation. Sideways learning includes:

1. an openness to novelty,
2. an alertness to distinction,
3. a sensitivity to different contexts,
4. an awareness of multiple perspectives, and
5. an orientation to the present in terms of being receptive to changes in an ongoing situation.

Attention and Distractions

"Clearly, we are more likely to remember something if we attend to it than if we do not attend to it. One may argue that memory is the most meaningful measure of attention" (Langer, 1997). While true, Langer is not retracting earlier conceptualizations regarding the importance of mindfulness. Rather, she has expanded her view to involve mindful attention. In a study comparing memory for a story, focused attention performance and mindful attention performance were examined. The results indicated that the mindful attention group, the group that had been given instructions to think about multiple aspects of each story, had better memory for the stories than did the focus group (Langer and Bayliss, 1994). Langer concluded that looking for novelty within situations enhances the ability to pay attention.

Attention is the novelty detector in the nervous system.

Distractions, therefore, do not hold the negative connotations for Langer that they do to many memory researchers. According to Langer, being distracted means that we are attracted to something else. What we call distractions may be a deliberate attending to something other than what we think is important. Neurologically, the brain is seeking novelty, and as a result, is increasing our ability to pay attention.

THE IMPORTANCE OF CULTURE AND CONTEXT

We often fail to recognize our contexts in our professional and private settings. This type of failure has the potential to lead to communication conflict and problems in understanding other people's views.

Have you ever encountered such a failure in communicating with a peer or parent? Could this lack of perspective have anything to do with it?

The mindful approach encourages the individual to be more open to alternatives, to see that there may be several disparate ways of accounting for information and that adhering to a perspective that there is only one way to perceive a situation eliminates the potential of drawing distinctions. By drawing distinctions, one is able to recognize that the event is situated in a context, and one can therefore appreciate and value the impact of other contexts. Recent research into the holistic versus analytical approach to thinking between Eastern and Western thinking patterns is a new area of investigation (Cohen and Gunz, 2001; Ji, Nisbett, and Su, 2001; Leu, Liu, and Nisbett, 2001). Information presented from a single perspective, as if it is true, is an approach that invalidates different contexts, cultures, values, and views.

Langer (1997) extends this view to encompass entire cultures. By adopting the limited and culturally restricted view of a problem, event, or life situation, we get locked into single-minded views but we also reinforce these views for each other until the entire culture suffers from the same mindlessness. A study by Langer that appears later in the culture section clearly demonstrates this particular view.

This same perspective applies to the conceptualization of gender in learning and work situations. Gender differences in skill acquisition are often cited as being learned in an absolute or conditional manner. Social factors such as being taught to be a "good girl" translates into "do what you are told"—absolute approach to thinking. To be a "real boy" means to be independent of authority and "don't listen to all you're told"—conditional approach to thinking. Such social training has an impact on learning ability and willingness to take new and different ways of thinking about information.

What approach do you take to your education?

EVERYDAY PROBLEM SOLVING AND WISDOM

Everyday or Practical Problem Solving

Probably, the most significant contributions to the study of everyday problems have come from the works of Nancy Denney and her colleagues. Much of the everyday problem solving research was driven by her conceptualizations of **unexercised abilities** and **optimally exercised abilities.** It was her belief that individuals should be expected to perform better on practical or everyday problems than on abstract problems such as those typically found on standardized or psychometric tasks. One finds little disagreement among researchers regarding the fact that performance on everyday tasks is not only better than performance on standardized tests but also that everyday thinking ability increases across adolescence into middle age (Denney and Pierce, 1989; Denney, Pierce, and Palmer, 1982). Disagreement arises regarding the age-related timing of declines in practical or everyday problem solving. While Denney and her colleagues would argue for a postmidlife decline, other researchers find continued improvement at least until around age seventy (Cornelius and Caspi, 1987; Cornelius, 1990). As researchers continue to explore the age-related changes observed in late life, it is sufficient for our purposes to note the peaking of these particular processes in midlife.

WISDOM

As Baltes (*The Aging Mind*, 1990) said "**Wisdom** comes with age; but not all old people are wise." One should assume that the wisdom made evident in old age had its roots in midlife.

Young adults are rarely seen as wise primarily because experience has been limited to them. It is during midlife when finally, one is able to examine one's life experiences, the workings of the world, and to attempt to put that information into a context. The observant individual is, in effect, balancing the present with the past and extrapolating to the future. The perspective available during midlife allows the individual to establish the beginnings of wisdom. But just as all old people are not wise, not all midlifers become students of their present and past.

More theoretical papers on wisdom exist than do empirical research pieces. There is little agreement as to how to operationally define wisdom, how it would be manifested and behaviorally measured, and what groups (who) might best display wisdom (Schaie and Willis, 1996). Therefore, in contrast to much work on the later phases of the life span, the domain of wisdom is theory rich and data poor. Most recently, Smith and Baltes (1992) have outlined five cognitive skills hypothesized to be involved in the development of and enacting of wise behavior and knowledge. They include:

1. *factual knowledge* regarding the current situation and available options;
2. *procedural knowledge* referring to the ability to access relevant information and as to how best to offer advice if requested;
3. *life span contextualism by putting* the other individual into a context, for instance, where he or she came from, expectations of self and others, the person's status in the community and the society, and so on;
4. *relativism* regarding the religious, spiritual, and cultural influences on the individual; and
5. *uncertainty* in focusing on the outcome of a series of actions and a readiness to enact an alternative plan.

These skills sound strikingly similar to those put forth in Langer's theory, don't they?

Wisdom may be colloquially thought of as interpersonal (everyday) problem solving, which requires dealing with individuals in a variety of circumstances. Clearly, a lack of personal experiences and an inability to evaluate experiences in a dispassionate light renders the individual incapable of wisdom. The inexperienced or dogmatic individual does not manifest wisdom in the later years or demonstrate such a potential in the middle years.

Midlife serves as the beginning in the establishment of the aforementioned cognitive skills. The dispassionate midlifers, able to evaluate where they are and where they are going, are on their way to wisdom.

What is the difference between wisdom and common sense?

Wisdom—Women and Men Across Cultures and Time

Wisdom carries with it positive overtones and connotations. Knowledge, know-how, awareness of cultural values and contexts, in addition to reasonable alternatives to situations, constitute the characteristics of the wise person.

Historically, women who held the title of wise women were women considered to have a strong tie to nature. These women often filled the niche as healer in the society. They were sought out on spiritual matters as shaman and what would be called today sources for alternative medicine. These women, who played an important role in most societies for over three centuries, became feared and persecuted as witches during the height of Protestantism in Europe and the American colonies. These women were either killed or driven into hiding.

Only recently has there been a resurgence of and increased public interest in the wise woman. Midlife and postmidlife women are defying the negative stereotypes associated with the title and are showing themselves to be women of power and presence. Today's wise women continue the tradition of strong generative and interpersonal ties with others as a way of giving back to the community. Additionally, these women have a sense of intrapersonal wisdom. In caring for themselves, they are increasing their own quality of life in the present and for the future. They are serving as wise models for the younger generations that they touch. Although one may feel a need to conceptualize a wise woman as being in some other culture other than our own, one need only listen to individuals speak of their mothers and grandmothers within our Western culture.

In contrast, the wise man has been equated with power and kings. If not the person in power, the wise man can be seen as belonging in a political arena by serving as counselor to the king or chief. There is a Budje saying from East Africa, "The exercise of power is the business of wise men." Today, as in the past, wise men serve predominantly in the political arena. There is little mention of their tie to nature or inter/intrapersonal ties to others or themselves. The wisdom sought from them is of a more immediate and public nature.

There exists within any culture the potential for a reversal of the traditional male and female role to encompass the medicine man or the woman behind the throne. However, the most common manifestation of the wise person has been presented. Wisdom has always been valued and in some cases feared. Wisdom has always accompanied the successful wielding of power. As in the past and currently, not all individuals will achieve wisdom. However, wisdom is still culturally valued. The arenas may vary. The need for such people is still desired. The midlife person of perspective and experience is the wise person in training.

PSYCHOMETRIC MEASURES OF INTELLIGENCE

The nature of intelligence has been long and hotly debated among scholars. Most recently, Baltes (1993) along with his colleagues have built on the Horn and Cattell's work on fluid and crystallized intelligence by proposing a view of intelligence that can be separated into two types of intellectual processes: mechanics and pragmatics (Baltes, Dittman-Kohli, and Dixon, 1984; Dixon and Baltes, 1986).

The **mechanics** of intelligence can be compared to that of fluid intelligence. This type of intelligence is basic and physiologically determined, as a result are subject to age-related decline due to their close link to neurological functioning. The **pragmatics** can be seen, although built on the basic foundation of mechanics, as involving a wide range of accumulated, culture-based knowledge, skills, and expertise, closely paralleling that of crystallized intelligence.

Baltes (1993) states that the middle-aged adult is likely to show improvements in the pragmatics of intelligence due to learning that occurred in educational settings and through work and other life and cultural experience. Baltes goes so far as to say that pragmatic intelligence often outweighs the brain's mechanical condition. Hence, there is an accommodation for the subtle neural changes that occur with age by way of experience and life knowledge. It is therefore not uncommon to find an average midlifer manifesting the general experiences in life, who can outperform an average, neurologically younger adult lacking pragmatic knowledge and experience (Baltes, 1993).

The Seattle Longitudinal Study

The Seattle Longitudinal Study is the classic and most commonly cited study of adult intelligence. This study, conducted by Schaie and his colleagues, has spanned over 30 years and provides the definitive view of the psychometric changes that occur in adult intelligence (Schaie, 1979, 1983, 1989a, 1989b, 1990, 1994; Schaie and Hertzog, 1983). Five hundred participants, between the ages of 20 and 70, began this study in 1956. Of the many findings that have resulted from this work, three findings are of particular relevance to the study of midlife. First, for most fairly healthy adults, no significant impairment of intellectual abilities is noted until after the age of 60 (some research suggests not until after age 70). Second, intellectual gains continue through the late 30s to early 40s, then, appear to be stable until the mid-50s or early-60s. See these depicted in figure 9.2. Finally, the losses that do show up (in one's 80s and 90s) have mainly to do with tasks that are unfamiliar, highly complex, or stressful (Schaie, 1990, 1994).

These tasks seem to tap mechanic intelligence and not that much of the pragmatics.

Gender Differences in Cognitive Abilities

The primary domains frequently cited in manifesting general gender differences focus on verbal, spatial, and mathematical abilities. Unger and Crawford (1996) provide a comprehensive examination of these particular skills from birth onward. Again, while the literature is abundant in childhood and adolescence, almost none exists on the midlife adult. One is left to extrapolate back from the findings of the older adult. Findings indicate that both men and women peak on inductive reasoning, spatial orientation, vocabulary, and verbal memory in midlife. Men, in general, tend to peak in these abilities around age fifty, while women show peak performance closer to their sixties (Willis and Schaie, 1999).

Keep in mind when you think about the life tasks confronting the individual at this time.

The implication from the research that does exist on the midlife adult suggests that midlife is a period of stability to slight growth in the intellectual skills used most often. It appears that, intellectually, midlife adults are at the prime of their cognitive life. Women and men show slight differences in the timing of their respective peak skills, however, the extent of these changes does not appear to be significant. The singular cognitive skill that does show continual decline from young adulthood on for men and women has to do with perceptual speed (Schaie, 1994). This speaks directly to Baltes' (1993) conceptualization of mechanics versus pragmatics in intelligence. Midlife adults who are milliseconds slower in their perceptual speed to respond to information (mechanics/fluid abilities) continue to increase in a myriad of cognitive skills typically honed and developed with education and life experience (pragmatics/crystallized abilities). Midlife adults can be seen to be less impulsive in cognitive processing with women and men showing a ten-year difference in their peak performance.

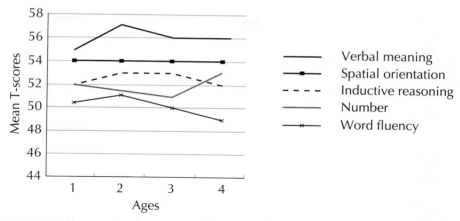

FIGURE 9.2. Changes in primary mental abilities between thirty-nine and sixty years of age.

GROUP 1—39 YEARS
GROUP 2—46 YEARS
GROUP 3—53 YEARS
GROUP 4—60 YEARS

Source: Shaie 1994.

Cultural Extrapolations to Psychometric Intelligence

No systematic cultural comparisons of psychometric intelligence have been noted in the literature. Only the most meager hypotheses can be put forth regarding subcultures within Western society and other non-Western cultures.

Why do you think this lack of information exists?

Several general findings regarding formal schooling and health factors, in particular, allow for cultural speculation. First, it was noted by Birren and Morrison (1961) that *educational level* played a significant role in general mental ability, with those having less formal schooling performing more poorly than those who had more schooling. However, when educational level was factored out of the equation, no differences were manifested between cohorts of individuals (Botwinick, 1978). Blackburn (1984) evidenced a similar finding when comparing the reasoning abilities of two cohorts of college-educated individuals. One can conclude from these findings that access to education is critical to better performance on standardized psychometric tests.

Health is another factor associated with cognitive performance. In general, healthier people do better on intelligence tests than do those in poor health (Botwinick, 1984). It has been suggested that improvements in nutrition and medical care would have a significant impact on diminishing differences due to health factors.

The cultural implications regarding the Westernstyle of standardized testing of individuals in different cultures are that recognition of factors such as availability to and quality of health care, education, and job opportunities need to be considered in the investigation. Additionally, other cultural factors such as trends in birth rates, advances in cultural technology, wars, plagues, famines, and so on will have an effect in the articulation of intellectual (psychometric) abilities.

Psychometric Measures of Intelligence versus Mindfulness

Since the early 1970s there has been an attempt on the part of the designers and testing services that norm and market standardized tests, to develop tests referred to as culture-fair if not culture-free. This attempt to strip away any aspects of culture leaves us with tests of what? What you get are measures of mental functioning devoid of expertise, training, interest or practical application. While legitimate in its attempts to attain a culture-irrelevant measure of intelligence (as defined by the tool), the rest is still subject to the two major points discussed in the previous section: education and health. The interactive potential of these factors is impressive. The debate on the psychometric approach to intelligence has been long fought in the developmental literature (Berk, 2001). It is not the point of this chapter to recount the debate, rather to point out another reasonable alternative to the understanding of intelligence.

Mindfulness (Langer, 1997) takes a sideways approach to defining an individual's intellectual abilities in that a mindful approach encourages evaluating a situation from multiple perspectives, taking the novelty of the situation into consideration, being aware of the situational context, and assigning relevant informational categories by which to understand the situation. See table 9.1 for a comparison of the psychometric intelligence and mindful approach. How then is intellectual functioning to be understood employing a multi-cultural perspective? As will be seen in the next section, one can make a culture-by-culture shopping list or begin to conduct research based on cross-cultural comparisons. The next section is a reflection of both approaches.

CULTURAL DIFFERENCES IN MEMORY AND INTELLIGENCE

Memory and Culture—What Adults Remember and How

Work by Wagner (1978, 1981) has indicated that people tend to remember that with which they are familiar and in which they have an interest. This was indicated when it was shown that uneducated Moroccan peasants and rug sellers

TABLE 9.1. Differences between Intelligence and Mindfulness

III. Intelligence	IV. Mindfulness
Corresponds to reality by identifying the optimum fit between individual and environment	Controls reality by identifying several possible perspectives from which any situation may be viewed
A linear process moving from problem to resolution as rapidly as possible	A process of stepping back from both perceived problems and perceived solutions to view situations as novel
A means of achieving desired outcomes	A process through which meaning is given to outcomes
Developing from an expert's perspective, which focuses on stable categories	Developed from an actor's ability to experience personal control by shifting perspectives
Depends on remembered facts and learned skills in contexts that are sometimes perceived as novel	Depends on the fluidity of knowledge and skills and recognizes both advantages and disadvantages in each

Source: Langer (1997).

performed superior to Moroccan scholars in a recognition memory test of rug patterns. It was concluded that familiar, culturally relevant material is remembered better than culturally irrelevant, foreign information (Cole and Scribner, 1974; Wagner, 1978). Another example of what may be termed as personally relevant memory is reflected in the classic study by Bartlett (1934) in which a Swazi cow herder was able to remember the minute details of a year past sales transaction that included information regarding the cost of a cow and relevant markings of the sold animal.

In cultures that rely on a strong oral transmission of information from generation to generation (i.e., Yugoslavian bards, the Kpelle of Liberia), different memory techniques to organize the information is used than in Western cultures (Cole and Scribner, 1974; Dube, 1982; Lord, 1982). That individuals' performances tend to conform to culturally valued and encouraged forms of cognitive processing is not surprising. It becomes a bone of contention when the standards of one culture are used as the marker by which to evaluate the abilities of individuals from other cultures.

> *Remember, culture can refer to persons in geographic regions distant from the majority culture, or it may reflect groups within the majority culture (i.e., the undereducated, the elderly, or nonmajority representatives).*

The limited research in this area points to a clear need in the research literature.

Cultural Expectations About Memory

There is a belief within American culture that memory decline is inevitable. It is not uncommon to hear this view expressed in young adulthood and increase in frequency to and through midlife. While this view is supported in Western research programs, there is debate as to the extent of this decline. Nonetheless, decline is observed. Work by Langer (1997) suggests a strong self-fulfilling prophecy that is culturally driven. Her conclusion derives from a study that involved deaf American adults, mainland Chinese adults residing in San Francisco, and mainstream hearing Americans. The deaf adults and Chinese adults were selected for their cultural differences except that both of these groups share a positive view of aging and hold few negative stereotypes and beliefs regarding aged individuals and the aging process. Langer stated that the Chinese people still speak of advanced years with pride and that the deaf individuals are not exposed to the "conversation that is the background of hearing life." It is Langer's position that subtle, negative messages about the aging process are conveyed from childhood onward, which result in an antiaging culture.

> *How many times have you heard someone say that he or she is unable to engage in some pursuit because they are of a certain age? Or perhaps you've heard someone belittled for engaging in an age-inappropriate activity.*

Briefly, her findings indicated that cultural beliefs about aging played a role in determining the degree of memory loss that people experience in old age, and the performance of the Chinese and deaf Americans were comparable to each other and superior to that of the hearing sample of Americans. It was concluded that the rigid mindsets that we hold about ourselves affect our performance. This is a finding regarding memory performance, but could probably be extended to many of the beliefs we hold in general regarding the impact of age on our potential.

Cultural Views of Intelligence

Logical thinking ability is frequently looked upon as a marker of intelligent thought. Should we assume that when individuals fail to answer simple, logical questions that they lack intelligence? However, researchers (Botwinick, 1978; Denney, 1974) have found cultural differences in response to the classic Luria (1976) logical deductive question resulting from the following information: In the far north, all bears are white. Novaya Zemlya is in the far north. What color are the bears there? The general findings showed that the unschooled peasants of central Asia and, less well-educated older Western adults were unable to answer this and like questions. Some of the typical responses were to talk to someone that had been there because one does not speak of that which he has not seen.

Imagine the difficulty if, in a testing situation, you were tacitly expected to adopt the view of a farmer of the Chinese highlands, a Peruvian plantation owner, a coal miner of Appalachia, or an Italian industralist. How might you perform if culture relevant approaches (not information) were required to obtain a correct answer?

Tasks of classification skills in the Kpelle people of Liberia show similar findings (Glick, 1975). Although they could be elicited, the expected Western responses were not necessarily the first or the preferred response. Luria (1976) found similar classification differences in peasants of Uzbekistan. In an attempt to explain these findings, Labouvie-Vief (1985) proposed that the definition of problems in different cultures might differ as a result of prior experiences and prior knowledge that reflects a correct response for that culture. What are reflected in these findings are different, culturally relevant interpretations of the question, not necessarily a lack of intelligence.

Summary and Comments

Relevance to the Midlife Adult

It may be difficult for many midlife adults to see themselves in the prime of their cognitive lives. This view may reflect the stress that accompanies demands placed on them by personal and/or professional responsibilities; poor sleep, nutrition, or exercise *habits;* or a variety of chemical dependencies, to name a few. The midlife adult may report increasing memory problems such as a loss of words or forgetting why he or she walked into a room. The most common and irritating memory complaints can be handled by increasing one's level of mindfulness.

The literature, in general, indicates:

1. that memory abilities tend to be relatively sound and robust during midlife;
2. intelligence, as measured by Western tests of ability, shows an increase in midlife, with continued increase in crystallized skills through midlife into early old age;
3. everyday problem solving is more reflective of the type of activity commonly encountered by the midlife adult and shows an increase in efficiency with experience, and
4. wisdom begins to develop over the course of midlife with increasing opportunities for a variety of life experiences, the increased opportunity for contact with a myriad of diversity in one's life, and an increased potential to demonstrate different kinds of intelligence and a mindful approach to daily activities.

The cross-cultural findings suggest that all is not as one might think, coming from a Western society. Marked differences are found on tasks of memory and intelligence. They indicate:

1. that memory is relative, primarily driven by that which is familiar and relevant to the individual's life; experimental tasks may lack personal relevance and thereby be reflected in poor performance;

2. cultural values and life tasks frequently dictate the type of cognitive activity most commonly employed in day-to-day commerce; and

3. cultural values and expectations for human behavior are frequently transmitted via informal communication.

The previous sections have highlighted the aspects of the successful midlife adult, one who is traversing this phase of the life span with relative ease and minimal distress. The cognitive approach taken to many of one's personal and professional situations is often reflected in the quality and satisfaction one expresses with one's life. This is not meant to say that an individual who takes a rigid, limited, and inflexible approach to thinking and acting in the world is unsuccessful, unhappy, or dissatisfied with his or her life. It only suggests that this individual must exert more cognitive effort in maintaining his or her perspective on the world as change, differing views, and differing expectations are introduced.

One can conclude that while experiencing some of the greatest demands on time, effort, and mental skills, midlife adults manifest some of the best cognitive skills that they will ever have. The existing empirical findings suggest the midlife adult is cognitively at the peak in life. Midlife adults should recognize these skills and capitalize on them to maximize their later years.

I was 18 years old in 1969, and . . . the world was full of mysteries, dangers, and opportunities. But above all, it was full of questions.

The Vietnam War polarized society completely. Everything—international attributions to Americans, national policy, movies, music, religion, personal preferences—was forced into two categories: pro-war and anti-war, pro-establishment and anti-establishment. The country had not been so divided since the Civil War/War Between the States.

Sex, drugs, & rock & roll: Easily obtained transportation, widely available birth control pills, a general tendency to question authority or challenge the parental generation, and honest fear that their lives might be very short combined to bring about a revolution in sexual behavior in teenagers and young adults. Basically, the "revolution" was in the attitudes and behavior of young women. Drugs were widespread and easily available, but most people either stayed away or only experimented to see what all of the fuss was about. Like now, alcohol was the biggest problem drug. Rock & roll, along with folk music, was the sound of the anti-establishment element in society. Folk music made you internalize, made you think about injustices and personal responsibility. Rock & roll made you externalize, made you jump up and down and want to do something about something. It was contagious.

Boys were thinking about . . . the war, which made them think about girls.

Girls were thinking about . . . boys, which made them think about the war.

VOICES OF OUR PARENTS 9.1

How my life was supposed to be. Two versions: The pro-establishment version is that I was suppose to pursue a path of becoming a loyal citizen and a good Christian, supporting God and country, shunting the anti-establishment movement that eroded the moral [*sic*] fabric of our society and threatened our way of life. The anti-establishment version is that I was supposed to liberate myself from the role of loyal citizen and good Christian that the establishment had provided for me, a role that was designed only to keep the rich rich, the poor poor, and the middle class working like crazy to reach unattainable goals.

My Identity: An all-pervasive sense of guilt about everything prevented a healthy, adaptive identity from emerging.

Where I was and wasn't going. I didn't know where I was and wasn't going. Uncertainty about college, the military draft, the changing nature of male-female relationships, and the general expectation that I (and the majority of my middle-class age peers) would not follow in the footsteps of our parents made it impossible to know.

Confidence and certainty: There was no confidence. There was certainty in family and friends, who despite having doubts regarding my sanity at times, provided unwavering financial (family) and emotional (both) support.

What I now know, for sure. I now know for sure that knowing things for sure is elusive. I would say that I know for sure that I love my partner and kids. I would say that I know for sure that there is beauty in nature–the sky, the oceans, the mountains, the forests, the deserts. I would say that I know for sure that I am very cynical about everybody and everything else. Nevertheless, I also know with some degree of certainty that I will never stop trying—but I don't know for certain why that is so.

PERSONAL PROFILE

Age:	51
Region raised in:	Texas
Any military service:	No.
Any college:	9 years; Ph.D. —*Major:* Psychology.
First career opportunity:	Visiting Assistant Professor.
Current career:	Full Professor.
Changes in career in between then and now:	growing old.
Marital history:	First—7 years; divorce. Second—23 years; success.
Children:	3, ages: 18, 14, 10.
Pets:	4 dogs belonging to various family members

VOICES OF OUR PARENTS 9.1 (continued)

CHAPTER 10

The Recognition: Identity, Self, and Psychological Forces at Work in Midlife

Wholly unprepared we embark upon the second half of life. . . . We take the step into the afternoon of life; worse still, we take this step with the false assumption that our truths and ideals will serve us as before. But we cannot live the afternoon of life according to the program of life's morning— for what was great in the morning will be little at evening, and what in the morning was true, will at evening will have become a lie.

—An Open Life
M. Toms (1990)

The only thing I'm sure about is that nothing is sure.

—42-YEAR-OLD HAIRDRESSER

At midlife there is a crossing over from one psychological identity to another. The self goes through a transformation.

—M. Stein (1994)

What did she mean "You're going to have to act differently (now because of your period). You're growing up"? I was just getting the hang of playing baseball with my brothers.

—24-YEAR-OLD COLLEGE STUDENT REFLECTING ON PUBERTY

OVERVIEW

At some point in midlife there comes a recognition—a recognition that life is changing in a way that puts you in a new status position. It may be that people now seek you out for your opinion, or people younger than you are ignoring you. The bumps, bruises, sports injuries, and minor illnesses that never slowed you down before are now taking longer to repair or may be laying you up for the first time. Sometimes you find yourself worrying about the plight of the younger generation and you begin to use your generation as a model for how it was and how it should be.

A story has been told about a man in his mid-20s and his son. From the time his son was 3 years old, he and his father would have playful wrestling matches every Thursday night. Both father and son looked forward to those evenings. Because of his larger size and strength, the father always pinned the young boy. With each passing year, the son grew and became stronger. The father, however, continued to win the wrestling matches even though it took him more time to win. After 14 years of weekly matches, the son pinned the father. There was never another Thursday night match. The father offered many excuses. The son eventually left home.

It can be said that on the night of his loss, the father experienced the *recognition*. Life had changed. He was no longer the person that he had been. His son had become a man. Both had made a shift, perhaps hardly noticeable to the younger man, but to the midlife man. . . .

The focus of this chapter revolves around the pivotal point in life when you can look back with years of experience behind you and look forward to the number of years ahead of you. This looking forward and back is different from other points in life in that at this time, one possesses the perspective, experience, and ability to evaluate the paths taken by you and others, that only comes with the passing of years. Now, more than at any other time in life, is the adult capable of meaningful and insightful self-examination, self-review, self-evaluation, and self-analysis.

The midlife adult frequently encounters the numerous occasions to engage in this internal and personal form of examination. Events that may precipitate an early form of life review may include:

1. the death of a friend or close family member (e.g., parent, sibling, or grandparent),
2. experiencing a divorce or marriage,
3. participating in a love affair,
4. experiencing one's child's many "firsts" (e.g., leaving home, graduating from school, getting married),
5. having one's first child at midlife,
6. attempting to have a child at midlife,
7. experiencing an unplanned pregnancy at midlife,
8. dealing with one's own first real life-threatening illness,
9. choosing a new career option, or
10. unpredictable life events occurring.

The Organization of the Chapter

First, the concepts of **identity** and **self** will be introduced. These concepts will be presented as they are discussed in the literature and as they are contrasted to each other. Second, comments will follow regarding the active nature in the construction of the self. Third, the differential impact of midlife on the identity process for women and men will be discussed. Finally, a brief review of general psychological functioning at midlife will be presented.

WHAT IS IDENTITY?

Identity has been defined in terms of how one finds meaningful interpersonal connections and pursuits within the larger cultural milieu (Kroger, 2000). This definition allows for the continuous development of one's identity over the course of the life span as one's societal and behavioral context expands. Young adults may feel constrained in their access to the larger world community by the older generations. Midlife adults may be experiencing maximal contact with and within the larger sociocultural milieu. Both young and midlife adults are undergoing numerous changes in their roles and responsibilities in society. Yet how well these new opportunities are incorporated into their identity and sense of self will dictate the ease of transition for these individuals.

HOW IS IDENTITY OBSERVED
AND INVESTIGATED?

Identity can be studied using the following approaches:

1. Historical—the focus of this approach is on the conditions that precipitate contemporary interest in one's identity. That is, when is the individual, not necessarily the time in history, of interest?
2. Stage-based—explained by developmental change.
3. Sociocultural—allowing for an examination of the role of society in shaping identity.
4. Narrative-based—transmitted via personal stories of identity.
5. Psychosocial—reflected in the integration of roles along with the psychological, biological, and social changes in life. This particular approach to identity is a good link to the ecological model of development.

Midlife identity is said to be achieved when the comments of others can serve as sources of reflection rather than rules to live by (Kroger, 2000). There are a variety of contexts that can influence the course of identity development, including family life, the work place, and the community. Each of these contexts will be explored in greater detail in later chapters.

WHAT IS THE SELF?

The development of what we call self is the result of cognitive and social construction. This construction begins preverbally as an infant and proceeds through the life span becoming more refined and defined. The self is a reflection of how we think about ourselves (thus, the internal cognitive component) from our earliest relations onward to the incorporation of societal expectations (thus, the external social component) as we mature (Harter, 1999). As we proceed through the life span, our personal notion of self becomes less dependent on others' evaluations and comes to reflect a core set of inner attributes supposedly reflecting one's "true self."

The development of self reflects the attempt to make sense of the personal and physical environment in the context of one's life. William James (1890) provided some post-Aristotelian thought on the nature of Self by proposing a duality in development. The duality contrasted the *I-self* and *me-self*. Components of the I-self include:

- Self-awareness—reflecting an appreciation for one's internal states, needs, thoughts, and emotions
- Self-agency—reflecting a sense of ownership/authorship over one's thoughts and actions
- Self-continuity—the recognition that one remains essentially the same over time
- Self-coherence—knowing that there exists a stable sense of self, both single and coherent

Components of the me-self include:

- The material me—how I live and where I live
- The social me—who I am to others in a variety of contexts
- The spiritual me—what are my beliefs

This dual system serves to distinguish between the self and identity. It has been proposed that the I-self is subjective—requires personal evaluation, dynamic in that it reflects a sense of personal control and personal agency, existential (Who am I?), the "ideal me," and involves the machinery of self. These views are set up to contrast with the me-self, which reflects objective definition by external standards (e.g., the good mother, the hardworking father), static specification indicating that the self is an object of one's knowledge and evaluation, categorical (identities to assume at certain ages), the "real me," and the result of the construction by self and others (Harter, 1999; Lewis, 1991, 1994).

The success of the self is in creating a balance for the individual. It is not suggested that balance does not occur by retreating into an autonomous, independent, self-focused orientation in which one constructs impenetrable boundaries between the self and others. Rather than a model of autonomy, independence, separateness, individualism, and distinctiveness, the focus across the life span should be on healthy adaptation reflecting an integration of autonomy and connectedness (Harter, 1999).

As will be highlighted now and in future sections, individuals who assume the extreme positions on this dimension, that is the overly separate and overly close, suffer the most psychologically, especially at midlife.

With the distinction drawn between the concept of identity and self, the reader will come to understand that midlife is very much an experience of the self—a personal evaluation and reconstruction. There may or may not be dramatic external manifestations (e.g., career change, divorce, or the decision to eat better and exercise more) of the internal work being conducted at midlife. With this in mind, theories that address more of this internal work will be discussed in the next section. It is at this point that one finds clear gender lines being drawn. The theories that address midlife changes in women better articulate this period of personal transition than do the theories that reflect the man's transition during this period. Reasons for these differences will be made apparent as they are discussed.

THEORIES OF SELF AND IDENTITY IN MIDLIFE

Jung's Contribution to the Understanding of Midlife

Jung's (1933) theory is rife with the use of symbolism and the presence of archetypical figures that serve as guides during times of unrest or transition. Jung envisions midlife as a time of great transition that results in a greater sense of **individuation** and personal integration along with the potential for greater introspection. He states that this period is a time for greater exploration of needs and reintegration of aspects of the self not integrated into the younger person (i.e., a sense of independence, masculinity, or femininity that may have previously been stifled in the individual). It is the time of **liminality,** the time to cross over a psychological threshold. By the time midlife comes, a person has usually settled into familiar psychological patterns involving work, family, and self. There comes a time however, when many facets of life are found to be lacking some unidentifiable, critical element that once made them meaningful. For this reason Stein (1994) describes midlife as a crisis of the spirit when old selves are lost and are replaced by new ones. The sense of self at midlife goes beyond a crisis in cosmetics to a keen and growing sense of limits and of the inevitability of one's death.

> *Do you know of anyone that you would say is clinging to the past? Why might this be so?*

In symbolic terms, the Greek god Hermes is presented in Jungian theory to serve as the guide out of this dark night of the soul to the other side. This other side represents the person you will become as you proceed through the post-midlife course. You are said to emerge with a greater understanding and control over balancing the factual world and the world of feelings and emotions. As shown in figure 10.1, Jung believes that individuation is achieved when the world of facts and judgments is in balance. When this is accomplished, one comes to enjoy and know the full range of one's capabilities, including self-knowledge.

In this theory, inner conflict and neurotic disturbances arise when one attempts to carry an earlier phase of development over into midlife. The psy-

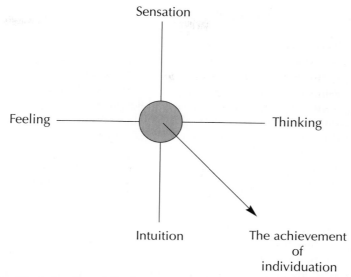

FIGURE 10.1. The balancing of the four aspects of life. Individuation occurs when the individual has command of these four elements.

chological stress brought by not letting go of an earlier self can be manifested in a variety of hypochondriac symptoms, denial, or self-destructive acts. As would be predicted from a Jungian standpoint, Kotre and Hall (1990) identified that midlife could be represented as (1) a time of shifting perspective from young to middle adulthood, (2) an increase in the sense of personal power, and (3) a reclaiming of opposite sex qualities (e.g., developing the nurturing, intuitive self). From this perspective, midlife can be a time of personal reorganization due to an increasing awareness of one's mortality.

WOMEN AT MIDLIFE

Approaches With a Strong Female Focus

The Work of Jean Shanoda Bolen

As with Jung's theory of midlife development, Bolen's (1994) interpretation of midlife experience is filled with symbolism. She conceives of midlife as a period of self-examination and self-exploration. This process is sometimes referred to as a quest or a voyage, an exploration of that which is meaningful to life. Spirituality increases in its significance to the midlife adult. The midlife adult engages in considerable personal evaluation. During this time of spiritual realignment, it is not uncommon for the midlife adult to encounter and deal with bouts of uncertainty, disillusionment, lost purpose, feeling lost, depersonalization, and conflict with oneself and others. The level of intensity of these feelings is said to reflect the degree to which your life is not as you would have liked it to be.

Bolen (1994) envisions the midlife transition as an active process with a heightened awareness of life events and their unfolding and an increased sensitivity to **synchronicity** (the right thing at the right time combined with feelings of fear and uncertainty). Bolen emphasized a need or an uninterrupted time of self-examination and self-discovery. Bolen, like Greer (1991), sees this as a time of passage with no rite of passage. The beginning of midlife ushers the individual into status in which one is no longer who she was before, but is not yet who she is becoming. The woman at this time may experience a sense of her life as being on a threshold, with an awareness of a gateway and the opportunity to step through it. At this time she has the potential to have experiences that will result in permanent change.

According to Bolen (1994), a woman encounters the opportunity to take a figurative pilgrimage, to new levels of self-understanding with each encountered body change. Over the course of her life, from adolescence onward, changes in her body are viewed as an invitation to a changing awareness of potential transitions and thresholds. The types of change referred to include entrance into puberty, loss of virginity, labor and delivery, menopause (all of the previous referred to as blood mysteries), general changes in bodily appearance, and dying. As a woman encounters each of these bodily changes, she has the potential for greater experiences of enlightment—an illumination that will add to a better understanding of her life and life in general.

In her discussion of the midlife woman's passage, Bolen (1994) also employs the physical landscapes to denote times of challenge, uncertainty, and clarity. Some of the landscape allusions include the forest, the plain, the mountaintop, and being "out of the woods." Emotionally, there exists a time of doldrums; of rigid attitudes; of a resurgence of the issues of aging, attractiveness, power, and potency. Accompanying these emotions, are feelings of a stifling of spontaneity and emotionality (Bolen, 1994). The midlife woman who successfully navigates this period emerges with greater feelings of **authenticity** and energy to face the next phase of her life.

Ruth Ann Josselson's Contribution to Midlife Understanding

Josselson's (1996) work has a slightly more specific focus than the global one presented by Bolen. The focus of her work has to do with the development of identity in a group of women spanning a twenty-year period. To Josselson, identity is the ultimate act of creativity, what we make of ourselves, who we are in the context of all we might be. Midlife allows one to see life in a continuous perspective both in retrospect and prospect. The experience of identity is reflected in meaningful continuity over time. Ordinarily, living our identities is like breathing, in that we don't have to ask ourselves everyday who we are. Josselson stated that we become aware of our identity when we are about to make or remake its acquaintance such as when past ways of behavior no longer feel gratifying or when inner changes or social dislocation bring about a shift in our perceptions of ourselves.

In following a group of college women from age twenty-one to forty-three, Josselson (1996) was able to identify four kinds of women based on their level of commitment to an identity and to the amount of exploration invested in the attainment of this identity. Four basic personality styles were identified through a number of personal interviews:

1. Pathmaker—women who experienced a period of exploration or crisis and then made an identity commitment on their own terms.
2. Guardian—women who made identity commitments without a sense of choice, carrying forward the plans for their life mapped out in childhood or designed by their parents.
3. Searcher—women in an active period of struggle or exploration, trying to make choices but not yet having done so.
4. Drifter—women without commitments and not struggling to make them, vacillating between feeling lost and following the impulse of the moment.

Although some of the women that she followed to their middle years changed dramatically, she noted marked continuity in the maintenance of their earlier young adult identities.

The Contribution of Kathleen Norris

Along the same lines of Bolen and Josselson, Norris (1996) focuses on the internal quest of a woman and the need to identify with something greater than herself. This personal pilgrimage, to create a clearer sense of self, aligns nicely with the conceptualization of Brandtstadter and Lerner (1999) that action is critical to the development of self. Norris sees this time at the beginning of midlife as better defining a sense of self and purpose to a woman's marriage, family, community, and commitments. As posited in the previous works, this woman's midlife journey is a positive one. The products of her efforts are more internal and reflect a stronger sense of self and sharper sense of agenda in the world. Again, the emphasis is on the *internal* work of the individual.

Women: History, Society, and the Construction of Their Identity

Today's American midlife adult (boomer) was brought up in a time when women's roles were sharply defined and prescribed, clearly and unquestionably specified. These women were brought up with the following givens:

1. her mission was to marry and raise children,
2. she could have a "woman's" job (teacher, nurse, secretary) prior to marriage but should not expect to continue until after her children were grown,
3. her social place and value were defined by her husband,
4. her identity was defined largely by attractiveness, and
5. her goal should be to entrap a man and ensure herself as the center of his life.

The ideas of a right to self-fulfillment, to a sense of personal identity, productive contribution, and independence were as foreign to many of the young women of the time as they were to their elders.

From this perspective, Josselson (1996) states that societies limit what is possible and impossible for the individual. Cultures are said to lay out an array of enabling potentials along with a set of constraining boundaries beyond which the construction of a new self or identity is not likely (Shotter and Gergen, 1989). These relatively rigid and impenetrable parameters shape the individuals contained within them who eventually come to compose the society. Essentially, these parameters compose the contexts for identity formation.

How should one conceptualize the impact of U.S. society, prior to the 1960's, as constraining parameters during the youth of today's midlife women? The best word is strained. Three powerful forces brought all walks of life to rally to these causes. These three forces included the Civil Rights movement, the opposition to the Vietnam War, and the women's liberation movement. To the observer of the times, it was clear that change was coming. The societal prohibitions, constraints, and limits could not contain the flood of ideas, ideologies, and demands. Not only were individuals' identities transformed, but also the identity of the entire society was transformed.

Women moved through this period with a sense of greater possibility and potential in society. At midlife, many of these women may be experiencing a new type of revolution, one that requires a greater strength for some, for this revolution represents a revolution of the soul, of the self, and a reevaluation of one's standing in society. Many of these women are reawakening to the idea of sisterhood. This involves a growing sense that a bond is required with whom you are traveling this road. Women can serve as guides for other women. Their stories can bring to others enlightenment, perspective, or courage. Women with no guides on this journey or pilgrimage can remain lost in the "forest of midlife" (Bolen, 1994). The ideals of this Western society run counter to the notion of sisterhood and its power. Our society imparts to its people the importance of self-definition and self-determination, which have the power to limit and empower. At this point in life, it appears that women need to begin to talk to each other again to successfully emerge from midlife with a continued and strong sense of energy, zest, and purpose.

MEN AT MIDLIFE

The general comments regarding identity and self apply equally to men and women. Self-examination and evaluation are no less important an endeavor for the midlife male. However, little has been written regarding this process in men. It may be that men in Western cultures, particularly the men in the United States, are given much less latitude in expressing and acknowledging a range of emotions. Men are not given permission to demonstrate a variety of feelings, so the midlife man experiences uncertainties in life, alone, without models and guides to ease the transition and without any socially sanctioned means of

expressing emotions. Theories that address men at midlife are strikingly analytical and devoid of the emotional tenor of those theories that address the
midlife woman.

Theories with a Predominately Male Focus that Address Midlife-Related Issues

Jung's theory, outlined previously, is equally meaningful in the discussion of
the man's transition through midlife. The issues of liminality and individuation
also apply to the man's midlife experience. For the man, it is a period of identity reconstruction and self-evaluation alignment, the roles he plays and the resolution of the polar opposites described in chapter 3.

Erikson's Contribution to Midlife Development

Chapter 3 also provides a comprehensive presentation of Erikson's (1950/
1963) theory of psychosocial development. The crisis of **generativity versus
stagnation and self-absorption** is the Eriksonian crisis most commonly cited as
the crisis of midlife. In more contemporary analyses, the crisis of generativity is
said to have implications for both the young adult and the midlifer. In young
adulthood, generativity is said to be manifested by the establishment and
maintenance of a family. This process is said to be reflective of hope for the
future and an investment in the future through your children. In midlife, a
man's generative feelings are noted by his concern for the future generations
via his investment of time in mentoring younger individuals. With perhaps his
children gone, the man reaches out to younger individuals in his work setting
or in the larger community. This reaching out by the midlife man provides that
he will have, at some level, continued influence in the future.

The alternative to generativity is stagnation and self-absorption. The non-
generative man's focus is reflective of limited demonstrations of closeness and
involvement with others with the personal agenda of self-aggrandizement.
This individual has little to offer the future and little desire to do so. The generative man, with his new perspective on life—a middle-of-life perspective—
can envision himself going into the future through his contact with and
contribution of wisdom to the younger generation. Many men seen working
with youth in a variety of contexts are demonstrating generativity (e.g., coaching, involvement in after-school programs, or teaching a new employee how to
cut through the 'red tape').

As was also mentioned in chapter 3, the concept of **revisitiation** has been
little studied in the literature. However, as will be seen in the discussion of the
midlife crisis, the crisis of **identity versus role confusion** (commonly discussed
as the crisis of adolescence) is confronted again (i.e., revisited) by the midlife
man. For any number of reasons (social, personal, work-related), the midlife
man is faced with a crisis of self. At this time, he must incorporate the notion of
"time left to live" into his understanding of himself and in his presentation of
his newly formulated identity to others. Otherwise, the man will be set adrift
without a clear conceptualization of himself. His old roles, old dreams, old

identities stemming from adolescence have the potential to be reviewed and updated given the current circumstances of his life. It is not uncommon to find a total revamping of one's personal identity. However, the man who takes the time to revisit this earlier-resolved crisis usually emerges with a stronger and more coherent sense of who he is at midlife.

Levinson's: The Seasons of a Man's Life

As noted in chapter 3, Levinson's theory (1978) does not reflect the dynamic aspects of the aforementioned theories. Levinson's theory is a man's theory in its development and presentation. Central to Levinson's theory are the joint concepts of the career **dream** and life review. During midlife, the man evaluates how close he has come to achieving his dream. He also has the potential to engage in the life review process at various **turning points** during the midlife transition. Given that midlife can span nearly 30 years, the man has numerous opportunities to engage in these evaluations. Levinson blocks "turning points" as occurring in 5-year intervals. Thus, the midlife man has the opportunity to engage in potentially 6 different periods of reevaluation.

> *How might the evaluation of the dream and life review process differ between the thirty-five-year old and the fifty-year-old?*
> *Consider the issues at the other intervals.*

Despite its narrow boundaries in presenting the man's life and its limited application to other cultures, an important element, consistent with previous themes and theories, is the emphasis that Levinson placed on the internal evaluation of a constricted part of the midlife man's context, the workplace.

Again we see in Erikson's and Levinson's writings, the emphasis being placed on the individual's active processing of his stage in life. These evaluations involve the assessment of one's sense of identity as manifested in one's roles, contact and closeness to others, and achievement in life within the work and family contexts.

Men: History, Society, and the Construction of Their Identity

In a recent interview with the singer-songwriter, Billy Joel was quoted as saying,

> I don't even know who the hell I am right now, and I find that kind of interesting. I'm a musician, pianist, a guy from Long Island. A father most importantly. And right up there with father is composer. I'm 52, jumping around on-stage like I'm 21 and thinking—this is not right. (U.S. Weekly Magazine, 2001)

While not many men have the high profile life of Billy Joel, this quote aptly reflects the thoughts of many men in the middle of midlife. Many of the hard won achievements in changing society's view of men and their roles and opening the potential for greater nonviolent emotional expressivity have not been realized by the generation of men that made these advancements. For the majority of blue-collar and white-collar men, the emphasis is on being strong, being the breadwinner, and working the traditional 9–5 job, as it was for their fathers. Few men have taken the opportunity to identify themselves in nontraditional roles (e.g., homemaker, nurse, daycare provider). They have not moved much beyond the roles of their fathers. The major difference between the midlife men of a generation ago and today's midlife men is that today's men are aware of the potential opportunities available to them. That they cannot or have not taken advantage of the opportunities becomes even more distressful to them.

How do others perceive the midlife man? The midlife man is typically seen as being at the peak of his earning power, and peak performance is generally expected from him. His primary domain is the work world. While continuing to master this world, he has a heightened awareness of the stresses associated with midlife; the desire for new beginnings; and the reconsideration of old habits, dreams, behaviors, and goals. He is often preoccupied with the material security of his family, financial planning for the future, presenting what society expects as a "strong male image" (Tamir, 1982).

How the midlife man perceives himself. The midlife man perceives marked limitations on his future (Tamir, 1982). He sees himself as experiencing no more (positive) firsts in life. He must now view the pleasures, challenges, and the struggles of youth from the sidelines. He sees himself often bearing the brunt of decision making and responsibility for others. Morale plummets in the absence of concrete problems as he finds himself not as unique as when he was young (many of the joys and problems are much the same for his peers). He finds that his children have left or are leaving home, parents may die, and he is faced with his mortality (Borland, 1978). He is reluctant to admit to personal doubts and anxieties because he tends to be prohibited in the expression of deep-felt anxiety. As a result, coming to terms with these emotions is more turbulent and disturbing during this stressful period (Tamir 1982).

In many ways, the behaviors and events produced and encountered by the midlife man parallel those of the adolescent male. He manifests emotional instability, hormonal shifts, periods of introspectiveness, and a search for new roles and commitments. The one behavior that can be seen as benefiting the midlife man is the growing level of introspection. This increasing **interiority** (Neugarten, 1968) can result in greater self-knowledge and can lead to the understanding of the duality of life. As Levinson (1978) has indicated, the midlife man has the opportunity to come to terms with himself and with the contradictions that life presents. Coming to understand himself and the world results in a higher form of cognition (Riegel, 1973) and the opportunity to improve his future (Brim, 1976).

PSYCHOLOGICALLY-RELATED ISSUES AT MIDLIFE

This section touches on the four topics central to women's and men's psychological health at midlife. They include general well-being, both an internal and external sense of control, midlife crisis, and depression. Within these sections, gender-and culture-related information will be presented where appropriate.

General Well-Being

Well-being is a multifaceted phenomenon amenable to empirical investigation as well as to holistic interpretation (Ryff, 1985, 1989a, 1989b). The holistic/theoretical identification of well-being has been termed as self-actualization by Maslow (1968), as a fully functioning person by Rogers (1961), as individuation by Jung (1933), and as maturity by Allport (1961). Six dimensions related to positive well-being include self-acceptance, positive relations with others, autonomy, environmental mastery, purpose in life, and personal growth (see Ryff 1989a and 1989b for a review).

In an examination of these factors, Keyes and Ryff (1999) found

1. midlifers function particularly well in comparison to young or elderly adults,
2. autonomy and environmental mastery show marked improvement at midlife,
3. purpose in life and personal growth appear to be stable from youth to midlife but decline thereafter, and
4. self-acceptance and positive relations with others reflect stability across the life span.

Keyes and Ryff concluded that, with regard to these dimensions, midlife provides the most balanced perspective, compared to the young adult viewing life more prospectively and the older adult seeing life retrospectively. Midlife appears to be the temporal benchmark construed by young and elderly adults (in this sample) as the time that they will be or had been at their best, respectively.

Cultural Differences in Well-Being

According to the literature, there are two general approaches to the manifestations of culture—the individualistic and independent approach (predominantly a Western view) and the collectivist and interdependent approach (predominantly an Eastern view). When Korean and North Americans were compared, the two approaches held in their initial descriptions. A comparison of Korean and American midlifers on the six previously mentioned dimensions indicated that:

1. Korean midlifers showed a lower level of well-being on all six scales. These results were attributed to cultural differences in using a six-point scale where extremely positive statements were not endorsed. This is consistent

with the culture's belief in the individual being more self-effacing, with clear sanctions against self-aggrandizement.

2. Korean midlifers showed their highest scores on positive relations with others and lowest scores on self-acceptance.

3. North Americans scored the highest on personal growth and on positive relations with others.

Further comparisons of the two cultures indicated:

KOREANS	*NORTH AMERICANS*
Determined their sense of well-being, maturity, and fulfillment through the accomplishments and success of their children rather than through personal achievement.	Determined their sense of well-being and fulfillment through family and marital relationships. Personal fulfillment was defined through personal accomplishments rather than children's success.
A mature person was defined through interdependent qualities, namely, being honest conscientious, modest, respectful to others, faithful, and responsible.	The mature person was caring and connected with others (interdependent qualities), while also being confident, assertive, showing continual growth, and enjoying life (independent qualities).
The ideal person was defined as: One who does one's best. (Independent qualities? That is, an achiever?)	The ideal person was defined as: An individual who is caring and has deep friendships. (Interdependent qualities?)

Clearly, the distinctions are not as cut and dry as many might think. The heterogeneous nature of the composition of midlife adults in the United States and personally held values/public beliefs regarding the presentation of one's culture may be at odds in this set of data. Also, the interpretation of the Korean ideal person as being an achiever may be a misinterpretation. One may be doing one's best . . . for others, possibly. The theme then for the Korean midlifer would be consistent with cultural expectations and self-expectations for the individual. Nonetheless, particular cultural differences do evidence themselves with regard to well-being at midlife.

Internal and External Sense of Control

Do midlife adults find themselves jointly more in control of their lives as well as more **efficacious?** The existing research for midlife adults is rather meager. However, the gender and race differences can be summarized as follows:

- midlife women had higher external control beliefs than did men (Shannon, 1991),
- midlife women felt greater control over interpersonal projects, with men feeling control over instrumental projects (Simon and Ogilvie, 1992);
- African American women held greater external beliefs of control and lower overall efficacy compared to African American men and Caucasian men and women (Tashakkori & Thompson, 1991);
- *income* was positively related to a greater sense of perceived or internal control for African American women and Caucasian men, and
- *occupational status* was positively related to perceived control for both African American and Caucasian women (Adelman, Antonucci, Crohan, and Coleman, 1989).

Cross Cultural Influences on Perceived Control

Three general findings are of interest with regard to this issue. First, an investigation of Western Europeans indicated that there was greater variation regarding internal/external locus of control beliefs as a result of the home country rather than because of life cycle changes, gender, or social class (Jensen, Olsen, and Hughes, 1990). Second, Japanese and German midlifers scored lower on a perceived sense of internal control (Levenson, 1981). Finally, a comparison of control strategies in Eastern and Western nations pointed to an Eastern approach of employing what are called **secondary control strategies** as manifested in changing oneself rather than the environment. Not surprisingly, the Western approach was to employ the **primary control strategy** of changing the environment to fit ones needs (Peng; 1994, Weisz, Rothbaum, and Blackburn, 1984).

So, what can be taken from the control literature? The message again is in balance and becoming a well-integrated individual. It is important to balance the understanding that total internally driven control is not accessible to any of us. Becoming aware of that which is and is not controllable leads to a more efficacious and physically healthier midlife adult (Clark-Plaskie and Lachman, 1999).

The Midlife Crisis

The question has been raised as to whether the classic midlife crisis is a real and empirically defined phenomenon or if it represents a culturally sanctioned myth. It is difficult to provide a definitive answer. Not all midlife adults experience what would be called a crisis. Most, however, would admit to a disruption in their life plans around the ages of forty to fifty. For these individuals, there was an occurrence that required some degree of a personal evaluation of their life. Midlife crisis is not a marital crisis, economic crisis, or professional crisis, although it may manifest as any of these (Rosenberg, Rosenberg, and Farrell, 1999). Underlying this event is the concurrent re-evaluation of self, ongoing, perhaps, for different reasons. This deeper evaluation of oneself may produce disturbing results that the individual interprets as a call for a change in one's life. If one makes a change inconsistent with societal expectations, it is referred to as a crisis.

Although often considered a Western and predominantly male phenomenon, evidence of midlife crises in "middle and upper middle class" China (Shek, 1995a, 1995b, 1996, 1997,) and women (Gutmann, 1998; Lieblich, 1986; Wethington, 2000) have been reported. Perhaps the experience of self-disturbance has cross-gender and cross-cultural legitimacy; however, the extreme enactment of this crisis is much more of a male behavior. Why might this be so? Earlier in this chapter it was stated that men have less emotional license than do women. Therefore, when confronted with an emotional upheaval in their lives, men do not know how to respond. Their traditional lack of models and belief in self-reliance, emotional control, dramatic action (being a hero), and competition may result in stereotypical behavior (i.e., getting that hot new sports car, that hot new woman, or a drastic lifestyle shift) accepted for men experiencing an emotional problem. Unfortunately, the turmoil that precipitated the crisis behavior is not addressed and has the potential to resurface.

An investigation into the underlying cause of a midlife crisis in two different cohorts of midlifers (those in midlife in the 1960s and 1970s were compared to midlifers in the 1980s and 1990s) resulted in clear cohort differences (Rosenberg, Rosenberg, and Farrell, 1999). The idea of a midlife crisis was still a viable concept for both groups of men. The age of a reported crisis shifted downward to 50 for the midlifers of the '80s and '90s. This latter group expressed less of a family focus and emphasized their search for personal fulfillment. The midlifers of the '60s and '70s were more focused on escaping an oppressive and forced identity, while the younger cohort was dealing with a quest to find any adult identity.

Whether tied to age or life stage, it was concluded that the term midlife crisis is commonly used to describe regrets, setbacks, negative feelings, or anxiety about role change (Madigan, 1998; Rosenberg, Rosenberg, and Farrell, 1999). It is clearly tied to the thought patterns occurring at this time. The thought patterns include increased introspection, realization that time is passing, and regret for lost opportunities.

Depression and Related Psychological Phenomena

Contrary to popular belief, depression is not a major factor for the midlife adult nor is being a midlife adult a factor in the existing rate of depression (Samuels, 1997). Statistics do however indicate that women are twice as likely to exhibit depression as are men (Bhatia and Bhatia, 1999), socioeconomic status determines access to pharmaceutical treatment of depression (Sclar, 1999), and when socioeconomic status is held constant, African American women are 56 percent more likely to be assigned antidepressants (Sclar et al., 1998).

The last point is provocative. What are its implications?

Yet, compared to younger and older adults, the midlife adult is in relatively good shape (Kessler et al., 1992; Mirowsky and Ross, 1992). However, it is felt that the rate of depression in this group is not fully represented. With a

TABLE 10.1. Factors Contributing to Midlife Well-being

Factors Impacting Overall Functioning

	Men	Women
Depression	• Being married, low levels[1] • Low socioeconomic status ↑ levels[5] • Caregiving to spouse or others ↑ levels[5] • Being a member of a dual career couple ↓ levels[5] • Sexual dysfunction ↑ levels[10]	• Being married, high levels[1] • Children in home ↑ levels[5] • Caregiving to spouse or others ↑ levels[5] • Being a member of a dual career couple[5] • High-strain job with low authority and low autonomy ↑ levels[5] • Being African American, unmarried, with few social roles ↑ levels[6] • Falling short of career goals ↑ levels[8] • Decrease in life purpose ↑ levels[8] • Lower sense of control ↑ levels[9]
Extroversion	• Positively correlated with perceived social support[2] • Positively correlated with seeking support when stressed[2]	• Positively correlated with perceived social support[2] • Positively correlated with seeking support when stressed[2]

Social Relationships	Positively correlated with
	  —satisfactory peer adjustment
	  —little to no anger[7]
	  —mentor relationships in young adulthood[3]	

Identity		African American women derive positive identify from
		  —family support in career
		  —living an integrated identity
		  —constant evaluation of the context and changes[4]

[1]Earle et al., 1998

[2]VonDrass and Siegler, 1997

[3]Westermeyer, 1998

[4]Burke, 1995

[5]Erikson, 1998

[6]Brown, Cochran, and McGregor, 1996

[7]McQuaide, 1996

[8]Carr, 1997

[9]Nolen-Hoeksema and Grayson, 2001

[10]Male Depression, www.midlife-passage/depressant, 2001

thirty-year span of time between the oldest and the youngest midlifer, different historical factors impacting the expectations and aspirations regarding life may be significantly different so as to impact these two groups' depression rates differentially (Clark-Plaskie and Lachman, 1999).

There are, however, findings regarding midlife depression and associated factors that contribute to well-being. Table 10.1 provides a summary of these findings.

Summary and Comments

The primary focus of the chapter was on issues of identity and self during the midlife period. The emphasis was on the self work being conducted. It was emphasized that much of this activity is personal and not available to external scrutiny. Except in extreme cases of turbulence and trauma (midlife crisis), the friends, family members, and casual observer may be unaware of the evaluative thoughts of the midlife adult.

The selected theories of Jung, Bolen, Josselson, and Norris addressed the spiritual search of women at this time. Jung, Erikson, and Levinson were cited as theories that directly addressed particular aspects of men's transition through midlife.

The more general psychological issues of well-being, perceived control, midlife crisis, and depression were highlighted. Broad cultural differences, Eastern philosophy versus Western philosophy, gender differences, and racial differences were also elaborated upon.

Much of the personal evaluation and self-alignment that occurs during midlife sets the course for the rest of the individual's life.

I was 18 years old in 1975 and it was a time of disco and partying . . . alcohol was the way to go . . . I was never exposed to drugs until I was 21 years old. We had fake ID's and lots of guts. My family, being military, did not allow for many freedoms ironically enough. They were very strict.

As soon as I graduated from high school I went to Tech immediately made great friends at USC thru my life guarding job . . . all the jocks were staying at a local apartment complex where I worked and my boss was one of the cheerleaders . . . My parents would not let me go to USC. They thought I was too young.

Guys LOVE them, they're so much fun. And girls, they used me to get to my jock brothers, they were lots of fun.

My dream was to become an airline stewardess and learn to speak 5 different languages and travel the world. I was too young at 17 when I was recruited by Pan Am, I was to start when I turned 18. So my dad made me go to nursing school until I turned 18 and I had to finish, which he knew.

My identity was one of confidence and focus. I knew what I wanted and did my best never giving in to defeat. By the time I was 21 I had experienced life very fast. Drugs Sex and Rock and Roll. . . . My husband at the time was a real piece of work. I was infatuated by all the stuff and the power. It also came with a lot of violence both passive and aggressive. I was totally naive. I may have grown up with parents who were military, but my father never raised his voice to my mother and vice versa. Their

VOICES OF OUR PARENTS 10.1

arguments were done behind closed doors where we never heard them or my mom just would give you the silent treatment until she was ready to have some dialogue. I never thought that my life would ever experience what it did between the age of 20 to 24 and from 25 to 29. It was a concentrated dose of life. I had almost lost all of my confidence and courage. But hey ho life is good. I have absolutely no regrets for anything that I did or said during that period of my life. I would not be who I am today if I had not lived life in the fashion that I did.

WHAT I NOW KNOW FOR SURE. . . . Life is what counts. Ask yourself these questions and then seek the truth of life.

1. What does it mean to be a human being?
2. Am I Creating Value in everything I do or say?

PERSONAL PROFILE

My name is M A and I am 43 at the present time. I was predominantly raised in the southern states . . . Kentucky mostly and South Carolina. My father was in the Air Force and we moved every one to two years in the first 12 years of my life. After that we lived in the Washington D.C. area. My dad worked for the White House, I choose to never serve the military. I have two brothers who followed in my father's footsteps and took it even further in regards to education. My education is that of high school and Technical College. My first career opportunity was life guarding at the age of 14. I lied about my age to take the course. I looked much older. Ha! ha!. Since that time I have trained as a nurse, my specialty was pediatric oncology and I also flew stocks and bonds for a company, I've waited tables. And now for the past 16 years I have been a Cosmetologist. I absolutely love it.

I was married for 364 days, legally, when I was 20 years old. It was an experience that I have only begun to remember as of 5 years ago. It was very abusive. My ex-husband and his father both tried to end my life. I never biologically have had any children. I just became a legal guardian in Jan. of 2001, the oldest daughter of a friend of mine who died as a result of stomach cancer. It's is an incredible experience. We have 2 dogs and 2 cats.

VOICES OF OUR PARENTS 10.1 (continued)

Preface to Section III

Behind the social persona of the parent, spouse, adult child, coworker, and friend, lies the core individual from which the former selves derive. For this reason, it may be said that the keystone chapter of this section focuses on the construction and identification of the self. Many midlife adults experience a period of questioning and self-examination at this point in their lives. For some, a transient assessment of who he or she is to others and him- or herself is conducted. For others, a much more elaborate and fine-tuned analysis of all aspects of their lives is conducted. Both groups of individuals may experience profound and significant change in some, if not all, aspects of their lives.

Midlife provides the opportunity for the adult to conduct an evaluation as to where they are in life. This midpoint provides perspective for a meaningful analysis. Their location in life may relate to family, friends, work, or more personal goals to enhance themselves educationally or as a contributor to the community. It is at this time that changes may occur in the social and personal components of their lives.

Therefore, four primary social domains are presented in this section. Relationships with others are presented first and analyzed. Then, the work environment, its meaning and impact, are considered. The link between the ever-changing workforce and the need for reeducation/retooling is presented. However, not all educational pursuits are driven by work-related factors. For many midlife adults, the educational setting provides them with the opportunity to achieve avocational or personal goals shelved during young adulthood. Volunteerism can also serve as an outlet for the adult examining her or his role in the greater society and community.

Who the midlife person is to him- or herself and the nature of relationships and goals during this time serve as the foundation of this section.

CHAPTER 11

Relationships at Midlife

A large part of the despair, loneliness, and confusion to those individuals undergoing midlife is that they have no map that suggests post-normal, post-adult stages of life.

—SAM KEEN

Consider what you want to do later in life while you are still young. If you associate enough with older people who do enjoy their lives, who are not stored away in any golden ghettos, you will gain a sense of continuity and the possibilities for a full life.

—MARGARET MEAD

OVERVIEW

Relationships form the foundation of a culture. In midlife, it appears that the number of relationships, reflected in a variety of contexts, are at their maximum. The quality of these relationships reflects one's history, health, community status, and self-perception. It is not possible to present any discussion of the human without providing an account of their links to others.

Relationships at midlife are multidimensional, multicontextual, and multigenerational. Who is the midlife adult? Midlife adults, not to be facetious, are frequently the persons who are chronologically in the middle of the family. He or she may have one or two generations younger than they and one or two generations older. Because of their standing in the community, they may be looked up to and relied upon for guidance. They may be a senior employee or an employer. They may be someone's sister, brother, or friend. They may be someone's significant other. They may also be trying to find a place for themselves in their own lives.

Many of the social roles that give our lives meaning are those involving relationships. We live, learn, work, and try to solve problems together. Our lives are reflected in our memberships in families, teams, classes, clubs, unions, and other informal groups. The emotional and social changes of midlife take place within the context of family relationships, friendly relationships, work relationships, and community relationships.

This chapter is divided into four major sections:

1. families: marriage, parenting, elderly parents, and siblings;
2. friendships;
3. gender roles and crises; and
4. cultural differences in relationships.

FAMILIES: MARRIAGE, PARENTING, ELDERLY PARENTS, AND SIBLINGS

Family relations are a vital aspect of life. The family can be viewed as a dynamic system of interdependent relationships (Hill and Mattessich, 1979). The notion of what makes up a family has changed over the past three decades. The classic **nuclear family** plays less of a central role in the lives of many individuals today. The **blended family** and single-parent family are increasingly common. There has been a considerable increase in the number of single-parent households as a result of divorce (see tables 11.1 and 11.2). In these families, like the **beanpole families,** you find a drop in family size reflected in the fewer number of children in the home (Aldous, 1990) reflecting a tilt toward families to becoming adult-centered in contrast to child-centered. In these families you find more generations living simultaneously—children, siblings, parents, grandparents, great-grandparents. One characteristic of these families is that there are considerably fewer children (Gatz, Bengtson, and Blum, 1990). With this trend toward shrinking families and greater overall national mobility in Western societies, the midlife adult finds fewer family resources (i.e., sisters, brothers, cousins, aunts, uncles) on whom to depend when attempting to pursue nonfamily activities involving educational, work-related, or leisure activities. These nonfamily related desires may be in direct competition to feelings of familial obligation. However, it should not be ignored that families can also serve as a source of tremendous support for the pursuit of personal goals (Setterstein, 1999). In our culture, it is not uncommon for a woman in her forties to be dealing with several concurrent family cycles. She may be involved in the support of aging grandparents, retirement issues of her parents, launching her children, or perhaps becoming a grandmother. This example emphasizes the cross-generational nature and mutual interdependence found in the family of the midlife adult.

The Marital Relationship at Midlife

Marriage is considered to be a dynamic system in that it changes over time. Partners change over time as a result of mutually shared or individually experienced events, the family constellation changes (children, pets, or parents are

TABLE 11.1. Households by Type and Selected Characteristics: March 2000 (in thousands, except average size)

Characteristic	All Households	Family		Household Other Families		Nonfamily Households		
		Total	Married Couples	Male Householder	Female Householder	Total	Male Householder	Female Householder
All Households	104,705	72,025	55,311	4,028	12,687	32,680	14,641	18,008
Age of Householder								
15 to 24 years old	5,860	3,353	1,450	560	1,342	2,507	1,266	1,221
25 to 34 years old	18,627	13,007	9,380	886	2,732	5,620	3,448	2,172
35 to 44 years old	23,966	18,706	14,104	1,102	3,449	5,250	3,261	1,969
45 to 54 years old	20,927	15,000	12,792	712	2,299	5,123	2,583	2,541
55 to 64 years old	13,582	9,568	8,138	351	1,080	4,023	1,533	2,490
65 years old or over	21,744	11,587	9,437	418	1,735	10,157	2,530	7,626
Race and ethnicity of householder								
White	87,671	60,251	48,790	3,081	6,060	27,420	12,204	15,215
Non-Hispanic	78,512	53,066	43,865	2,468	6,732	25,753	11,278	14,475
Black	12,848	8,664	4,114	706	3,514	4,185	1,876	2,309
Asian and Pacific Islander	3,301	2,506	1,996	179	231	831	432	399
Hispanic (of any race)	9,319	7,561	5,133	658	1,769	1,758	974	783
Presence of related children under 18								
No related children	67,350	34,670	28,919	1,628	3,924	32,660	14,641	15,031
With related children	37,355	37,366	26,248	2,202	6,752	(x)	(x)	(x)
One raised child under 18	15,491	15,486	9,892	1,321	4,275	(x)	(x)	(x)
Two related children under 18	14,020	14,000	10,567	644	2,809	(x)	(x)	(x)
Three related children under 18	5,510	5,510	4,235	155	1,067	(x)	(x)	(x)
Four or more related children under 18	2,332	2,332	1,660	52	591	(x)	(x)	(x)

TABLE 11.1. (continued)

Presence of own children under 18								
No own children	10,100	37,420	30,062	2,242	5,116	32,660	14,641	19,033
With own children	34,606	34,806	25,382	1,788	7,571	(x)	(x)	(x)
With own children under 1	2,639	2,939	2,264	174	501	(x)	(x)	(x)
With own children under 3	8,786	8,786	6,784	441	1,561	(x)	(x)	(x)
With own children under 8	14,066	14,586	11,383	706	2,867	(x)	(x)	(x)
With own children under 12	25,885	25,885	19,082	1,226	5,568	(x)	(x)	(x)
Size of households								
1 person	26,724	(x)	(x)	(x)	(x)	26,724	11,181	15,543
2 people	34,553	29,834	22,589	1,730	5,206	4,632	2,507	2,225
3 people	17,152	16,805	11,213	1,105	4,086	746	570	177
4 people	15,309	15,064	12,455	652	1,927	245	179	86
5 people	6,961	6,894	5,723	307	864	87	70	17
6 people	2,445	2,413	1,916	130	355	32	26	8
7 or more	1,400	1,416	1,106	78	237	13	6	5
Average size	2.62	3.24	3.26	3.16	2.17	1.25	1.34	1.77

(x) Not applicable

Note: Data are not shown separately for the American Indian and Alaska Native population because of the small sample size in the Current Population Survey in March 2000.

Source: U.S. Census Bureau, Current Population Survey, March 2000.

TABLE 11.2. Percentage of Divorce Rates in Selected Countries

Country	Divorces (as % of marriages 1996)
Belarus	68
Russian Federation	65
Sweden	64
Latvia	63
Ukraine	63
Czech Republic	61
Belgium	56
Finland	56
Lithuania	55
United Kingdom	53
Moldova	52
United States	**49**
Hungary	46
Canada	45
Norway	43
France	43
Germany	41
Netherlands	41
Switzerland	40
Iceland	39
Kazakhstan	39
Luxembourg	39
Austria	38
Denmark	35
Slovakia	34
Bulgaria	28
Israel	26
Slovenia	26
Kyrgyzstan	25
Romania	24
Portugal	21
Poland	19
Armenia	18
Greece	18
Turkmenistan	18
Spain	17
Azerbaijan	15
Croatia	15
Cyprus	13
Tajikistan	13
Georgia	12
Italy	12
Uzbekistan	12
Albania	7
Turkey	6
Macedonia	5

Source: Aldous, 1990.

added to the equation), and personal and historical events impact the relationship (Newman and Newman, 1995). Newman and Newman write that there are three requirements to a successful marriage:

1. a commitment to growth as an individual and as a couple,
2. effective communication, and
3. creative use of conflict situations.

Which of these three elements do you consider to be critical in relationships and why?

Can it be said that marriage at midlife is bliss or the blahs? Kerckhoff (1976) states that it is difficult to assess, especially when evaluating the marriage from the perspective of the wife or the husband.

Women in Marriage Relationships

Three observations have been made regarding midlife women's perceptions of marriage:

1. Women tend to begin to publicly express the inadequacies of their spouse (Duvall, 1977).
2. Women appear to be reassessing their roles as wives and mothers and are beginning to concentrate on their individuality (Alder, 1990).
3. The midlife woman is also working on the rebuilding of the marriage relationship and on maintaining kin ties with older and younger generations (Duvall, 1977).

Men in Marriage Relationships

Marriage is the strongest and most intimate human relationship experienced by a man (Lowenthal and Robinson, 1976). Midlife men have reported the following responses regarding marriage:

1. Their job is no longer *the* means of self-fulfillment and life satisfaction regardless of their life status. Of increasing importance are intimacy needs and the value of their marital partnership (Tamir, 1982).
2. They report being more attuned to affiliative needs (Brim, 1976).
3. They also report receiving less pampering from their spouse (Lowenthal and Weiss, 1976).
4. They feel that the positive feelings they feel toward their wives are significantly related to their overall life satisfaction (Tamir, 1982).

Interesting sidelight: According to researchers in Scandinavia, the number of couples choosing to live apart, yet remain married, has doubled since 1993. Newlyweds fifty and older often choose this arrangement to avoid the hassles of giving up a home or uprooting children from a previous marriage (My Generation, 2001). This yet unnamed category can be added to the existing blended, single-parent, beanpole, and nuclear family.

Parenthood at Midlife

Parenthood at midlife can fall into three categories: parents of children in their late childhood to young adulthood, parents of newborns, and parents of adult children returning home.

Parenthood at any age is a demanding, difficult learning experience in that every child is different, and parenting requires different skills and different levels of commitment compared to other relationships (Newman and Newman, 1995). Statistics indicate that midlife parents have few, if any, children living in their homes (Aiken, 1998). Only 10 percent of parents in their early fifties have households that contain children under the age of eighteen years (Saulter, 1996).

What is the nature of your family structure?
Are there any more children to be launched?

It is said that middle-aged parents spend an average of approximately seven years in the launching of all of their children (Duvall, 1977). During this launching period, there is a shift in the parent-child relationship. Both the parent and the child are changing places in the family structure. Those changes include the adoption of new identities, new roles, and new responsibilities (Hagestad, 1982, 1987). Frequently, parents use this time of transition for their child to evaluate their own accomplishments as parents (Ryff, Schmutt, and Lee, 1996), as well as to review their own personal development (Newman and Newman, 1995).

Have you noticed a change in roles between you and your parents? Elaborate either way.

However, this launching process begins later in working-class and non-white families due, typically, to a larger family size (Barber, 1989).

Launching has already been referred to as a positive time when the children in the family move on (Antonucci, Tamir, and Dubnoff, 1980). Launching can be contrasted to what has been colloquially referred to as the empty nest. The empty-nest syndrome is most frequently seen as occurring in full-time mothers who view their child/children's departure with feelings of depression, sadness, and crisis. For many, the whole of their identity is wrapped up in their children's lives (Neugarten, 1970). Interestingly, this negative reaction toward the departure of the child has been attributed to a corresponding unhappy marriage (Bee, 2000). Whether viewed positively or negatively, the departure of the last child from the family begins the post parental period in the midlife adult's life. Although one is always a parent, the day-to-day role changes (Bee 2000), regardless of whether this period is met with depression or feelings of rejuvenation (Neugarten 1970).

During the period of prelaunching, 75 percent of midlife males with adolescent children report moderately tense relationships (Borland, 1978; Brim, 1976). These fathers report experiencing a values clash with their adolescent son, envy of youth and a youthful child, and a revisitation of their own adolescent crisis along with their original adolescent struggle (Levinson, 1978).

They Do Come Home Again

A surprise to midlife parents today—and a relatively recent phenomenon—is the increasing number of adult children returning home after the parent thought that the adult child had gone (Barber, 1989). Data suggest that young adults are leaving home later and are more likely to return. Data also indicate that of parents aged 45–54 who have adult children, 45 percent have an adult child living at home (Aquilino, 1990), about 15 to 20 percent of adult children between the ages of 20 and 30 live with their parents, and an additional 10 percent of these individuals are over 30 (Ward and Spitze, 1996).

Do you view this tendency to return home to be good or bad?

What may be the long-range implication for the returning young adult?

What has accounted for this not-so empty nest? Many of these adult children return because they are experiencing a divorce or separation, have never married, are unwed mothers, or find that their salaries do not provide the lifestyle to which their parents had made them accustomed (Glick and Lin, 1986; Ward, Logan, and Spitze, 1992). This return can have two possible results. On the one hand, there exists a potential for conflict with regard to employment status (usually unemployed), lifestyle choices, forms of dress, and choice of friends (Aquilino and Supple, 1990). On the other hand, the positive results from the return of an adult child are that household responsibilities can now be shared along with the sharing of leisure activities. The older the returning child, the better the generational interaction (Suitor and Pillemer, 1988).

Grandparenthood at Midlife

Grandparenthood comes to the midlifer who married early and started a family as a young adult, who married into an already existing older family structure, or who is a member of a family where a teenage pregnancy is a reality. In the last case, many middle-age grandparents take on the responsibility of caring for and raising the grandchild (Cherlin and Furstenberg, 1986). Three-fourths of midlife adults become grandparents before they are sixty-five years old, with half of the women becoming grandmothers before the age of fifty-four. There are many ways to be a grandparent, not all requiring the same level of involvement or responsibility. Three styles of grandparenting have been identified in the literature:

1. remote—in which the grandchild is seen infrequently and contact is limited,
2. companionate—in which a warm and caring relationship is developed, and
3. involved—in which day-to-day care is central to the relationship. These children are typically brought up by their grandparents because their mother was unwed and financially unable to care for them, the child is the result of a divorced household and has no parental care, or both parents work to the extreme and are unable to care for a child.

What type of grandparenting do you recall or are you experiencing?

There is a tendency for the younger grandparent to fall into the category of companionate, with older grandparents being remote. Also, it has been shown that African American and Hispanic grandparents are closer to their grandchildren and have more frequent contact than is the case with white, non-Hispanic grandparents (Newman and Newman, 1995).

The Sandwich Generation or The Middle Generation Squeeze

What is the sandwich generation, and what is happening to create such a situation? Midlife adults are experiencing the stress and change associated with the departure of their child or children and in some cases, the return of these adult children, as well as possibly adopting the new role of grandparent. These demands represent one side of the life facing the midlife adult, who may also be feeling, for the first time (in a while), personal aspirations during this postparental period when the psychological, physical, and financial pressures of frail or elderly family members (usually parents) arise. The empty nest has the potential to be refilled (quickly) by two different generations, one older and one younger (Aizenberg and Treas, 1985; Clemens and Axelson, 1985).

What complicates this situation is the increasing number of women, the traditional caregivers and **kin keepers,** entering or returning to the workforce. Over half or the women between forty-five and fifty-four years of age are in the workforce and are relatively unavailable to be involved in or participate in their traditionally expected roles (Gatz, Bengtson, and Blum, 1990; Treas and Bengtson, 1987). The older women have typically come from larger families and have an extended network of relatives and relationships upon which they can rely for support. Baby boomers, typically coming from smaller families, will have limited support available when needed (Aizenberg and Treas, 1985).

While feeling a need to respond to their own children's life situation, the top ten activities that midlife adults feel are expected of them as it relates to the care of elderly family members include:

1. helping to understand resources available in the community,
2. giving emotional support,
3. talking over matters of importance,
4. making room in home in an emergency,
5. sacrificing personal freedom,
6. giving care when the elderly family member is ill,
7. being together on special occasions,
8. giving financial help,
9. giving the parent advice, and
10. adjusting the family schedule to accommodate helping (Hamon and Blieszner, 1990).

Typically, in our society, the daughter or daughter-in-law is expected to serve as the primary caretaker. Duties taken upon by this woman can reflect an expectation of direct hands-on medical care, to providing food, housekeeping, and/ or transportation for the older parent. The impact of this caregiving takes its toll on the midlife adult physically, financially, and emotionally; especially if the caregiver is attempting to hold down a job, care for a spouse, and assist her own children or grandchildren (Cicirelli, 1980, 1981, 1989; Rossi and Rossi, 1990; Chappell, 1990; Aiken, 1998, Finley, 1989; Frank, Avery, and Laman, 1988). An attempt at parity in familial responsibility was legislated by the Family Medical Leave Act in 1998. As described by this act, the most immediate family member to the individual requiring aid is to assist in this effort. Therefore, it is the son who must take off time from the job to assist in the care of his mother or father. It is not the responsibility of the daughter-in-law.

The Sibling Relationship at Midlife

After a time of separation, and the development of the many aspects of their identities, middle-age siblings often make attempts to establish new ties and do away with old conflicts and rivalries (Cicirelli, 1980; Scott and Roberto, 1981). Cicirelli reported that 85 percent of middle-age Americans feel close or very close to their siblings.

Sibling relationships have been characterized in five ways:

1. intimate—extremely close, confidants, best friends;
2. congenial—close and affectionate but lacking empathy;
3. loyal—based on belonging to a family rather than affection;
4. apathetic—indifferent to each other; or
5. hostile—characterized by anger, enmity, and resentment (Gold, 1989, 1990).

The test of any relationship, not only a sibling relationship, comes usually at a time of crisis, usually over the care of an elderly parent or an inheritance.

These are particularly difficult if the relationship has not been good. While having the potential to be a great source of support, siblings are also a great source of interpersonal stress (Suitor and Pilleman, 1988).

FRIENDSHIPS

Next to relatives, friends are our closest companions and confidants (Dickens and Perlman, 1981; Larson, Mannuel, and Zuzanek, 1986). Critical to the formation of friendships are feelings of mutual trust and the knowledge that friends will be there to share the good times and that they will serve as a source of psychological and physical support at times of stress (Levinson, 1986; Sarason, Sarason, and Pierce, 1989; Hirsch, 1981; House, Robbins, and Metzner, 1982; and Cohen et al., 1997).

A look at midlife friendships indicates that they are fewer in number compared to young adults. However, the midlife adult has more "old friends" whom they may not see often but on whom they feel they can rely (Hess, 1972).

Women and Friendships

Women tend to have more friendships than do men. Their friendships can be characterized as deeper and long lasting and were actively sought out to have relationships outside the family (Dickens and Perlman, 1981). Women's friendships are more self-disclosing, are represented by a sharing of feelings and concerns, and show a willingness to give and receive emotional support (Fox, Gibbs, and Averback, 1985; Reisman, 1981). The vast majority of these friendships are woman-woman friendships and are most fully engaged during times of stress (Fooken, 1985).

How many friends does your mother have? How does she define a friend?

Men and Friendships

Men of all backgrounds experience a change in their lives during midlife. Typically, it is reflected in a shifting of priorities and values (Tamir, 1982). Friendships in men are manifested differently than are friendships in women. Their friendships are based on shared interests and activities carried out in the form of "mini-competitions" (Tannen, 1990). Compared to women, men have fewer friends, tend to confide less in others, and fail to establish relationships of equal intensity (Lowenthal and Robinson, 1976). Men's friendship networks are small and tend to be less supportive during times of stress. When surveyed, men asserted that their spouse was their closest confidant (Tamir, 1989). College-educated and noncollege-educated men express this period of transition differently when it comes to friendships. Noncollege-educated men who lacked a sense of social connectedness also lacked in self-esteem. They visited neighbors less and lacked an overall zest for life. When anxious, they tended to talk to family members and relatives less often. College-educated men experienced more psychological immobilization at midlife, resulting in the greater use of social support systems of friends and relatives (Rubin, 1976; Tamir, 1985). The greater the life-stress situation, the harder it was to establish and maintain any relationships (Tamir, 1989).

How many friends does your father have? What is the nature of their friendships?

Closing Comment on Friends

While both men and women spend less time currently with their close friends than they had formerly, the strength of the relationships and expressed levels of self-disclosure were reported to increase with time (Fiebert and Wright, 1989). Overall, however, midlifers often find themselves alone during crises due to geographic distance from family members and friends, a feeling that they don't know each other well enough "to impose" on the friendship, and increasing reliance on public agencies for help. Reliance on individual resources and social resources has increased in importance for the successful coping with critical life events. It is, however, that interpersonal contact that makes crises bearable.

GENDER ROLES AND CRISES AT MIDLIFE

During this time, an interesting series of changes have been observed in the midlife woman and man. The middle-aged man is often depicted as experiencing role strain. The man at this time is said to be attempting to reintegrate his multiple roles in the work context, community, and home (Tamir, 1989). Men and women show a reversal of personality characteristics by assuming the characteristics of the other gender. However, the behavior being observed now is nothing new. Rather, women and men are just beginning to more fully express features of their personality that were always present but that were being closely modulated and controlled by society during young adulthood. During times of stress and change, we all begin to manifest fundamental characteristics of our personality that we have successfully monitored and controlled in the good times.

There are certain life events that begin to accumulate at this time that add to personal stress. They include divorce, illness, widowhood, parenthood, and caregiving and related expectations (usually for the woman) (Lemme, 1999; Green and Boxer, 1986). Although more women have entered the full-time job market, among other inequities encountered by women, one particular stressor that affects her quality of work and the quality of her family life is the lack of parity found in caregiving. Few men are stepping up and assuming a caregiving role that would have ordinarily fallen to the wife (Finley, 1989). This lack of parity leads to a spillover of stress by the woman. Only recently with the implementation of the Family Leave Act has the issue of parity in caregiving been addressed in a widespread manner.

An Expansion of Gender Roles in a Variety of Cultures

Local and cross-cultural gender roles have been examined and have indicated the expression of more masculine qualities and more pacific qualities in midlife women and men in the United States, respectively. The Native American woman at midlife is allowed to participate in tribal council affairs due to her greater "manly-heartedness." Midlife Japanese women are depicted as being freed from many of the constraining social proscriptions exemplified by their ability to make bawdy jokes in mixed company. Finally, middle-aged Lebanese women are found to be more bawdy, aggressive, and controlling than younger women in the society (Gutmann, 1987; Huyck, 1994; Nash and Feldman, 1981; Valliant, 1977).

Are you aware of other cultural differences in gender and family relationships?

CULTURAL DIFFERENCES IN RELATIONSHIPS

Research into cultural differences has been scattered and lacking any unified theme(s). First, readers of this text may be looking for a more extensive review of homosexual relationships at midlife. What may surprise many individuals is that the data that exist on the creation of homosexual friendships and more permanent unions mirror, very much, the patterns of establishing these same types of relationships in the heterosexual community (Bliss, 2000). Relationships are established at work, in educational settings, and in community organizations. Beyond this summary statement, it can be added that midlife homosexuals experience nearly all of the same issues as do midlife heterosexuals, with the additional stressor of discrimination directed toward them for their sexual orientation. More detailed information regarding midlife homosexuals is limited because the volunteers for surveys are primarily white, typically representing one partner in the relationship, and are anonymous self-reports (Huyck, 1995). Until greater acceptance is afforded homosexuals in our culture, a clear and balanced picture will be difficult to obtain.

The remaining findings regarding cross-cultural patterns in gender roles and friendships will be arranged by geographical region and/or particular cultural representation in lieu of any other organizing strategy.

Korean, Korean American, and Vietnamese Marriages

A number of Korean, Korean American, and Vietnamese women have chosen to marry outside of their cultural group. This behavior has been termed **out-marrying.** The data support the initial assertion that women outmarry at higher rates than do males. In fact, male outmarriage is relatively rare (Rhee, 1999). The impact of outmarriage for the woman is critical and devastating to the maintenance and creation of relationships. Problems encountered include disapproval by the family, isolation by the community, language difficulties between the husband and wife, conflicts due to cultural differences, and identity problems in the children of interracial marriages (Rhee, 1999). The midlife outmarried woman is not immune to the stressors previously mentioned, and these are encountered with a greater depth of crisis management in the absence of familial support.

Is outmarrying a possibility in our culture?

Marital Patterns in Nigeria and Bajju Cultures

With greater educational opportunities afforded them, more Nigerian women are seeking alternatives to marriage, delaying marriage, and actively reducing the number of children they bear (Isiugo-A banine-Uche et al., 1993). This finding parallels the beanpole families observed in Western cultures, suggesting the potential to carry comparable problems regarding support relationships with it.

In the Bajju culture, marriage is determined via wife-capture or wife stealing, thereby requiring the woman to leave her clan and establish new familial attachments. Depending on the new clan traditions, the woman may have to establish new familial, friend, and community relationships (McKinney, 1992).

Filial Piety as an Eastern Concept

Filial piety is exemplified by the expression of responsibility, respect, sacrifice, and family harmony. Filial piety is reflected in the practice of family care and support for parents resulting in cohesive ties between family members, family responsibility, interdependence between members, harmony, and the pooling of the individual members' resources to promote the well-being of the parents and the family. Of all the elements of filial piety, respect is the most important (Sung, 1998). This approach is in direct contrast to the individualistic philosophy of the West in which one is responsible for all aspects of one's life. Filial piety is the (ideological) foundation of family support in Eastern cultures. With this as the guiding family philosophy, along with the considerable intergenerational interdependence, the notion of the sandwich generation is an unlikely experience in Eastern cultures.

African American Marriages

Factors that have been found to contribute to success in African American marriages include a sense of emotional support from one's partner; having fewer children with correspondingly decreased childrearing worries; the ability to express individuality within the relationship; and as job satisfaction increases for the African American woman, so does her satisfaction with her marriage. Researchers emphasize that more information is required on the extended kin network of African American families, the impact of religion in the life of the married couple, and a better sense of the contribution of community to their lives (Broman, 1993; Clark-Nicholas and Gray-Little 1991).

Summary and Comments

Relationships exist in a variety of settings in a variety of ways. For most midlife adults, the primary relationships that they have are with family members. As would be expected from the ecological framework, immediate family (the microsystem) serves as the first and most enduring set of relationships. They include the midlife adult's parents, grandparents, siblings, spouse or partner, children, and possibly grandchildren. The next circle of relationships in the mesosystem include extended family—nieces; nephews; cousins; aunts, or uncles; as well as friends, neighbors, or fellow church members. At the exosystem level, relationships exist with coworkers, employers or employees, trades people, and professionals in the community. The midlife adult probably has established some profession-related relationships at a national or international level (macrosystem level), for example, the Lion's Club member who regularly attends the national meeting or a quilter who shows her or his work at regional, national, or international exhibits. Many more relationship opportunities exist for individuals in all walks of life.

Relationships at all of these levels can be supportive, helpful, frustrating, troublesome, or competitive. We tend to tap different relationships with different types of information, such as adopting a new pet. You may share that with a friend or relative but not necessarily your mechanic. Depending on the event, we may be more selective with whom we share information. We may not share information regarding an incontinence problem with our grocer but might share that information with a close friend or family member.

Across all ages, relationships play a critical role in our development. At midlife, the number of relationships that have been developed are many and varied. Nonetheless, these relationships are important to the great number of roles adopted by the midlife adult.

Special Relationship Note

For the individual interested in obtaining a better understanding of the impact of ethnicity and cultural diversity on the family structure, you are referred to *Family Ethnicity: Strength in Diversity* (McAdoo, 1993). In this volume, African American families, Mexican and Spanish families, Native American families, Muslim families, and Asian American families are discussed.

Growing up in the 60's and being the middle child of eight was a challenge. My mother had 4 children when my father died; I was four at the time. Two years later she met and married a man with children of his own and together they had four more children. With the children from my step father's first marriage, my brothers and sister from my mother's first marriage and the children from their marriage together, there were 14 children altogether.

I believe that growing up with this many siblings was a benefit. There were so many of us that it was always easy to get out of trouble, but being in the middle had its disadvantages as well. The responsibility of the younger kinds fell on us because the older ones soon left home.

Not having a father of my own, I believe that I took on the ideas and beliefs of my step dad. Growing up I learned the family business. A business that today, I own.

I grew up in a small town in the south. Living in a rural area had its advantages. We were not exposed to the drugs like the big cities. Sex before marriage happened, but not as much as today's society. Drinking was something that you hoped that your Dad never found out you did.

After graduation from high school, I enlisted in the Air Force and gave Uncle Sam four years of my life. Then I returned home to my mother and younger sister and brothers. I continued working with my Dad until his retirement. One of my younger brothers and myself continued the business.

I never married. I remained home with my mother until her death a few years ago. Now I am too set in my ways to settle down with any one person. I enjoy my freedom and would not want to have someone conform to my ways.

What I know is that life is precious. Would I change anything in my life. . . . . .WHY?

PERSONAL PROFILE

Age: 42

Occupation: Independent businessman

VOICES OF OUR PARENTS 11.1

CHAPTER 12

Work at Midlife

I suppose that I'm in a bit of a rut, really. In the same job 13 years, getting on the same train at the same time every morning, press the same elevator button at the same point, still having someone checking the quality of my work after all this time. I'm not totally dissatisfied . . . I would like to be doing something different, but it's hard.

—60-YEAR-OLD MALE CITY ADMINISTRATOR
KROGER, 2000

These days I'm kind of in a holding period. . .I'm taking things slowly. I don't fight it as I would have in the past. I think that I will find something that will be the next stage for a new beginning, perhaps not just in terms of my career but in other things as well.

—55-YEAR-OLD SCHOOL ADMINISTRATOR
KROGER, 2000

I don't really feel I had a career . . . two jobs and I stopped to have a family. I'm in the process of trying to start my own business. Once that is off the ground, then *I would say that's a career.*

—40-YEAR-OLD FORMER HOMEMAKER
GROSSMAN AND CHESTER, 1990

OVERVIEW

The work environment provides one source of establishing new relationships and enhancing already-existing relationships. Coworkers can serve as a source of support and/or a source of stress. These relationships, along with others in the world, provide a picture of an increasingly well-rounded adult.

WORK AND ITS MEANING

The work setting represents one context familiar to both men and women. Nearly every man and woman in every culture across history has worked. **Work** has been defined as the production of services and goods of value to others (Fox and Hesse-Beiber, 1984). In the past, work was seen as a means of obtaining some payment for services rendered, excluding housework or rearing children. It also served as a vehicle by which one obtained a sense of purpose to one's life. The Judeo-Christian work ethic has been influential in Western culture and held that the ability to work was a blessing. The ability to carry out some occupation that benefited the self, family, and/or community was considered a gift from a higher power.

How many people do you know hold this view?

Conducting daily work activities was a "thank you" to one's God for being given life and health to carry out the tasks. In addition to the sense of purpose provided by the ability to work, it also served as a means of providing the individual with a sense of identity. It is not uncommon for individuals of every class and most cultures to define themselves, first and foremost, by their work. What we do is an added dimension to who we are. Working (being involved in a job or career) is the hallmark of well-being in life. It denotes that one's life has meaning and direction (Sheehy, 1992).

Is there a predominating work philosophy of which you are aware?

Havighurst's (1972) third developmental task highlighted "reaching and maintaining satisfactory performance in one's career." But, to what does Havighurst refer when he refers to the idea of a career? The terms vocation, career, and job have frequently been used interchangeably. However, these terms can be differentiated. A **vocation** is analogous to a calling, primarily a means of channeling one's efforts into activities while deriving a sense of personal fulfillment and having an impact (not necessarily monetarily driven, although recompense is possible). A **career,** in comparison, reflects a chosen path for one's life reflecting a planned, coherent, organized sequence of steps by which one can advance to a higher level within that context for which one usually receives monetary compensation for one's efforts and that may result in changes over the lifetime. A **job** is typically defined as an immediate work position to which the individual is willing to devote six–eighteen months before moving on. The move may be to another job or on to the attainment of one's career goals. Jobs reflect a means for monetary accumulation without a personal investment in or identification with the work. The distinction between a job and career is indicated by the level of professional investment and identity derived from one's efforts (Webber, 1998). Remember, one person's job may be another's career.

Indeed, it may also reflect a vocational calling. It depends on what personal meaning is derived from the efforts.

> *Are there individuals of whom you are aware that have moved from job, to career, to vocation?*
>   *To what level do you aspire in life?*

Values also play a part in determining one's work environment. Values give meaning to life. In addition, one's value system guides one's priorities and ambitions. Two paths have been identified as reflecting personal values systems. First, one's value system may give priority to work and its peripheral elements—travel, long hours, personal sacrifices, not developing close relationships, or not starting a family, to name a few. The second approach to work reflects a career/job choice in which friendships, family, work, and self-care are equally important in the broader context of one's life. Neither approach is better than the other. They offer different benefits and engender different costs to the person. The critical element is the derived meaning obtained through one's efforts.

> *Have you considered these issues as you move toward your chosen career?*

The meaning that one derives from his or her work context is translated into **job satisfaction.** While meeting one's personal sense of meaning is critical, external markers also have been identified to correlate with evaluated levels of job satisfaction. Job satisfaction increases with (1) one's status in the work context; (2) the amount of power one has and wields over others; and (3) the level of financial compensation afforded the individual, including salary, benefits, and discretionary funds. An examination of job satisfaction in three age groups of adults indicated that young adults and older adults showed greater levels of job satisfaction than did middle-aged adults (Warr, 1994). An explanation may be that both younger and older adults are glad to have a source of income, while middle-aged adults are much more aware of the long-term implications of the current work situation. The middle-aged persons are less satisfied given the financial responsibilities that loom in their lives. In midlife, the worker may be facing college funding for the children, supplemental help for aging parents, unexpected personal medical costs, the routine costs associated with living, and preretirement planning. The midlife adult, as will be seen, is actively reevaluating plans, dreams, and goals and determining the course for the next twenty–thirty years. The factors associated with job satisfaction rise in importance at this time.

This lack of satisfaction can be translated into accident rates in the work context. Workers who are unhappy, more anxious, less emotionally stable, and hostile toward authority are more likely to have accidents on the job (Hansen, 1989; Arnett, 1990; Montag and Comrey, 1987; Perry, 1986). This finding suggests that midlife workers are not only subject to personal evaluations of life progress, they run the risk of physical accidents due to distractions as they evaluate their life.

Do you see how one's perspective may change at midlife, with choices going in either direction? Can you think of an example or two?

Today's workers can expect to change jobs a minimum of five–ten times in their working life (Toffler, 1970). Job changes typically occur due to (1) *economic downturns* that impact the wealth and fiscal stability of the company; (2) *technological changes* that require new skills and/or equipment resulting in greater technical abilities of the worker; (3) *buyouts and mergers* resulting in corporate decisions to cutback on less profitable aspects of the work, reconfigure the hierarchy, and put "their own" people into place to convey the new business philosophy; (4) *competition* that shows itself as being more attractive to the public; and (5) *downsizing* in which businesses work within their structure to eliminate positions that they perceive as expendable to the overall functioning and well-being of the company.

These changes are new to this generation. What level of Bronfenbrenner's framework does it impact?

The midlife workers in middle-level work situations are particularly susceptible to unemployment and layoffs. Middle-age adults who have maintained a relatively stable history in a work context are typically individuals who have seniority, more extensive benefit packages, and higher salaries; in other words, they are the most expensive of the expendable workers. Layoffs can occur at all status levels, from the semi-skilled, to corporate executives, to professionals. The impact of layoffs and unemployment may be manifested in anxiety, depression, feelings of emptiness, a decline in health, an increase in alcoholism, or the possibility of suicide (DeFrank and Ivancevich, 1986; Kelvin and Jarrett, 1985). Joblessness has a direct impact on families (McLoyd, 1998) and poses a threat to the person's sense of competence, security, and control. The midlife adult is particularly susceptible to these feelings during this time of self-evaluation. However, as long as a layoff is not internalized as one's fault or interpreted as a societal rejection of one's value as breadwinner and as a human being (Malinckrodt and Fretz, 1988), the individual can move on to the next occupation.

How might internalizing this job situation impact the person and family?

THE MIDLIFE WORKER

Considerations

Midlife occurs over a long period of one's adult life. It was projected that the number of workers would increase 41 percent between the years 1985–2000, with the median worker's age being thirty-nine years (Report by the Secretary of Labor, 1989). Given that the literature assigns nearly thirty years to the portion of the life span called midlife (from start to finish), the midlife adults have a lot of time to try things out in finding their career identity (Newman and Newman, 1995). At midlife, the management of one's career becomes of central importance, impacting adaptation and individual development. Managing one's career is fluid, requiring constant evaluation of skills and talents in this ever-changing world (Hollander, 1985). When surveyed about the most important aspect of their lives, middle-aged adults emphasized jobs or careers (Ryff, 1989a). Furthermore, it was found that a greater percentage of midlife adults asserted that current and future goals regarding the work domain took precedence over any other life domain (Clark-Plaskie and Lachman, 1999). This approach to life was particularly present in the sentiments of white-collar workers (Howard and Bray, 1988).

Midlife represents a significant reorganization of personality. The focus is on generativity and achievement, involving an integration of skills and perspectives, along with a commitment of energy to the future (Newman and Newman, 1995). Midlife workers strive to find a balance between values and actions. The midlife adult finds no permanent balance with regard to these efforts. Instead, they find that constant adaptation is required. No single answer is correct for all times and situations. What is right for you at 39, may no longer be right at 49 or 59. There is a constant shifting of valences—general life domains or specific events that possessed little weight in the past have new importance in the present.

This reformulation of ambitions, goals, and competence is reflected in new manifestations of cognitive processing and social interactions. The bulk of the literature investigating cognitive performance and the impact of the work setting is unidirectional in that the work context is evaluated as to how it impacts the cognitive capabilities of the worker in later life (Denny, 1982, 1984, 1989; Salthouse et al., 1990; Schaie, 1988; Schooler, 1984). Typically, occupations supporting greater self-direction can have a significant impact on the level of intellectual flexibility observed later in life (Schooler, 1990). Few studies, if any, investigate the cognitive capabilities and sophistication that come with time in the workforce.

Langer's (1997), Denny's (1989), Gardner's (1983), and Sternberg's (1985) emphasis on learning that occurs in everyday life and the skills and knowledge that come from that experience are fruitful grounds for investigation. This is especially true given that new levels of competence are achieved by the midlife worker in the areas of working with others, working with authority, and responding to new skill demands. The midlife worker has the opportunity to develop wisdom within this context and to transmit/share it with the younger, less experienced worker. This constitutes generativity at work. This more sophisticated way of thinking about one's work experience and work setting along with the impact of self-directedness go hand in hand with the impact of perceived control in one's occupation. Clark and Lachman (1994) found that midlife workers' perceived sense of internal control was higher for goals in the work context than it was regarding family, health, leisure, and financial goals. Also, Andrisani and Nestel's (1976) study of 3,000 middle-aged men indicated that internal control systematically influenced work success.

Changes in Careers at Midlife

A number of external forces precipitate job changes at any age in life. Still other factors may facilitate a change in one's work focus during midlife. These factors include (1) the fact that some careers, based on strength, speed, and endurance, end at midlife; (2) the realization that the career is not as it was envisioned during one's youth in that it no longer meets one's personal needs, thereby resulting in boredom or frustration; (3) the sense that one has gone as far as possible in terms of advancement without retraining; (4) dissatisfaction with all aspects of the job; and (5) being a woman in that most women enter, for the first time, or reenter the workforce at midlife (Howard and Bray, 1988; Aiken, 1998; see Avolio and Waldman, 1990, for a multilevel Bronfenbrennerian review of white-collar workers). Several personal reasons for seeking change have been articulated by midlife workers. These reasons include an unwillingness to settle for the status quo; a lack of satisfaction with "just having a job"; no sense of fulfillment in the current work situation; and discovery of more negative than positive aspects of the work context during one's examination of personal, financial, and social aspects of life (Howard and Bray 1988; Aiken, 1998).

In the United States and many European nations, discrimination by age in any form, in any context, is a violation of law. Most relevant for workers between the ages of forty and seventy years of age, this violation can take the form of failure to hire, failure to promote, or termination without just cause. The Age Discrimination in Employment Act (ADEA) was passed in 1978 as a means of protecting the worker against arbitrary age-based decisions regarding hiring and firing. Although most people consider this legal protection to be most applicable to adults in late life, it is the middle-aged adult that is particularly susceptible to age discrimination. Typically, workers in midlife have reached a fairly high level of seniority with resultant financial costs to the company or organization (Aiken 1998). The midlife adult also faces the personal concerns of feeling out of date, being insecure regarding requisite retraining to upgrade or retool skills, and facing the prospect of being unable to find a comparable position while at the same time being too far from retirement (Aiken, 1998; Merriam, 1980). The pattern of corporate take-overs so common in the late twentieth century exacerbates feelings of insecurity. Such takeovers frequently lead to downsizing and substantial layoffs of employees at all levels, blue-collar, sales, and management. Stress associated with these concerns and burnout resulting from the job not only impact the physical and emotional health of the individual but also affect general cognitive capabilities (Avolio and Waldman, 1990).

Contemporary Workforce Patterns

The way one measures personal success has been through meaningful work. This view was espoused by 50 percent of the individuals participating in a survey of 7,200 business managers (Goddard, 1991). Having an interesting and meaningful job was more important to these workers than was advancing up the career ladder. The attitudes of the midlife managers paralleled the attitudes and goals of contemporary new, young workers. This new generation of workers was interested in solving worthwhile problems and was looking toward continuous change and improvement in their lives. These preferences of the young worker were markedly similar to the responses of a group of midlife workers. Seventy-five percent of the midlife workers wanted to continue working in meaningful roles and 50 percent desired and expected a continual upgrading of skill throughout their careers (Paul and Townsend, 1993). The midlife worker of today has the potential to be an active agent in designing the nature of his or her work and ideally should take on that responsibility with an air of excitement and enthusiasm.

Why do you see this generational skip in attitudes and goals?

THE MIDLIFE WOMAN AND WORK

Today's midlife woman was socialized to prepare for work experiences that could be interrupted and easily resumed. Primarily, women were expected to prepare for marriage and motherhood. Careers, as such, were only relevant to single women (Betz and Fitzgerald, 1987 and Crites, 1980). If a career was encouraged, it was in the context of selecting something that one could fall back on should the need arise, as in the case of widowhood or divorce (James, 1990). The **traditional woman** (Tangri and Jenkins, 1992) was expected to displace career achievement to her husband. If she selected a career, she was to make certain that it did not interfere with running a house or raising children. Given the traditional roles, this type of career choice was one that the husband did not have to make. He could have his career, wife, and children. Many midlife women felt that they had to choose between a career and being a wife and mother (Grossman and Chester, 1990). This approach to women and work was a culturally sanctioned form of career **foreclosure** (Helson and Wink, 1987). This attitude was directed most specifically at the middle-class, white woman and women of prestige and power. There has never been any question that poor, black women (including many African American and recent immigrants) would be part of the workforce in the United States (Sanchez, 1997). Due to their race and ethnic origin, their contribution to the workforce has been underestimated and de-emphasized.

Despite the wide range of opportunities for young women today, is the attitude any different?

All but the wealthiest of women work outside the home. For those women who work at home, most of their work is unpaid and is considered to be less important than jobs performed by someone earning a wage. Also, women's unpaid work has been considered less central to their definition of self and personal identity. The unpaid work a woman performs usually involves the care and maintenance of the household and family—labor over the course of her life span equivalent to approximately $1 million in wages (Dunleavy, 2001; Grossman and Chester, 1990). Nevertheless, expectations regarding women's working outside the home changed dramatically during the late twentieth century in America. It is estimated that 65 percent of women age 45–54 participate in the paid workforce (Grossman and Chessler, 1990). Of this number, only 1 percent reported being a full-time homemaker over a 10-year period, with 79 percent reporting that they were able to combine a career and family successfully (Betz and Fitzgerald, 1987; Osipow, 1973).

Why Women Work and What Work Means

A number of surveys involving women working outside of the home indicated that women work for the same reasons as do men, to earn a living and to be seen as making a positive contribution to society (Astin, 1984; Fitzgerald and Crites, 1980; Oppenheimer, 1982; Osipow, 1973, 1987). What work means to a woman is a more complicated question. The work setting selected by women often is not chosen as function of prestige or the economic value attached to the setting by the wider culture (Stewart, 1990). The meaning that work takes on for women is complicated by the different meanings society attaches to women and to women's work. Women in contemporary American society are viewed through a series of complex interpretive filters involving sex role expectations, work and family role ideologies, and occupational stereotypes (Stewart, 1990). As a result, women who work outside the house are consciously or unconsciously viewed slightly more negatively because they are violating long-held expectations regarding what a woman is.

Stewart (1990) further questions whether it is possible to determine the meaning that work holds for women outside of their personal definition. This question derives from the observation that career development for women is a much more complex phenomenon due to differences in the socialization process of women (Diamond, 1997). In a review of women's career development, Fitzgerald and Betz (1983) state that *occupational development for women is a comparatively recent area of investigation*. For example, in contrast to men, women over forty-five find their desire for promotion to be at its lowest. They also have less desire to change jobs as compared to men (Ornstein and Isabella, 1990). A comparison of homemakers versus career-oriented women indicated that homemakers indicated higher needs for acceptance and affection, while career-oriented women showed higher achievement needs (Eadwins and Mellinger, 1984). Josselson (1996) stated that even when she is employed, a woman's sense of self is more anchored in her relational than her occupational life. It appears that women tend to deal with a wider array of spheres within which to resolve identity than do men, whose self-definition is typically more confined to the occupational domain (James, 1990). Other sources (resources) of identity for women include volunteer work (Gora and Nemerowicz, 1985), involvement in political causes (Schenkel and Marcia, 1972), and development of and involvement in a variety of philosophical stands (Tesch and Whitbourne, 1982).

Job Stress

Although studies of women in midlife are relatively rare, findings from the work of Abush and Burkhead (1984) and Eadwins and Mellinger (1984) indicate that for women between the ages thirty to fifty-five, the greatest source of work-related stressors were a lack of affiliation with other workers their own age and an external (as opposed to internal) locus of control over their lives. Other factors that yielded greater job stress include:

- being a **type A personality,**
- having little autonomy,
- obtaining little feedback on work performance,
- feeling that their job is less significant than other jobs, and
- having fewer friendships.

Job stress is more common in married, female workers who experience greater work and nonwork stress (by their husbands). This type of stress is termed **multiple-role strain** (Repetti, Mathews, and Waldron, 1989) and is evident when the role of worker interferes with the role of wife and mother. Repetti, Mathews, and Waldron (1989) have suggested that the direction of stress moves from the job to the family, thereby creating family problems yielding cognitive distractions and resulting in increased on-the-job accidents. Multiple-role strain is especially high in mothers who have young children in the household. Remember, it is not unlikely that the midlife woman may have a number of young children in her household due to choices made in delaying the start of a family. Overall, women experience more job stress than do men in comparable work situations (Greenglass and Burke, 1988).

Another stress-related factor is the result of being a single-working mother. Statistics indicate that 60 percent of American children spend at least some time in a one-parent family. The majority of these families are headed by women (Kotre and Hall, 1990). The single parent, usually the mother, typically has the least favorable options for work and the least time to spend with her children. Often, these women lack the financial and educational resources to obtain a job that will be able to support the family. Many of them attempt to hold multiple low-paying jobs, with consequences for the children. It should not be overlooked, however, that more educated, midlife, single mothers face many of the same mental and physical stresses, as do their less-advantaged cohorts.

Dual Career Couples at Midlife

When both spouses work outside the home, today's midlife women report that they (1) work with the permission of their husbands; (2) are limited by their husbands regarding their level of involvement in their jobs; (3) put the careers of their husbands ahead of their own; (4) continue to do the bulk of the house–work after a full day's work, and (5) frequently experience conflict between career aspirations and family commitment, thereby limiting their own competitive, achievement-oriented strivings (Baruch, Baruch, and Rivers, 1983; Heckman, Bryson, and Bryson, 1977; Hochschild, 1989; Pina and Bengston, 1993; and Rogers and Rogers, 1989).

How can parity be gained in dual career marriages?

Those factors that aid in decreasing the level of work-related stress for women in a dual career family include the stability of the marriage, joint planning of careers by partners, development and use of coping skills, support from nearby relatives, and awareness that any individual's time and energy are limited (Newman and Newman, 1995).

THE MIDLIFE MAN AND WORK

Men's career development choices are most influenced by parental career aspirations for them (King, 1989). Career paths or patterns are easier to discern for men. Four primary paths have been identified:

1. *Conventional:* typical career path from a trial experience to a stable choice. These paths are typically represented in managerial, skilled, or clerical positions.
2. *Stable:* this path is most common among professionals in which the young man goes directly from college or graduate school into a profession. (73 percent of white-collar and 46 percent of the blue-collar workers fall into these two categories.)
3. *Unstable:* the young man invests in a trial career, is relatively stable, then moves to another trial career.
4. *Multiple-trial:* this style is reflected in frequent job changes with no one type predominating (Hayslip and Panek, 1993; Miller and Form, 1951; and Slocum and Cron, 1985).

At midlife, men frequently encounter feelings of dissatisfaction and restlessness associated with their work (Osipow, 1973). Across all levels, unskilled to professional, dissatisfaction is related less to wages and benefits and more to the work being dull and meaningless and to their efforts going unrecognized and unappreciated (Roth, 1991). Restlessness is frequently followed by what researchers call stability. This type of stability may be seen in terms of men who, if they haven't "made it" by age forty-five, begin to coast. These men want to make it to the end of their careers without making a mistake. They are "resigned to the fact that they had lost the game" (Hayslip and Panek, 1993).

Three factors have been shown to have a more positive influence on a man's midlife evaluation of his career. First, there is achieving the dream established in young adulthood (Levinson, 1978). This achievement is positively related to the midlife man's mental health (Drebbing and Gooden, 1991). Second, the midlife male's college experience has been shown to be critical in the development of self-worth and intellectual maturity. College-educated men exhibited greater self-knowledge, awareness of the impact of time in their lives, greater self-esteem, and greater self-worth than those not having attended college (Smith, 1997). Third, men who have a healthy family life cope more successfully with job stress (Barnett, Marshall, and Pleck, 1992). This is especially true as men find themselves more vulnerable to job loss during midlife (Lajer, 1982).

Job Hunting is the Latest Boomer Challenge

Hundreds of thousands of jobs have recently been cut at companies ranging from dot-coms to Fortune 500 firms. Thousands of people are looking for work, including many baby boomers, individuals born between the years of 1946–1964. While there is no evidence that individuals in their forties and fifties are being disproportionately affected by layoffs, counselors are saying that they are hearing from a lot of clients in that age group. An increasing number of vocational services are advising individuals in this age bracket to consider a variety of options that may include possible career and lifestyle changes, going back to school, entering the nonprofit world, or scaling back to spend more time with the family

The important thing for midlifers is to figure out what they want and where they want to go.

CULTURE AND THE VALUE OF WORK

What constitutes work, its meaning, its value, and its distinction from leisure and play varies by culture. The bulk of the research literature that addresses the concept of work emanates from the United States. If the United States were to have an unofficial motto, it might be "Work is U.S." Workers in the United States and Canada are characterized by others in the world as working too hard and too much. In Australia, visiting workers receive 6 weeks of mandatory paid vacation per year; while nationals receive nine weeks of paid vacation per year. To American ears this may sound like Utopia, but many Aussies feel that this is not enough time and consider the two weeks that Canadians and U.S. workers take to be absurd. It is the Australian view that you have a better product and a better worker if the workers have time to enjoy their lives (Kelly, 2001).

In Japan, the midlife adult need not face the threat or fear of potential joblessness. While formal policy exists in Japan's major national corporations, an informal approach to work, workers, and productivity exists throughout the nation. There is an approach of continually restructuring the workforce in all settings to accommodate the changing needs of the workers, their lifestyle situations, and the differing types of contributions workers of different levels of status and age may contribute.

While 56 percent of the late midlife adults (age sixty to sixty-four) in the United States are working, one finds that 75 percent of the same-aged individuals in Japan continue to work. This difference reflects the willingness of multinational companies, local and national government, and local businesses to acknowledge the specialized skills of the worker—skills that have been honed over the years, skills that continue to have value within each work setting (*Working Age*, 1988).

An even more direct comparison of the meaning of work comes from a stark contrast between high-caste Hindu and high-status Nepalese men and Gusii men of Kenya. The high-caste Hindu men (fathers, grandfathers, teenage brothers, and uncles) take over the feeding, washing, and nurturing of the children. These behaviors go beyond playing with the small child, do not jeopardize masculinity, and are interpreted as a form of leisure activity. It was seen in a group of high-status Nepalese, that the more educated men worked to "cut better deals" that would allow them to spend more time caring for the young children. In contrast, the Gusii consider caring for a baby to be of low status such that men and teenage girls do not even become involved in those activities (Langer, 1997).

Summary and Comments

Beginning with the last section of this chapter, it is clear that that the Bronfenbrennerian framework serves as an excellent vehicle for examining the concept of work.

- Work is as the culture sees it,
- the worker is more than the sum of his or her years of service, and
- a philosophy that work interwoven with play enhances the overall effectiveness of the work environment.

The stereotypic midlife work crisis is less common in women than in men. Where most midlife men have defined their self and perhaps entire adult identity (as early as their college years) in terms of their job/career, many midlife women have defined themselves less unidimentionally than men and find in this particular time of life a new beginning. Women find that many opportunities will avail themselves during this time. Often, skills they have acquired as stay-at-home moms can be spun into contemporary work-related abilities.

This in no way suggests that a midlife woman, entering the workforce for the first time or reentering after a time, will be greeted by most businesses with open arms.

These women usually begin at entry-level positions, face a diminished probability for promotion, and encounter a new type of stress as they attempt to balance work and home life. Well-developed coping skills and a supportive spouse and extended family, as well as a strong sense of self-worth, are particularly important during this time of transition. It is not uncommon to find that midlife women, rather than working within the constraints of the work-a-day world, will step out of the box and invest themselves in entrepreneurial activities, where their success is dependent upon themselves, their ideas, and their initiative. This approach leads to a greater sense of control, direct and immediate feedback as to progress, and the potential to develop a congenial workforce. Stress does not disappear but it is a different type of stress.

The midlife man, who typically has laid out his life defined by his career choice, has a constrained frame by which to evaluate his goals and achievements. The midlife man is typically not as energized as the midlife woman. Because of this linear approach to life, he is aware of the beginning and end of his career and is more disrupted by the ever-changing job market. Rather than seeing this as a time of potentials and possibilities (as do many women), the midlife man often shows himself as being more resistant to the now proforma expectations of retraining, retooling, or reeducating oneself. As the midlife man traverses this period, he too is in need of a supportive spouse, a supportive extended family, and a strong sense of self.

Work is critical to the identity of the typical American. It serves as a daily organizer as well as the marker of one's status and success. At midlife, work becomes pivotal in evaluating one's past and in planning one's future. Not surprisingly, success and satisfaction for the midlife man often spring from the same sources as those mentioned for midlife women entering and reentering the ever-changing world of work, in investing themselves in new and personally valued enterprises in which their experiences, interest, and initiative are assets.

I was 18 years old in 1962 and was expected to do what was right. Sex and girls was all I had on my mind. I was supposed to go to college and get a job. I had lost my identity and was going nowhere. What I know for sure now is that—I WISH I HAD DONE THINGS DIFFERENT.

PERSONAL PROFILE:

Age:	56
Region raised in:	South
Military service:	None
Any College:	None
First Career Opportunity:	Mechanic
Current Career:	Mechanic
Career Changes:	None
Marital History:	39 years married now
Children:	4
Pets:	2

VOICES OF OUR PARENTS 12.1

CHAPTER 13

Reentering the Educational Setting at Midlife

I hated my time as a traditional student. I was bored out of my mind—I wanted to be a mechanic. I was more interested in cars, smoking, drinking, and chasing girls. (After dropping out and spending nineteen years as a sheet metal worker, this man earned his Ph.D. in history.)

—NONTRADITIONAL STUDENT AT AGE 41

I read an article about setting goals and wrote my impossible goal—Getting a College Degree. I placed this in my wallet and carried it around for several years. I then decided to go for my impossible dream.

—MIDLIFE MAN RETURNING TO SCHOOL

Divorce put me on the "gotta" path. College was the answer.

—COMMENT FROM MIDLIFE WOMAN

Why do we continue to learn? In the discovery of the answers, we reach our personal and spiritual human core.

—J. GIULIANI, COLLEGE STUDENT

OVERVIEW

The return to some type of formal education is often motivated by the ever-changing workforce (as noted in the previous chapter). Often, however, the midlife adult rediscovers an intellectual or vocational passion that until now was unattainable due to work or relationship responsibilities. The midlife adult may find today's educational settings markedly different from one previously encountered or previously heard of. Nonetheless, more midlife adults are becoming stable fixtures in educational settings everywhere.

REASONS UNDERLYING THE RETURN TO THE EDUCATIONAL SETTING

Why would you go back to school, especially when you're forty or fifty years old? Where do you go back to school? Today and future midlife adults face inevitable changes in their lives. Individuals who find themselves disenfranchised, downsized, lateralized, divorced, disenchanted, or in need of new challenges in life find themselves pursuing a GED, picking up new technical skills, starting a new degree of study, finishing an old degree program, or seeking out a new major area of study. While some decide that their time is better spent in volunteer activity, on personal development, or in spiritual pursuits, many choose to hit the books. This decision may be made to update skills to hold onto a job, to maintain a record of continuing education credits, or to escape a current life situation by earning the next highest degree. These individuals are realizing that their lives are much more cyclical than that of the linear lives of their parents. They are realizing that the current employment context may require that the individual start over again. This reason, accompanied by greatly increased life span, has caused the individual to ponder and act in response to these new challenges. Individuals may pursue these efforts in technical colleges, junior colleges, special workshops, or traditional colleges or universities. This return to education has at its foundation in two main categories: employment and personal.

Without the life opportunities of the midlife adult and without already achieving a first career, if you had to choose a second career, what would it be and why?

Employment

The emergence of a global marketplace, rapidly changing technology, and continual restructuring of employment is driving the need for more education (Noumair, 1996). The Consortium for Higher Education (2001) said the average worker will explore an average of four different careers during a lifetime. Of new jobs being created, more than half will require education beyond high school. It is anticipated that jobs in the future will require much higher math, language, and reasoning capabilities than do current jobs. Jobs that require a bachelor's degree are expected to grow the most quickly in the twenty-first century. Many midlife and older adults are planning to or are postponing their retirement and are looking toward college courses to acquire knowledge to maintain credibility in their current positions.

Have you noticed more returning students in your classes? Do you know why they are there?

Data from a recent research project conducted by the American Association of Retired Persons (AARP) (2001) revealed that eight in ten baby boomers plan to work at least part time during retirement. Five percent indicated that they will continue to work full time and 17 percent stated that they would be starting their own businesses.

It is widely recognized that the job market is changing and that workers need to return to school if they want to succeed. The momentum behind this movement is the striking impact of technology. Workers realize that they must do something or be left behind. Even professionals, such as physicians, dentists, and nurses, are enrolling in courses to stay current in their professions. Maintaining certification in teaching, real estate, paramedical skills and the law are requiring continued certification. Many individuals feel that continuing education is a protection against job obsolescence and a source of increased job security (Knable, 2001).

Personal

One common objective of many midlife adults returning to college is that they want to obtain some formally recognized academic achievement beyond a high school diploma or its equivalent. Additionally, individuals may have encountered an event that sparked an interest that can be pursued only at a university or local community college. The rising divorce rate has also impacted an increase in college and university enrollment. Women, in particular, are returning to institutions of higher education as a result of a change in their marital status. Midlife adults are faced with frequently changing goals and values in what they find important in their lives. Many find that further education is the way to define, make concrete, and pursue these changes.

Statistics from Colleges and Universities

Contemporary data from the National Center for Educational Statistics (1995) from 2-year institutions, 4-year institutions, and professional schools indicate that 25 percent of 2-year college institution enrollment was comprised of individuals over 35 years of age. The areas of study for these groups were primarily business, computer science, mechanics, and transportation. Approximately 12 percent of students in 4-year institutions were comprised of individuals over 35 years of age who primarily focused their studies in public administration and social work.

> *Notice the emphasis areas of study. Do you think that they reflect a shift in values or an articulation of a generation forced into careers to which they were never committed?*

Perhaps most surprisingly, 33 percent of graduate and professional students were over 35 years of age, emphasizing studies in education and human relations. A further comparison of full-time and part-time attendance at institutions of higher education by women and men indicated that there were 48 percent more women as part-time and 47 percent more as full-time students. Since 1998, institutions of higher education have seen a 95 percent increase in women's attendance as both full-time and part-time students. Men, in contrast, have shown a 93 percent drop in both full-time and part-time attendance (U.S. Department of Education, 1999). One explanation for the drop in men's attendance in public institutions focuses on the fact that many men, who realize the need for upgrading skills, take classes provided by their employers (Sapiro, 1999).

Despite corporate sponsored training, might there be any other reason underlying the lack of men attending colleges and universities?

Many women, on the other hand, stopped formal education or never began a secondary education, in order to marry and raise a family. Some of these women realize at midlife that their future may lie in obtaining some formal documentation of skills and education.

Middle Aged Women in Classes

Where opportunities for self-expression are limited in their current context, many women will seek out a new line of work, often one requiring more education. This movement toward educational settings is a sign of women's movement toward restructuring their sense of vocational identity at midlife (Hornstein, 1986).

What might limit women's access to education?

An interesting conflict exists between women who return to the classroom. Some women express a need for structure in the classroom. Their desire is for a clear-cut course with externally imposed structure, a class with a clearly articulated curriculum. They had three primary complaints about educational settings: (1) free-form classes were undisciplined and self-indulgent, (2) younger students who arrive late to class are irresponsible and seen as eroding the academic environment, and (3) being asked to create their own structure was too much of a burden given home demands. Accompanying these views suggesting a need for structure, these women expressed a shaky feeling that they had knowledge, too, and desired a two-way street between the student and professor to demonstrate that (Belenky et al. 1986).

In an attempt to explain the response of these women, Steinem (1993) felt that the midlife woman today was taught to undervalue herself, resulting in a plummeting of her intellectual self-esteem. Gilligan, Lyons, and Hanmer (1990) felt that this loss of confidence began as adolescence approached for these women. Unfortunately, this pattern continues in today's adolescent girls (Unger & Crawford, 1996).

In contrast, some midlife women entering college want to be set free with the opportunity to establish their own structure and to find their own timetable. Both groups of women coexist in numerous educational settings. What may differentiate them is the course of study that they pursue. The latter group may choose a course of study that meets their need for freedom and lack of need for constraint.

What Returning Students Bring to the Setting

The one thing that all returning students bring to the educational setting is experience. Some of this can be in the form of postformal thinking, a distinctly adult way of cognition. Postformal thinking requires the process of encapsulization, reliant upon specialized knowledge that the adult finds easier to access, add to, and use (Hoyer and Rybash, 1994; Rybash, Hoyer, Roodin, 1986). Postformal thinkers are capable of seeing shades of gray, which allows them to look at things in unaccustomed ways (analogous to Langer's [1997] sideway thinking) and to come to look at knowledge or values as relative (Labouvie-Vief, 1990a, 1990b). Just as wisdom is not attainable by all adults, not all adults attain postformal thought (Labouvie-Vief, 1982, 1990a, 1990b). The criteria for postformal thought include the ability to mentally shift gears, to be able to understand multiple causality and to suggest multiple solutions, to possess a level of pragmatism, and to be aware of paradox in life (Sinnott, 1984).

In the classroom, midlife adults are capable of integrating what they already know to the newly presented information (Grossman and Chester, 1990). This knowledge allows for the translating of truths about the human condition into symbols that the younger generation can turn to for enlightenment (Gutmann, 1977). The midlife adult can bring a form of integrative thinking to the classroom that has both an established emotional and societal component to it (Main, 1987; Schafer, 1980). As Denny and Palmer (1981) state, the adult's form of thinking is at its best during the adult's forties and fifties.

Learning Styles

What more educators have come to realize is that the experiences and thinking styles brought to the classroom by the returning student require an adjustment in instructional approach. There has been a growing emphasis in understanding learning styles with a related emphasis on general student evaluation. With regard to evaluation, essay exams and active experimental projects are replacing and/or supplementing the traditional multiple-choice exams.

Adult learning research has focused on a number of different aspects of the domain of study (Brookfield, 1995). The primary areas of research on adult learning include:

1. *Self-directed learning*—focusing on the process by which adults take control of their learning in terms of how they:
   a. set their learning goals,
   b. locate appropriate resources of information,

    c. decide on learning methods, and

    d. evaluate personal progress.

2. *Critical reflection*—considered to be a distinctively adult form and process of learning, based on three interrelated processes:

    a. questioning and reframing a previously unquestioned common sense assumption,

    b. taking an alternative view of a previously taken for granted idea, action, way of reasoning, or ideology, and

    c. understanding the impact of the dominant culture and its values on the minority cultures in that context and attempting to make meaning of their personal experiences in light of the dominant culture.

3. *Experiential learning*—a continuing process of evaluating experience, representing teaching grounded in the adult's experience via simulations, case studies, and internships, for example.

In a recent study, Justice and Dornan (2001) investigated the learning styles of traditional and nontraditional students in a variety of classes. The results of this study indicated that the older women reported more intrinsic motivation in courses taken than did young men, young women, or older men. Nontraditional students tended to more accurately assess their memory abilities and to employ higher-level cognitive strategies such as hyperprocessing that increases comprehension and an integration of the material (Richardson and King, 1998). In particular, Justice and Dornan state, "as non-traditional age students become a permanent part of the college population, our ability to provide appropriate academic experiences will depend on understanding the factors that affect their learning." The challenge in educating midlife adults rests in designing a curriculum that can allow them to exercise the information and experience they have accumulated and weave those opportunities into a format that can facilitate learning in the traditional student.

Cross-Cultural Adult Learning

One can describe the existing literature that addresses cross-cultural adult learning as minimal at best. However, there is evidence that the interest is increasing (Cassara, 1990; Ross-Gordon, 1991). Two important suggestions for productive research in the area have been suggested. First, adult educators from the dominant American, European, and northern cultures need to examine their assumptions regarding education and education styles congenial to other cultures. For example, a study by Podeschi (1990) indicated that the Hmong people of Laos found self-directed teaching to be anxiety producing, in that their culture promotes cooperative work and a looking to their teachers for direction. Second, there was a greater feeling of comfort if educators were drawn from their culture to instruct the adult students. While this may not always be possible, it is an important element in providing greater educational access to all individuals.

Summary and Comments

The parents of today's midlifers frequently emphasized the importance of obtaining an education. In retrospect, this encouragement reflected a pragmatic view of life (wanting something better for their children) and a clear valuing of the educational process and of educated people. As stated several times in earlier chapters, the baby boomers in the United States represent a generation of well-educated individuals. As these individuals find themselves focusing on an ever-changing job market or some void in personal goals, they are drawn in increasing numbers to a variety of educational settings. Men and women are making this step for many reasons and as a result of the returning students, educators are finding new and interesting challenges in their well-worn classes.

Not only is the midlife student retooling, so is the midlife instructor. This is being done to make the educational experience meaningful for all. New learning styles are being explored; new approaches to educating individuals from nonmajority cultures are being recognized.

Given the lack of stability and predictability in today's job market, educators can expect to see more faces of experience in their classes.

I was 18 in 1968 and I intended to go back to college when my youngest child started school full-time. I thought I wanted to be a teacher. I love working with kids, even the difficult ones. I went to work straight out of HS, worked 10 years as a secretary. Don't want to do that again. We did foster care for 10 years. We adopted 4 children with mild to moderate needs. That changed me. I began fighting with myself on whether I wanted to be a teacher or a social worker. I finally figured out that I needed to become a school social worker. Then my (then) husband cleared out our bank account, left me with 2 months past due bills, and he moved in with someone else. My youngest was only 4 at the time. I worked 3 different part-time jobs that all allowed me to remain at home with my kids when they were home. One job I did only on wekends they were with their Dad. One job was only 8 hrs per week during the school day; the 3rd was an in-home typing job. My youngest was held back in Kindergarten and started 1st grade 1 year late. So I followed the weird working schedule an extra year. When she hit first grade I (perennial procrastinator) began searching for schools. Divorce put me on the "gotta" path. Personal choice put me on the path of education. I'd rather sacrifice during these years, get a degree I want, do a job I really want to do rather than work where I'm only earning a buck and not doing what my heart is leading me to. My only concern is how many years will it take to pay back student loans? I'll probably end up working 'til the day I die!! But at least I'll be where I wanted to be.

VOICES OF OUR PARENTS 13.1

I can only speak for myself, but here goes. . . .

I'm a boomer born in 1955–

After a fits and starts undergraduate career (Bachelors Degree in Education 1981 followed by one year of postgraduate language training in Taiwan '81–'82), returned to University of Washington, Seattle, Washington USA in 1991 for a Masters Degree, as an in-career transition/training tool. (Shifted from one career field to another with the same employer, who paid for the degree.)

Am now enrolled with University of Leicester, UK in Doctor of Education program, researching education management. This is a transition degree, as I retire from my current employer in two years, and intended to go into adult education management. I have work related jobs with my present employer, but need the credentials to get into the academic sphere with an adequate income.

Bottom line is that for me, my return to universities following undergraduate completion has been tied to career transitions. I am now entering my third different career focus since graduation with a BA. Each subsequent transition has been marked by return to university for "retooling."

I was the victim of downsizing after 27 years with a major corporation. I had worked my way up through the ranks and had held a managerial position for the last 15 years of my employment. When I went job hunting, having a degree was a big deal. My experience did not seem to be as important. I was hired into another major corporation in an entry-level call center position. In six months, I was promoted to an exempt position; however, I was told that additonal promotions, were not possible. I do not ever want to be in the posiiton of having to start from the bottom again. I am now just about even in pay to what I was earn(ing) before I was downsized, before but in reality I have lost 7 years of superior power. Why did I go back to school? Because that degree counts more in the market place than experience counts. In nine weeks, I will have my degree and while I am not planning on changing careers, there are no guarantees in life.

I started my BA at the age of 42, have earned two Masters degrees (one in Anthropology, the other in Pastoral Studies). I took a two year hiatus and I'm now in the second year of a Ph.D. program in Educational Studies.

Once I accepted that I was never going to be a mother, I decided to take the chance and return to school. I will probably be 59 before I obtain that degree and don't expect to have many job offers at that age. However, there is certain satisfaction in the process of learning and doing new things and stretching oneself. I feel that lifelong learning is "the only way to enjoy getting older."

VOICES OF OUR PARENTS 13.2

CHAPTER 14

Volunteerism at Midlife

Volunteer work was the process of bringing something new into being as the result of an intense meaningful encounter with the world.

—MAY, 1975

I feel my volunteer activity jump started the second half of my life.

—55-YEAR-OLD PROFESSIONAL VOLUNTEER

Instead of rushing at life and producing furiously, I wanted something more meaningful. Taking a year's leave of absence from business, I've (dedicated) myself to the National Woman's Hall of Fame. They honor women's achievements. I signed on, pro bono, as my legacy to my daughter and granddaughter.

—50-YEAR-OLD BUSINESSWOMAN
SHEEHY, 1995A

OVERVIEW

Thus far, we have covered information reflecting the midlife adult in family relationships and work and educational environments. This chapter focuses an midlifers in the context of volunteerism. An increasing number of midlife adults have expressed desires to have a broader impact on society. They may frame this desire as giving back or serving in some way. The benefits derived from reaching out to others are usually outside the family but can also reflect greater extended family involvement. Whoever the recipient of these efforts, the midlife adult is moving beyond the home and work setting to develop a unique set of relationships in potentially diverse arenas.

MOVING BEYOND THE CURRENT CONTEXT

At midlife, there is often a desire to contribute to a greater whole (Galinsky, 1993). It is not unusual for men and women in adulthood to change values in terms of what they find important in their lives (Harker and Solomon, 1996). As with other aspects of the self, again, one can tie Erikson's (1950/1963) view to an increased tendency toward volunteerism through which generativity may be expressed. **Volunteerism** is a form of generativity that allows one to foster creative productions and share knowledge and talents to the benefit of the community (Kroger, 2000). Two dimensions of importance in the development of volunteerism are (1) *perspective:* the capacity to put aside personal views and self-interest in the service of a broader outlook and (2) *connectedness:* a vital, deep, and meaningful involvement with family, friends, and community (Hearn et al., 1998).

THEORETICAL EXPLANATION FOR THE RISE OF VOLUNTEERISM AT MIDLIFE

By the time most people reach midlife, they are beginning to make an important discovery: life has not always been what they were led to expect (Hunter and Sundel, 1989). How is this circumstance linked to volunteerism? According to the **growth task model of development,** human growth is conceptualized as a cluster of developmental tasks that form cyclical themes throughout the individual's life (Weick, 1983). Weick (1983) along with Erikson (1950/1963), views volunteerism via the concept of generativity, as an opportunity to experience one's creativity and to transcend personal concerns.

Contrast generativity and creativity.

This model recognizes an array of capacities some based on independence but also on a continual need to create the world. Growth, from this perspective, is part of a naturally occurring process of change expressed in a variety of ways, physical, emotional, spiritual, within the context of the social environment (Weick, 1983).

How can creativity be exploited in volunteer situations?

The primary assumption here is that human growth always occurs in a social context. Two principles hold that all human beings grow and develop within the context of community and that the idea of community embraces interlocking circles of connection among all human beings and ultimately, all forms of life and matter. This view is consistent with the Bronfenbrenner (1979) framework. It establishes a complex view of the community; brings the matrix of relationships in our lives into sharper focus; and expands the notions of person-in-the-environment, person-in-the-community, and person-in-the world.

The growth task model centers not on what society expects of people but on what people can come to learn about themselves. One thing that the midlife adult comes to recognize from volunteerism is that a side effect of this activity is energy. This energy impels growth and yields power. Reaching out to others stimulates his or her power and enables the volunteer to act in the world. The real challenge for the volunteer is learning to recognize and express power without dominating or ignoring others. To be productive means to express talents in ways that contribute to and sustain community life. Finding ways to do this throughout the life span is the challenge of productivity.

> *How might you begin to contribute now in your youth rather than waiting until midlife?*

To be culturally productive is considered to be much richer than the more limited version of paid work (Hunter and Sundel, 1989)

FORMS OF VOLUNTEERISM

Local and Regional Volunteerism

There exists within our society a number of what can be called professional volunteers. These individuals serve as the organizers, coordinators, and core figures in volunteer organizations such as the Red Cross, Salvation Army, and VISTA. In some cases, the participation of these individuals serves such critical roles to these organizations as to merit a paid volunteer position (Herzog, 1989).

Most volunteer activities, however, fall into the unpaid category. By definition, volunteerism is considered to be a giving freely of an individual's time, talents, and energy (Anderson, 2000). The greatest benefit of having volunteer workers is the low-cost and high-quality effort from these individuals. The greatest drawback is the lack of people to volunteer. Unfortunately, volunteerism is an overlooked and underrated experience in a woman's or man's life by our society. It is estimated that 89 million Americans were engaged in some sort of volunteer activity in 1990 (Anderson, 2000). Results of a survey by the U.S. Department of Labor (1990) indicated that these millions of Americans find that volunteerism helps them broaden their skills while extending their social contacts (Moen, 1997; Moen and Fields, 1998).

Volunteerism takes many forms. Individuals are involved in

- religious organizations and causes;
- schools or in educational programs such as adult literacy programs (Center for Statistics—ED/OERI, 1986; Anderson, 1989) or becoming a mentor to a child by way of scouting;

- civic and political organizations such as the effort in Quebec directed toward those experiencing financial crisis in the public sector (LaRochelle, 1992);
- environmental monitoring groups that collect relevant information for civic decision making, provide public education, monitor the quality of water in areas, and engage in local environmental surveillance (Lukasik, 1993; Sheehy, 1995b);
- hospital- and health-related organizations such as those providing community support for the reintroduction of individuals leaving mental institutions (Denner, 1974) or those engaged in the health promotion of mammograms in rural communities (Anderson et al., 2000);
- social organizations directed toward the support for women musicians and conductors (Miller, 1997) or focusing on reducing sex-role stereotyping and expanding options in education, work, and lifestyle (Ingram and Boethel, 1979);
- sports or recreational involvement via coaching; or
- focusing on a particular family member or friend.

A particularly poignant example of high profile, and ultimately a high-profit venture that began in the form of volunteering one's knowledge, skills, and passion for children, is the work of Joan Ganz Cooney the founder of the Children's Television Workshop that produces the now-famous *Sesame Street*. This effort, on her part was to give something to children since she had no children. As a result of her effort, she touched millions of children's lives.

International Volunteerism

One of the most well-known international volunteer organizations is the Peace Corps. Volunteers describe their Peace Corps experience as the most significant and the most challenging in their lives. Currently, more than 7,300 Peace Corps volunteers are serving in seventy-five countries (see Table 14.1) to bring clean water to communities, teach children, help start new small businesses, and stop the spread of AIDS (Peace Corps, 2001).

A parallel international organization is known as Cross Cultural Solutions. The goals of this organization are to educate others back home regarding different cultures, personal learning about another culture, engaging in cultural exchange, and providing hands-on impact in foreign communities (Cross Cultural Solutions, 2001). Volunteers to Cross Cultural Solutions are primarily composed of women who are currently divorced or widowed and are former career professionals. The dual goals of the volunteers are service to others and travel to foreign environs. The number of volunteers increased from 550 members in 1996 to 1,000 volunteers in the year 2000. This organization carries the philosophy of the Peace Corps but is membered by significantly more midlife adults. The majority of the volunteers are 50 and older, who "wanted to join the Peace Corps when they were young but didn't take the chance at that time" (personal communication—Cross Cultural Solutions, 2001).

TABLE 14.1. Statistical Profile of the Composition of the Peace Corps

Current number of Volunteers
   7,300

Gender
   61% female   39% male

Marital Status
   2% single   8% married

Minorities
   14%

Age
   29 years old (average)

Volunteers Over the Age of 50
   7% (oldest volunteer is 82)

Education
   82% have undergraduate degrees
   13% have graduate studies/degrees

MEN, WOMEN, MIDLIFE, AND VOLUNTEERISM

The cyclical nature of life demands starting over during the middle years and beyond. This realization that careers and relationships are everchanging can lead the midlife adult toward the general idea of volunteerism (Sheehy, 1995a). Many midlife, divorced men become involved in community activities as a way to fill the hours between 5 P.M. and 9 A.M. This previously mentioned pattern for men emphasizes the linear, work/career focus, life structure for men.

Women's development, however, is more typically predicated on the relational bonds that they form and on the sense of responsibility they feel to others. Relational bonds are the content of the life structure for women rather than work or career (Gilligan, 1980, 1982). A woman's creativity is expressed through her active volunteerism. Mothers and nonmothers participate in similar levels of voluntary activities. Job-free women show greater sustained volunteerism than do career women. Volunteerism takes the place of paid employment for them; while career women and nonmothers often cite volunteer activities as a way to fill a vacancy in their lives (Mercer, Nichols, and Doyle, 1989). For all, however, increased feelings of efficacy, confidence, and strength have been reported by women having these experiences (James, 1990).

Summary and Comments

Freely giving one's time, talents, and self is seen as a hallmark element of volunteerism. Midlife is depicted as the time in the life span when perspective for time passed and time to come offers an opportunity for change. The changes that occur in the midlife adult are multifaceted, multicontextual, and multirelational. Often these individuals find a need to contribute in some way to the local or international community. This movement beyond home and personal concerns is consistent with the findings regarding the changing of the workforce for men and the entry or reentry of women into public, private, and entrepreneurial workforce. As individuals are asked to reconceptualize themselves in the career arena, midlife adults become more aware of their potentials in many different areas.

While statistics are not kept for many volunteer activities, available evidence suggests that a growing number of midlife individuals are investing themselves in the international level of volunteerism. As this generation of baby boomers traverses midlife moving toward their later years, one may speculate about increased participation in all forms of volunteerism. These individuals may enact the espoused philosophy of their youth—asking what they can do. Subtle signs of this helping philosophy can be seen as a greater number of corporations, private businesses, and institutions of higher education encourage volunteer activities. All one need do is to see who is making these additions to the systems. You will probably find that behind these programs are midlife adults who have risen to positions that impact more than their work settings.

Do you see this being enacted in any way in your life?

My story is very simple. I grew up in a Christian home. My parents expected me to be someone's wife and someone's mother. I was someone's wife for a short few years. I found that there was more to me than living the traditional life. At age 26, I joined the Peace Corps and loved every minute of it. Since then, I have chosen a "life of service," as they say. I give of my effort and give of my time. I have never had a child but have had an impact on hundreds of them. I have never been a mother, but have been a mother to many—to some my age or older. I love life and the life I lead. I know that I didn't envision myself here when I was 18. My life is good. Follow your dreams, live them, and love them.

PERSONAL PROFILE:

Age:	53
Region Raised in:	Iowa
Military Service:	None
Any College:	BS—Biology
First Career Opportunity:	Housekeeper
Current Career:	Captain in the Salvation Army
Marital History:	2 years and out
Children & Pets:	None

VOICES OF OUR PARENTS 14.1

CHAPTER 15

To Midlife and Beyond

OVERVIEW

This final chapter opens with a brief recounting of the main purposes of the previous chapters. Then, the importance that culture plays in the understanding of midlife will be presented. Finally, some general comments regarding the pivotal role midlife plays in the overall structure of the life span will be presented.

CONTENTS OF THE TEXT IN RETROSPECT

Chapter 1: Introduction—Hey, Read This Section!
- ✓ The period of midlife is introduced as a viable period of study.
- ✓ Myths of midlife are presented as reflecting the views of contemporary U.S. American individuals.
- ✓ An overview of each chapter is provided.

Chapter 2: Ecological Views of Development
- ✓ Developmental systems theory is presented as a way to conceptualize human development. Particular emphasis is placed on the importance of the interaction between the individual and the environment.
- ✓ Bronfenbrenner's ecological framework is put forth as the primary model to understand the period of midlife specifically and the life span generally.
- ✓ The individual is depicted as an active agent in the construction of his or her life.

Chapter 3: Nonecological Theories of Development Applicable to Midlife-Related Issues
- ✓ A number of theories that have particular relevance to the midlife experience are highlighted.
- ✓ Concepts from the theories of Jung, Maslow, and Erikson are argued to be of considerable relevance to the experiences of the midlife adult.

Chapter 4: Experimental Investigation into the Life Span Process
- √ The basic methods of data collection and experimental design are introduced for consideration.

Chapter 5: Culture, Context, or Place: Distinctions in Understanding the Life Span
- √ Culture is introduced as the broad and enduring influence on the individual's sense of belonging and identity.
- √ Historical events and their impact on each cohort are introduced as a means of explaining generational differences.
- √ An important element in the ease of the midlife transition is the development of a strong sense of self. The way one enacts self is very much influenced by the context and culture of the individual.

Chapter 6: Those Were the Times, Those Were the People
- √ The early twenty-first century group of midlifers, the baby boomers, is introduced.
- √ Specific demographics are provided to indicate the considerable number of midlife adults found worldwide.
- √ Reflections on youth in Asian, South American, and North American cultures are provided to demonstrate the impact of one's context on one's view of life.

Chapter 7: General Health in Midlife
- √ This chapter focuses on the shared health changes that occur in men and women beginning at midlife.
- √ Later sections focus on the specific gender related health concerns confronted by the midlife adult.
- √ Considerable emphasis is placed on the importance of lifestyle choices made by the individual from his or her childhood on.

Chapter 8: Fertility and Menopause
- √ A brief historical and cultural comment on women's health issues is provided.
- √ The impact of menopause on the lives of women and men is considered.
- √ The choices facing couples and singles regarding parenthood are also presented when considering midlife parenting.

Chapter 9: Cognitive Processes in Midlife
- √ Traditional views of memory and intelligence are provided as they apply to midlife cognitive abilities.
- √ Everyday problem solving, wisdom, and a new concept of mindfulness are presented as perhaps a more effective way in understanding the cognitive capacities of the midlifer.
- √ Midlife is repeatedly highlighted as the prime period of the individual's life.

Chapter 10: The Recognition: Identity, Self, and the Psychological Forces at Work in Midlife
- √ Issues of identity and self serve as the foundation to this chapter.
- √ Particular issues relating the psychological processes at work during this period of reflection and assessment are provided for both men and women.

Chapter 11: Relationships at Midlife
- √ This chapter highlights the multitude of roles adopted by and assigned to the midlife adult.
- √ The primary set of relationships at this point in the life span is the family. The roles of marriage partner, parent, and adult-child to aging parent are woven into the social fabric of midlife.
- √ Extended relationships are also presented as critical factors during times of stress.

Chapter 12: Work at Midlife
- √ The distinction between a job, a career, and a vocation is introduced in this chapter.
- √ The value of work in the life of the woman and man is discussed.
- √ Contemporary workforce patterns and challenges to the midlife worker are presented for consideration.

Chapter 13: Reentering the Educational Setting at Midlife
- √ This chapter explicates the challenges and benefits that the midlife adult encounters and brings to the educational setting.
- √ Gender differences, selected course of study majors, and types of institutions attended are reviewed.

Chapter 14: Volunteerism at Midlife
- √ Volunteerism is introduced as an emergent activity capturing the imagination and energy of the midlife adult.

Note: In all chapters, the impact of cultural and contextual differences is presented in as much detail and as comprehensively as possible.

A CALL FOR MORE CROSS-CULTURAL RESEARCH

This text has emphasized the importance of culture as one approaches, enters, and leaves the midlife phase of the life span. Culture is not only presented in the languages, food, and traditions provided by its members. It reflects a mindset of expectations and options afforded the individual. Cultural factors impact potential for education, suffrage, and health. Cultures, like the individuals representing them, are subject to change with the passage of time and reflect the level or stage of development of the culture. Cultures impact the adoption of values by their members, the interests they express, and the abilities they develop.

With increased access to other cultures via improved communication, transportation, and information sources, will we begin to understand and perhaps incorporate aspects of other cultures into a unified amalgam with the hope of contributing to a better life experience for all.

There are a variety of cultural influences that impact the quality of the life span. Perhaps a sharing and a blending of cultural elements will not only enhance the period of midlife but also positively impact the quality of the entire life span.

Much of human behavior and the way an individual traverses his or her life are dictated by cultural components of spirituality, health practices, nutrition, and economics. Taking a multicultural, transgenerational, contemporary historic perspective has the potential to benefit all. A strong acknowledgement of cultural influence in research today is critical to the generalizability of our theories and observations of behavior.

Summary and Comments

Midlife can be for most individuals a crystallizing and defining time that directs the rest of the individual's life. To the developmental researcher, midlife reflects one more period of the life span that merits investigation. To the midlife adults, however, this period presents an undeniable reality of the never-ending passage of time and of their place in its journey.

Midlife represents a unique turning point of evaluation, reflection, and planning. At no other time in one's life does one have the ability to impact the quality of one's life with a limited guarantee of thirty–forty or more years to enact these changes. Accompanying this potential for possible growth is the potential for the unexpected, unplanned, or unwanted event. However, one of the many tools the midlife adult brings is the ability to adapt and gain life perspective. The changes that occur during this period have the potential to be monumental for the future of the individual. The changes that occur may be reflective of physical changes, marital status changes, parental changes, work changes, and so on.

The word *change* epitomizes the period of midlife. At no other period in the life span is change so apparent. The change encountered by this generation of midlifers will be similar but still different for each new generation of individuals entering this phase. As human beings, we walk down the same path, but the path changes with each generation.

As medical science continues to make more strides in combating deadly diseases, the stage of midlife becomes even more important because many of the lifestyle changes suggested by the medical community will have a longer-lived impact on the individuals of that period. Medical advances, moves toward greater cultural understanding, and the personal control one exerts over one's lifestyle will insure a greater influence of the period of midlife and the potential for global and local contribution by individuals of this age group. Midlife is a period to look forward to rather than run from.

Appendix: Voices of Our Parents

This appendix serves as an example of the questions presented to survey participants. All individuals could answer any of the below or produce their own narrative. Here are the points that I would like you to address. You can answer them as an essay, individually, or selectively. I do appreciate your help. Also, pass it along to anyone you might think is interested or might be interesting. Please have them e-mail the answers to me.

1. I was eighteen years old in 19___ and . . .
2. The impact of the sociocultural milieu during my young adulthood.
3. Sex, drugs, and rock and roll.
4. Boys were . . .
5. Girls were . . .
6. How my life was supposed to be.
7. Identity.
8. Where I was and wasn't going.
9. Confidence and certainty.
10. What I now know, for sure.

PERSONAL PROFILE (OPTIONAL)

Age

Region of the country in which you were raised

Any military service

Any college

—Major

First career opportunity

Current career

Changes in career in between then and now

Marital history

Children

Pets

Glossary

adrenal gland One of a pair of ductless glands located above the kidneys.

adulthood Does not begin at any particular age. It is a period characterized by financial and emotional independence from parents and by acceptance of responsibility for one's actions.

age differences Observed differences between individuals representing different age groups.

age norms Expected behaviors and growth standards anticipated for the average member of a designated group.

age-related changes Changes observed in variables of concern as represented by individuals of increasing age.

age spots Deposits of increased pigmentation usually occurring on the hands and face as one ages.

alzheimer's disease A dementia-related disease resulting in loss of cognitive function and ultimately, death.

amenorrhea Absence of the menses.

andropause Synonym for male menopause.

anovulatory cycles Monthly cycle in the female in the absence of a viable egg.

atropic urogenital changes A thinning of the vaginal lining due to a lack of estrogen.

attention A concentration of the mind on an idea or thought.

authenticity A true understanding of one's self.

autonomy Freedom of will and actions.

baby boomers Colloquial name given to the generation of children born between the years 1949 and 1962.

beanpole family A family consisting of the parent or parents and one–two children. The number of extended family members is limited.

being present Being aware of one's immediate experiences.

between subject differences A comparison of behaviors between different individuals.

bioecological framework An approach whose focus is more concerned in the context in which an individual develops.

blended family The joining of two previously divorced-widowed families into a new single family unit.

bodily-kinesthetic intelligence A form of intelligence postulated to rely on the awareness and use of established motor patterns.

carcinogen Any substance that tends to produce cancer.

career A deliberate chosen path for one's life with an organized and coherent plan for advancement.

case study A thorough and comprehensive investigation of an individual.

chronic ischemic heart disease Chronic obstruction to arterial blood flow.

chronosystem Patterns of stability and change over time/history.

climacteric A period of decreasing reproductive capacity in men and women culminating in women at menopause.

coconstruction The individual development of a psychological perspective guided by the person's social world.

cohort-sequential designs A design that follows two or more cohorts over time.

collagen A protein that yields gelatin on boiling and is contained in connective tissue and bones.

componential element A single element comprising a multifactored cognitive process.

congestive heart failure A condition in which the heart fails to pump blood adequately to either the systemic or the pulmonary arterial distribution.

constructs A concept typically represented by a set of variables.

context The social relationships, the features of the culture that promote growth, and the social institutions that regulate the individual's beliefs and behaviors.

contextual element An element comprised of the parts of the surrounding required for a cognitive event.

correlational study A comparison of measures to determine the strength of the relationship, not the cause between the two measures.

critical period Is a time frame associated with the emergence of new structure-function relationships. A time during which damage may occur to structures or functions in the prenatal phase; also, a point during prenatal development that serves as a window of opportunity for the enhancement or impairment of specific behaviors.

cross-sequential designs An experimental design using the same individuals across prescribed times of measurement.

crystallized intelligence A form of intelligence best represented by verbal processes.

cultural revolution The period of radical change in the culture of China to the communist reign. During this period the intelligentsia were taken to camps for reeducation and removal from the cities to an agrarian way of life.

culture A group of people who belong together by virtue of shared features; or semiotic mediation that is part of the system of organized psychological functions.

data Observable, and measurable points that can be quantified and subjected to some form of analysis.

dementia Cognitive decline in memory and related intellectual functioning.

demographic trends Reflect basic descriptive information regarding a particular population and the changes that occur over time with regard to the measures observed.

developmental contextualism Individual changes across life are both products and producers of the multiple levels of context within which the person is embedded.

developmental systems theory A view that emphasized systematic person-context relations and interactions across the life span.

developmental teratology The area of developmental biopsychology and medicine dedicated to the study of environmental influences on atypical prenatal development.

DHEA Steroid hormone produced by the adrenals; implicated in sexual functioning.

diabetes mellitus A disease that impairs the ability of the body to use sugar.

distal processes Information processing relying on external mnemonics and skills.

dopamine Hormone implicated in sleep behavior.

dream Levinson's conceptualization of a man's career plan during the course of his life.

dynamic interaction The active impact two or more agents have on each other thereby resulting in a change in all agents involved.

ecological transitions Changes in settings experienced by the individual.

efficacious Capacity for producing a desired effect.

empty nest Time and trauma referred to when all grown children have left home thereby leaving the parent(s) alone.

encode Mental storage of information for later use.

estradiol An estrogenic hormone causing a thickening of the tissues and blood vessels of the endometrium.

estrogen One of a group of female hormones that induce estrus.

estrone Estrogenic hormone produced by ovarian follicles and found in pregnancy urine.

exosystem The environmental system that includes broader and professional community relations.

experiential element Different approaches to familiar or novel tasks.

extreme groups design In this design, only the greatest age-disparate groups are compared, with generalizations spanning those two age groups.

fertility The ability to produce offspring.

fertility rate The number of offspring born to a prescribed generation.

filial responsibility The Eastern belief of devotion, dedication, and caring for elderly family members. In these cultures, the eldest son is given the responsibility for the care of the elderly parent(s).

fluid intelligence Form of intelligence implicated in procedural and speeded processes.

follicle stimulating hormone Hormone produced to induce the production of an egg.

foreclosure The premature commitment to a career path with no extensive exploration or choice.

generativity vs stagnation The Eriksonian crisis of midlife in which the individual invests efforts toward the future generations as a model or mentor, in contrast to a path of self-absorption.

grip strength The amount of power in one's grip as measured by a dynamometer.

growth task model of development The conceptualization of human growth as a cluster of developmental tasks that cyclically form throughout the course of one's life.

hormone replacement therapy A medical regimen employed to provide men and women the hormones depleted during menopause.

hot flashes Rapid fluxuation in body temperature resulting in discomfort.

hypothalamus The portion of the diencephalons forming the floor of the median ventricle of the brain.

hysterectomy Surgical excision of the uterus.

identity The finding of meaningful interpersonal connections that define the individual across the life span.

identity vs role confusion Erikson's crisis of adolescence.

incidence The rate or range of a behavior.

individuation The process of bringing thinking and feelings into balance; Jung's conceptualization of the balance of cognition and intuition.

insight Instance of apprehending the true nature of an event.

intelligence A measure of intellectual ability.

interiority Increasing awareness and concern for the functioning of the self.

interpersonal intelligence Intelligence used in the understanding of others.

interviews A series of one-on-one conversations conducted by an experimenter to elicit information of empirical concern.

intrapersonal intelligence Intelligence used in the understanding of the self.

i-self William James' conceptualization of what one is to one's self.

job An immediate work position to meet current life demands.

job satisfaction Confident acceptance of one's current job situation.

kin keeper The individual in a family who serves as the organizer of family events and the touchstone of family information and connection.

launching The period in the family from the start of the first adult child's departure to the last child's departure from the family home.

leutinizing hormone Hormone implicated in the stimulation of ovulation.

life events approach An attempt to understand the behavior of the individual by taking into account and incorporating life experiences into the understanding of the purpose.

life expectancy The number of years a particular group of individuals, born in a particular year, is projected to live. Life expectancy is often contrasted to life span, the maximum projected life duration of a species.

life review A period of purposeful reminiscence that involves a reconsideration of previous experiences and their meanings.

life span development Views the complexity of human change and underlying factors with the perspective that development is a lifelong process reflecting a multidirectional blend of biological, psychological, and social forces.

lifestyle A relatively permanent structure of activity and experience; the balance struck between work and leisure and family and social relationships.

liminality Jungian term used to denote the process of transition from one psychological threshold to another.

linguistic intelligence Intelligence manifested in strong verbal skills.

lipids Any group of organic compounds that are greasy to the touch and insoluble in water; serves as the chief structural component of living cells.

liposuction A medical procedure used to remove subdermal fat deposits usually from the stomach, hips, and thighs.

logicomathematical intelligence Intelligence reflected in superior performance in the conduct of logical mathematical abilities.

longitudinal studies The study of the same individuals over repeated testing times.

macrosystem The most global of the environmental system reflecting societal or cultural influences.

male menopause Psychological and physiological changes brought about by hormonal changes in men between the ages of thirty five and sixty five.

mechanics Basic processes involved in the process of cognitive activity.

melanin The dark pigment in the hair and epidermis of the body.

menopause The period of the permanent cessation of menstruation.

me-self The persona presented to others.

mesosystem The level of the environment that reflects the connections among microsystems.

microsystem The lowest level of the environment that includes the setting for individual behavior and activities, participants, and roles in that setting.

middle age A situation resulting from an accumulation of life events rather than a recorded number of years.

mindfulness Active awareness of the current events and the demands of the situation.

mindlessness Form of behavior reflected in automatic responses with little, if any, thought given to the act.

multiple intelligences Position arguing for a constellation of specialized intellectual abilities beyond the traditional verbal and mathematical skills.

multiple role strain Tension experienced in the conduct of numerous and different role expectations.

musical intelligence A specialized form of intelligence reflected in musical skill.

myocardial infarcts Area of the heart tissue that is dying due to deprivation of blood supply.

myopic Nearsighted; objects are seen clearly when held close to the eye.

myth A traditional story without a determinable basis of fact or natural explanation.

naturalistic observation A form of investigation that does not employ any experimental manipulation but rather reflects the behaviors noted in a natural setting in which the subject is commonly found.

nephrons A structural and functional unit of the kidney.

night sweats Phenomenon encountered by menopausal women that results in excessive sweating during sleep.

nuclear family Traditional family consisting of mother, father, and child(ren).

optimally exercised abilities Cognitive abilities used frequently and successfully.

outmarrying The marriage between individuals of different cultures, often resulting in one of the partner's abandonment or rejection from his or her home culture.

ovarian follicles A small cavity or sac of the ovary containing undeveloped human eggs.

oxytocin A polypeptide hormone that stimulates the contraction of the uterus.

pace The speed of change observed in a society.

perception The ascription of meaning to sensory input.

perimenopause The stage prior to the completion of menopause.

person–process–context–time (PPCT) The most recent conceptualization of Bronfenbrenner's framework that incorporates all aspects of the interactions proposed to influence the individual.

place A location or physical setting identified with an object or event.

plastic surgery A medical procedure employed to modify or correct physical defects.

population pyramid Demographic representation of the individuals of different ages in a nation. The base of the pyramid is represented by the younger age groups with a decreasing number of individuals in the older age brackets.

postmenopausal zest Period of renewed energy.

postmenopause One year after the last menstrual cycle.

postparental period The period referred to after all children have left home.

pragmatics The practical point of view.

pregnenolone Hormone using cholesterol for its manufacture, playing a role in memory and cognitive functioning.

presbycusis The loss of hearing in the high frequency range.

presbyopia The drying of the vitreous humor resulting in decreased retinal flexibility and decreased ability to see near objects.

prevalence The measure of how widespread an event is.

primary control strategies Changing the environment to fit one's needs.

prostate gland The muscular, glandular organ that surrounds the urethra of males at the base of the bladder.

proximal processes Behaviors reflecting the fundamental biological processes relying on internal sensory input required for basic behavioral functioning.

reciprocal activity and interaction The impact of the individual on the environment and the impact of the environment on the individual's future behavior.

rectangular population profile The near equal number of individuals in a nation representing all age brackets, youngest to eldest.

research design The structure of a research project, including characteristics of the participants, the experimental manipulation (if any), and the schedule for testing-observation.

retrieve The accessing of cognitively stored information for use.

revisitation Eriksonian concept of reexperiencing earlier crises upon encountering or completing a new psychosocial crisis.

sandwich generation Descriptive of the midlife adult caught between the needs of their adult children and their aging parents.

secondary control strategies The change of one's self (rather than the environment) to fit one's needs.

self The personal sense of who one is to him or herself and to others; the compilation of roles.

self-actualization The process of reaching one's full potential on personal and professional fronts.

self report surveys A series of questions answered by the individual under investigation that reflect the individual's personal interpretations.

semiotic mediation The way in which a culture conveys information regarding its identity through organized psychological functions within the culture.

semantic memory Memory reflected in verbal scripts of a general nature.

sensation The stimulation of one or more sensory organs due to some external or internal cause.

sequential designs Experimental designs whose purpose is to disentangle the confounding effects of cross-sectional and longitudinal designs.

sideways thinking Approaching a problem in a different way or using a different form of thought.

silicone implants Polymer packets inserted into the body for reconstruction purposes.

social age clock An internalized calendar, learned from society, which tells us about when in our lives we should be doing what.

synchronicity The coincidence of events in time.

synovial fluid A lubricating fluid secreted by membranes of the joints.

tacit knowledge Understood without being openly expressed.

testosterone Hormone secreted by the testes.

time-lag studies A particular experimental design allowing for inferences regarding longitudinal features and historical components.

traditional woman A woman's adoption of society's prescribed female roles.

turning point A time marked by a major change in life events.

type A personality A personality style resulting in high levels of stress and commitment to multiple activities.

unexercised abilities Mechanisms of thought not frequently used.

unstable angina A syndrome characterized by constricting pain below the sternum.

vasomotor flushes Periodic changes in the diameter of the blood vessels resulting in feelings of hot and cold.

vasopressin A chemical that raises blood pressure causing contraction of the arteriole muscles.

viropause Term used to describe the psychological and physical changes associated with male menopause.

visual-spatial intelligence The ability to represent and manipulate two-and three-dimensional forms.

vital capacity The power or force of the cardiac and respiratory system negatively impacted by coronary artery disease.

vitreous humor The transparent, gelatinous substance, behind the lens, filling the eyeball.

vocation A channeling of one's efforts into activities from which a sense of fulfillment is derived.

volunteerism A form of generativity allowing for the fostering of creative productions and a sharing of knowledge and talents to the benefit of the community.

wisdom Knowledge of what is true or right with our judgment as to what is right.

within individual changes Changes observed in a select variable produced by the same individuals.

working memory The aspect of memory in which information is brought into conscious awareness.

References

Abush, R. and Berkhead, E. J. (1984). Job stress in mid-life working women: Relationships among personality type, job characteristics, and job tension. *Journal of Counseling Psychology*, 31, 36–44.

Adams, P. F., and Benson, V. (1992). Current estimates from the National Health Interview Survey (1991). *Vital and Health Statistics*. National Health Statistics. Hyattsville, MD.

Adelman, P. K., Antonucci, T. C., Crohan, S. E., and Coleman L. M. (1989). Empty nest, cohort, and unemployment in the well-being of midlife women. *Sex Roles*, 20, 173–189.

Agoestina, T., and van Keep, P. A. (1984). The climacteric in Bandung, West Java Province, Indonesia. A survey of 1025 women between 40 and 55 years of age. *Maturitus, 6*, 327–333.

Aiken, L. (1998). *Human development in adulthood*. New York: Plenum Press.

Aiken, L. R. (1997). *Psychological testing and assessment* (9th ed) Needham Heights, MA. Allyn and Bacon.

Aizenberg, R., and Treas, J., (1985). The family in later life: Psychosocial and demographic considerations. In J. E. Birren and K. W. Schaie (Eds.), *Handbook of the psychology of aging*. 2d ed. New York: Van Nostrand Reinhold.

Alban, S. (2001). Later adulthood in Finish Individuals. Paper presented in the Psychology of Aging, November.

Aldous, J. (1990). Family development and the life course: Two perspectives on family change. *Journal of Marriage and the Family, 52*, 571–583.

Alder, A. P. (1990). Identity, intimacy, and marital satisfaction in midlife marriages. Ph.D. diss., *Abstract in Dissertation Abstracts International* 52: p. 24 Univ. of Michigan.

Allen, M. J. (2000). Teaching non-traditional students. *APS Observer*, September.

Allport, G. W. (1961). *Pattern and growth in personality*. New York: Holt, Rinehart, and Winston.

American Association of Retired Persons. (2001). *Life in the middles: A report on multicultural boomers coping with family and aging issues*. Washington: Author.

American Cancer Society. (1994). *Cancer facts and figures*. Atlanta: American Cancer Society.

American Heart Association. (1994). *Heart and stroke facts: 1994 statistical supplement*. Dallas, TX: American Heart Association National Center.

Anderson, D. (1991). Retirees: Community service resources. In *Resourceful aging: Today and tomorrow*. Washington DC: American Association of Retired Persons.

Anderson, E. E. (1989). Adult basic education programs in Canada. In M. C. Taylor and J. A. Draper (Eds.), *Adult literacy perspectives*. Malabar, FL: Krieger Publishing Co.

Anderson, K. (1988). A history of women's work in the United States. In A. H. Stromberg & S. Harkness (Eds.), *Women working: Theories and facts in perspective*. Mountain View, CA: Mayfield.

Anderson, M. R., Yasui, Y., Meischke, H., Kuniyuki, A., Etzioni, R., and Urban, N. (2000). The effectiveness of mammography promotion by volunteers in rural communities. *American Journal of Preventive Medicine, 18*(3), 199–207.

Andres, R., Muller, D., and Sorkin, J. D. (1993). Longterm effects of change in body weight on all-cause mortality. *Annals of Internal Medicine, 7,* 737–743.

Andrisani, P. J., and Nestle, G. (1976). Internal-external control as contributor to and outcome of work experience. *Journal of Applied Psychology,* 61(2), 156–165.

Antonucci, T. C., and Akiyama, H. (1991). Social relationships and aging well. *Generations, 15,* 39–44.

Antonucci, T. C., and Mikus, K. (1988). The power of parenthood: Personality and attitudinal changes during the transition to parenthood. In G. Y. Michales & W. A. Goldberg (Eds.), *The transition to parenthood: Current theory and research.* New York: Cambridge University Press.

Antonucci, T. C., Tamir, L. M., and Dubnoff, S. (1980). Mental health across the family life cycle. In K. W. Black (Ed.), *Life course: Integrative theories and exemplary populations.* Boulder, CO: Westview Press.

Apter, T. (1996). Paths of Development in Midlife Women. *Feminism and Psychology, 6,* 557–562.

Aquilino, W. S. (1990). The likelihood of parent-adult child coresidence: Effects of family structure and parental characteristics. *Journal of Marriage and the Family, 52,* 405–419.

Aquilino, W. S., and Supple, K. R. (1991). Parent-child relations and parent's satisfaction with living arrangements when adult children live at home. *Journal of Marriage and the Family, 53,* 13–27.

Arlin, P. K. (1984). Adolescent and adult thought: A structural interpretation. In M. L. Commons, F. A. Richards, and C. Armon (Eds.), *Beyond formal operations.* New York: Praeger.

Arnett, J. (1990). Drunk driving, sensation seeking, and egocentrism among adolescents. *Personality and individual differences, 11,* 541–546.

Astin, H. S. (1984). The meaning of work in women's lives: A sociopsychological model of career choice and work behavior. *The Counseling Psychologist, 12,* 117–126.

Atkinson, R. C., and Shiffrin, R. M. (1971). The control of short-term memory. *Scientific American,* 225(2) 82–90.

Avis, N. E. (1999). Women's Health at Midlife. In S. Willis and J. Reid (Eds.), *Life in the Middle.* San Diego: Academic Press.

Avolio, B. J., and Waldman, D. A. (1990). An examination of age and cognitive test performance across job complexity and occupational types. *Journal of Applied Psychology, 75,* 43–50.

Bachman, D. L., Wolf, P. A., Linn, R., Knoefel, J. E., Cobb, J., Belanger, A., D'Agostino, R. B., and White, L. R. (1992). Prevalence of dementia and probable senile dementia of the Alzheimer type in the Framingham study. *Neurology, 42,* 115–119.

Baltes, P. B. (1993). The aging mind: Potential and limits. *Gerontologist,* 33(5), 580–594.

Baltes, P. B., Dittmann-Kohli, F., and Dixon, R. A. (1984). New perspectives on the development of intelligence in adulthood: Toward a dual-process conception and a model of selective optimization with compensation. In P. B. Baltes and O. G. Brim (Eds.), *Life-span developmental psychology.* Vol. 6. New York: Academic Press.

Baltes, P. B., and Nesselroade, J. R. (1970). Multivariate longitudinal and cross-sectional sequences for analyzing ontogenetic and generational change: A methodological note. *Developmental Psychology, 2,* 163–168.

Baltes, M. M., and Baltes, P. B. (1986). *The psychology of control and aging..* Hillsdale, NJ: Earlbaum.

Bamford, J., Sandercock, P., Dennis, M., Burn, J., and Warlow, C. (1990). A prospective study of acute cerebrovascular disease in the community: the Oxfordshire Stroke Project–1981–1986. *Journal of neurology, neuroimagery, and psychiatry, 53,* 16–22.

Banner, C. (1992). Recent insights into the biology of Alzheimer's Disease. *Generations,* 16(4), 31–35.

Banner L. M. (1993). *The meaning of menopause: aging and its historical context in the twentieth century.* Milwaukee: University of Wisconsin Center for Twentieth Century Studies.

Barber, C. E. (1989). Transition to the empty nest. In S. J. Bahr and E. T. Peterson (Eds.), *Aging and the family.* Lexington, MA: Lexington.

Barnett, R. C., Marshall, N. L., and Pleck, J. H. (1992). Men's multiple roles and their relationship to men's psychological distress. *Journal of marriage and the family, 54,* 358–367.

Bart, P. B., and Grossman, M. (1978). Menopause. In M. T. Notman and C. C. Nadelson (Eds.), *The woman patient.* Vol. 1. New York: Plenum Press.

Bartlett, F. C. (1932). *Remembering.* Cambridge, England: Cambridge University Press.

Baruch, G., Barnett, R., & Rivers, C. (1983). *Lifeprints.* New York: McGraw-Hill.

Bee, H. L. (2000). *The Journey of Adulthood.* 4th ed. Upper Saddle River, NJ: Prentice Hall.

Belenky, M. F., Clinchy, B. M., Goldberg, N. R., and Tarule, J. M. (1986). *Woman's ways of knowing.* Basic Books.

Benedek, T. (1950). Climacterium: A developmental phase. *Psychoanalytic Quarterly, 19*(1), 1–27.

Benedek, T. (1959). *Psychoanalytic investigations.* New York: Quadrangle.

Bengtson, V. L., Rosenthal, C., and Burton, L. (1990). Families and aging: Diversity and hetero-geneity. In R. H. Binstock and L. K. George (Eds.), *Handbook of aging and the social sciences.* 3d ed. San Diego: Academic Press.

Berg, C. A., and Sternberg, R. J. (1992). Adults' conceptions of intelligence across the adult lifespan. *Psychology and Aging, 7*(2), 221–231.

Berk, L. E. (2001). *Development through the lifespan.* 2d ed. Boston: Allyn and Bacon.

Berkman, L. F. (1984). Assessing the physical health effects of social networks and social support. *Annual Review of Public Health, 5,* 413–432.

Betz, N. E., and Fitzgerald, L. F. (1987). *The career psychology of women.* Boston, Academic Press.

Beyene, Y. (1986). Cultural significance and physiological manifestations of menopause: A biosocial analysis. *Culture, Medicine, and Psychiatry, 10,* 47–71.

Bhatia, S. C., and Bhatia, S. K. (1999). Depression in women: Diagnostic and treatment considera-tions. *American Academy of Family Physicians, 7,* 1–16.

Birren, J. E., and Morrison, D. F. (1961). Analysis of the WAIS subtests in relation to age and edu-cation. *Journal of Gerontology, 16,* 363–369.

Blackburn, J. A. (1984). The influence of personality, curriculum, and memory correlates in formal reasoning in young adults and elderly persons. *Journal of Gerontology, 39,* 207–209.

Bliss, G. K. (2000). Self-disclosure and friendship patterns: Gender and sexual orientation differ-ences in same-sex and opposite-sex friendships. Ph.D. diss: *Abstract in Dissertation Abstracts International* 61: Univ. of Michigan 114–116.

Block, J. (1984). Gender differences and implications for educational policy. In J. Block (Ed.), *Sex role identity and ego development.* San Francisco: Jossey-Bass.

Blustein, D. L. and Noumair, D. A. (1996). Self and identity in career development: Implications for theory and practice. *Journal of counseling and development, 74*(5), 433–441.

Boesch, E. E. (1991). *Symbolic action theory in cultural psychology.* Berlin: Springer.

Bolen, J. (1994). *Crossing to Avalon: A women's midlife pilgrimage.* New York: Harper Collins Publishers.

Borland, D. C. (1978). Research on middle age: An assessment. *The Gerontologist, 18,* 379–386.

Botwinick, J. (1973). *Aging and behavior: A comprehensive integration of research findings.* Berlin: Springer.

Botwinick, J. (1978). *Aging and behavior: A comprehensive integration of research findings.* Berlin: Springer.

Botwinick, J. (1984). *Aging and behavior: A comprehensive integration of research findings.* New York: Springer.

Brandstadter, J. (1984). Personal and social control over development: Some implications of an action perspective in life-span developmental psychology. In P. B. Baltes and O. G. Brim, Jr. (Eds.), *Life-span development and behavior.* Vol. 6. New York: Academic Press.

Brandtstadter, J. and Lerner, R. M. (1999). *Action and self development: Theory and research through the lifespan.* Thousand Oaks, CA: Sage Publications.

Brim, O. G. (1976). Theories of the male mid-life crisis. *The Counseling Psychologist, 6,* 2–9.

Brim, O. G., Jr. (1992). *Ambition: How we manage success and failure throughout our lives.* New York:: Basic Books.

Brim, O. G., Jr., and Kagan, J., (Eds.). (1980). *Constancy and change in human development.* Cambridge, MA: Harvard University Press.

Brody, E. M. (1981). "Women in the middle" and family help to older people. *Gerontologist, 21,* 471–480.

Brody, E. M. (1985). Parent care as normative family stress. *Gerontologist, 25,* 19–29.

Brody, E. M. (1990). *Women in the middle: Their parent-care years.* New York: Springer.

Broman, C. (1993). Race differences in marital well-being. *Journal in Marriage and the Family, 55,* 724–732.

Bronfenbrenner, U. (1979). *The ecology of human development: Experiments by nature and design.* Cambridge, MA: Harvard University Press.

Brookfield, S. (1995). Adult learning: An overview. In A. Tuinjman (Ed.), *International Encyclopedia of Education.* Oxford: Pergamon Press.

Brown, D. R., Cochran, D., and McGregor, K. C. (1996). Race differences in the multiple social roles of midlife women: implications for mental well-being. *American Sociological Association,* Toronto, Canada.

Burke, P. C. (1995). Identity development in midlife: A qualitative study of professional women in the 1990s. Ph.D. diss: *Dissertation Abstracts International.* Univ. of Michigan.

Calandra, S. (2001). New trends in hair transplants in midlife men. *Andropause, 3,* 27–31.

Carlson, N. R (1991). *Physiology of behavior.* Boston: Allyn and Bacon.

Carr, D. (1997). The fulfillment of career dreams at midlife: Does it matter for women's mental health? *Journal of Health and Social Behavior, 38,* 331–344.

Caspi, A. (1998). Personality development across the lifecourse. In N. Eisenberg (Ed.), *Handbook of child psychology: Vol. 3 Social, emotional, and personality development* (5th ed). New York: John Wiley and Sons.

Caspi, A., and Moffitt, T. E. (1993). When do individual differences matter? A paradoxical theory of personality coherence. *Psychological Inquiry* 4(4), 247–271.

Cassara, B. (1990). *Adult education in a multicultural society.* New York: Routledge.

Cattell, R. B. (1965). *The scientific analysis of personality.* Baltimore: Penguin.

Center for Statistics (ED/OERI). (1986). Research report. *Adult literacy programs: Services, persons served, and volunteers,* 143. Washington, DC.

Chappell, N. L. (1990). Aging and social care. In R. H. Binstock and L. K. George (Eds.), *Handbook of aging and the social sciences.* 3d ed. San Diego: Academic Press.

Cherlin, A., & Furstenberg, F. F., Jr. (1986). *The new American grandparent: A place in the family, a life apart.* New York: Basic Books.

Chesler, P. (1972). *Women and madness.* New York: Doubleday.

Cicirelli, V. G. (1980). *Adult children's views on providing services for elderly parents.* Report to the Andrus Foundation, Los Angeles, CA.

Cicirelli, V. G. (1981). *Helping elderly parents: The role of adult children.* Boston: Auburn House.

Cicirelli, V. G. (1989). Helping relationships in later life: A reexamination. In J. A. Mancini (Ed.), *Aging parents and adult children.* Lexington, MA: Heath.

Clark, M. D., and Lachman, M. E. (1994). *Goals and perceived control: Age differences and domain effects.* Poster presented at the meeting of the American Psychological Association, Los Angeles, CA.

Clarke, J. I. (1978). *Self-esteem: A family affair.* Center City, MN: Hazelden Educational Materials.

Clarke, J. I. , and Dawson, C. (1998). *Growing up again: Parenting ourselves, parenting our children.* 2d ed. Center City, MN: Hazelden Educational Materials.

Clark-Nicholas, P., and Gray-Little, B. (1991). Effect of economic resources on marital quality in black married couples. *Journal of Marriage and the Family, 53,* 645–655.

Clark-Plaskie, M., and Lachman, M. (1999). The sense of control in midlife. In S. L. Willis and J. D. Reid (Eds.), *Life in the Middle: Psychological and Social Development in Middle Age.* San Diego: Academic Press.

Clausen, J. A. (1986). *The life course: A sociological perspective.* Englewood Cliffs, NJ: Prentice-Hall.

Clausen, J. A. (1995). Gender, contexts, and turning points in adults' lives. In P. Moen, G. H. Elder, and K. Luscher (Eds.), *Examining lives in context: Perspectives on the ecology of human development.* New York: American Psychological Association.

Clemens, A. W., and Axelson, L. J. (1985). The not-so-empty nest: The return of the fledgling adult. *Family Relations, 34,* 259–264.

Cohen, D. J., and Gunz, A. (2001). Differences in memory representation and emotion perception between Easterners and Westerners. Paper presented at the annual meeting of the American Psychological Society, Toronto.

Cohen, S., Doyle, W. J., Rabin, B. S., and Gwaltney, J. M. (1997). Social ties and susceptibility to the common cold. *Journal of the American Medical Association, 272*(24), 1940–1944.

Cole, M., and Scribner, S. (1974). *Culture and thought: A psychological introduction.* New York: Wiley.

Collins, J. G. (1993). *Prevalence of selected chronic conditions: United States 1986–1988 Vital Health Statistics.* Series 10, No. 182. (PHS 93-1510) Hyattsville, MD. National Center for Health Statistics.

Cornelius, S. W. (1990). Aging and everyday cognitive abilities. In T. M. Hess (Ed.), *Aging and cognition: Knowledge organization and utilization.* Amsterdam: North-Holland.

Cornelius, S. W. , and Caspi, A. (1987). Everyday problem solving in adulthood and old age. *Psychology and Aging, 2,* 144–153.

Costa, P. T., and McCrae, R. R. (1980). Still stable after all these years: Personality as a key to some issues in adulthood and old age. In T. E. Heatherton and J. L. Weinberger (Eds.). Can personality change? (pp. 21–41). Washington, DC. American Psychological Association.

Cowan, N. (1995). *Attentional memory: An integrated framework.* London, Oxford University Press.

Cowie, C. C., Harris, M. I., Silverman, R. E., Johnson, E. W., and Rust, K. F. (1993). Effect on multiple risk factors on differences between blacks and whites in the prevalence of non-insulin-dependent diabetes mellitus in the United States. *American Journal of Epidemiology, 137,* 719–732.

Crenshaw, T. L. (1996). *The alchemy of love and lust: Discovering our sex hormones and how they determine who we love, when we love, and how often we love.* New York: G. P. Putnam's Sons.

Crohan, S. E., Antonucci, T. C., Adelmann, P. K., and Coleman, L. M. (1989). Job characteristics and well-being at midlife: Ethnic and gender comparisons. *Psychology of Women Quarterly, 13*(2), 223–225.

Cross Cultural Solutions. (2001). Volunteer Programs. New Rochelle, New York.

Currier, A. A. (1897). *The menopause.* New York: Appleton.

Dannefer, D. (1984). The role of the social psychology in life-span developmental psychology, past and future: Rejoinder to Baltes and Nesselroade. *American Sociological Review, 49,* 847–850.

Dannefer, D., and Perlmutter, M. (1990). Development as a multidimentional process: Individual and social constituents. *Human Development, 33,* 108–137.

De Frank, R., and Ivancevich, J. M. (1986). Job loss: An individual review and model. *Journal of vocational behavior.* 19, 1–20.

Dement, W. C., Miles, L. E., and Bliwise, D. L. (1982). Physiologic markers of aging: Human sleep pattern changes. In M. E. Reff and E. L. Schneider (Eds.), *Biological markers of aging.* National Institutes of Health Publication, No. 82-2221. Bethesda, MD: National Institutes of Health.

Denner, B. (1974). Returning madness to an accepting community. *Community Mental Health Journal, 10*(2), 163–172.

Denney, N. W., (1974). Classification ability in the elderly. *Journal of Gerontology, 29,* 309–314.

Denney, N. W., and Palmer, A. M. (1981). Adult age differences on traditional and practical problem-solving measures. *Journal of Gerontology, 36*(3), 323–328.

Denney, N. W. and Pearce, K. A. (1989). A developmental study of practical problem solving in adults. *Psychology and Aging., 4,* 438–442.

Denney, N. W., Pearce, K. A., and Palmer, A. M. (1982). A developmental study of adults' performance on traditional and practical problem-solving tasks. *Experimental Aging Research, 8,* 115–118.

Denny, N. (1974). Clustering in midlife and old age. *Developmental psychology, 10,* 471–475.

Denny, N. (1982). Aging and cognitive changes. In B. Wolman (Ed.). *Handbook of developmental psychology* (pp. 807–827). Englewood Cliffs, NJ. Prentice-Hall.

Deutsch, H. (1945). *The psychology of women.* Vol. 2. New York: Grune & Stratton.

Diamond, J. (1997). *Male menopause.* Naperville, IL.: Sourcebooks.

Dickens, W. J., and Perlman, D. (1981). Friendships over the lifecycle. In S. W. Duck and R. Gilmour (Eds.), *Personal relationships:2 Developing personal relationships.* New York: Academic Press.

Dixon, R. A., and Baltes, P. B. (1988). Toward lifespan research on the functions and pragmatics of intelligence. In R. J. Sternberg and R. K. Wagner (Eds.). *Practical intelligence: Nature and origins of competence in the everyday world.* (pp 203–235). New York: Cambridge University Press.

Dixon, R. A., Hertzog, C., and Hultsch, D. F. (1986). The multiple relationships among metamemory in adulthood (MIA) scales and cognitive abilities in adulthood. *Human Learning Journal of Practical Research and Application, 5*(3), 165–177.

Donahue, E. M., Robins, R. W., Roberts, B. W., and John, O. P. (1993). The divided self: Concurrent and longitudinal effects of psychological adjustment and social roles on self-concept differentiation. *Journal of Personality and Social Psychology, 64,* 834–846.

Doress, P. B., and Siegel, D. L. (1994). *The midlife and old woman.* New York: Simon and Schuster.

Drebbing, C. E., and Gooden, W. E. (1991). The impact of the dream on the mental health functioning in the male midlife transition. *International journal of aging and human development, 32(4),* 277–287.

Dube, E. F. (1982). Literacy, cultural familiarity, and "intelligence" as determinants of story recall. In H. C. Trandis and A. Heron (Eds.), *Handbook of cross-cultural psychology: Developmental psychology.* Boston: Allyn and Bacon.

Dunleavy, K. (2001). Job choice and personality. *Journal of Allied Health, 30*(2), 75–82.

Duvall, E. M. (1977). *Marriage and family development.* 5th ed. New York: Harper and Row.

Eadwins, C. J. and Mellinger, J. C. (1984). Mid-life women: Relationship of old age and role to personality. *Journal of Personality and Social Psychology, 47,* 390–395.

Earle, J., Smith, M., Harris, C., and Longino, C., Jr. (1998). Women, marital status, and symptoms of depression in a midlife national sample. *Journal of Women and Aging, 10,* 41–57.

Elson, M. (1984). Parenthood and the transformations of narcissism. In R. S. Cohen, B. J. Cohler, and S. H. Weissman (Eds.), *Parenthood: A psychodynamic perspective.* New York: Guilford Press.

Erikson, E. (1968). *Childhood and society* (4th ed.) New York: Norton.

Erikson, E. H. (1968) 2nd Ed. Adulthood and world views. Unpublished paper prepared for Conference on Love and Work in Adulthood, American Academy of Arts and Sciences, Palo Alto, CA.

Erickson, M. A. (1998). Work, family and health trajectories: Their relationship to perceived health and depressive symptoms in late midlife. Ph.D. diss., *Abstract in Dissertation Abstracts International* University of Michigan Vol. 6, 27–28.

Evans, J. G., Goldacre, M. J., Hodgkinson, H. M., Lamb, S., and Savory, M. (1993). *Health and function in the third age: papers prepared for the Carnegie inquiry into the third age.* London: Nuffield Provincial Hospitals Trust.

Evers, H. (1985). The frail elderly woman: Emergent questions in aging and woman's health. In E. Lewin and V. Olesen (Eds.), *Women health and healing: Toward a new perspective.* New York: Tavistock.

Fiebert, M. S., and Wright, K. S. (1989). Midlife friendships in an American faculty sample. *Psychological Reports, 63*(3, pt2), 1127–1130.

Finch, J., and Mason, J. (1990). Gender, employment, and responsibility to kin. *Work, Employment, and Society, 4,* 349–367.

Finley, N. (1989). Theories of family labor as applied to gender differences in caregiving for elderly parents. *Journal of Marriage and the Family, 51,* 79–86.

Finley, N. J. (1989). Gender differences in caregiving for elderly parents. *Journal of Marriage and the Family, 51,* 79–86.

Fitzgerald, L. F., and Crites, J. O. (1980). Toward a career psychology of women: What do we know? What do we need to know? *Journal of Counseling Psychology, 27,* 44–62.

Fooken, J. (1985). Gender differences in mortality. *The journals of gerontology, 56B(4),* 246.

Ford, D. (2001). Georgia Reproductive Specialists, www IVF.Com

Ford, D. H., & Lerner, R. M. (1992). *Developmental systems theory: An integrative approach.* Newbury Park, CA: Sage.

Fox, M., Gibbs, M., and Averbach, D. (1985). Age and gender dimensions of friendship. *Psychology of Women Quarterly, 9,* 489–502.

Fox, M., and Hesse-Beiber, S. (1984). *Women at Work.* Palo Alto, CA: Mayfield.

Frank, S., Avery, C., and Laman, M. (1988). Young adults' perceptions of their relationships with their parents: Individual differences in connectedness, competence, and emotional autonomy. *Developmental Psychology, 24,* 729–737.

Galinsky, E. (1993). *National study of the changing workforce.* New York: Families and Work Institute.

Gardner, H. (1983). *Frames of mind: The theory of multiple intelligences.* New York: Basic Books.

Gatz, M., Bengtson, V. L. and Blum, M. (1990). Caregiving families. In J. E. Birren and K. W. Schaie (Eds.), *Handbook of the psychology of aging 3rd ed* (pp. 404–426). New York: Academic Press.

Gillian, C., Lyons, N. P., and Hanmer, T. J. (1990). *Making connections: The relational worlds of adolescent girls at Emma Willard School.* Cambridge, MA: Harvard University Press.

Gilligan, C. (1980). Restoring the missing text of women's development to life cycle theories. In D. G. McGuigan (Ed.), *Women's lives: New theory, research, and policy.* Ann Arbor, Michigan: University of Michigan, Center for Continuing Education of Women.

Gilligan, C. (1982). *In a different voice: Psychological theory and women's development.* Cambridge, Massachusetts: Harvard University Press.

Glick, J. (1975). Cognitive development in cross-cultural perspective. In F. Horowitz (Ed.), *Review of child development research.* Vol. 4. Chicago: Chicago University Press.

Glick, P. (1977). Updating the lifecycle of the family. *Journal of Marriage and the Family, 39,* 5–13.

Glick, P. C., and , S. L. (1986). More young adults are living with their parents: Who are they? *Journal of Marriage and the Family, 48,* 107–112.

Gold, D. T. (1989). Sibling relationships in old age: A typology. *International Journal of Aging and Human Development, 28,* 37–54.

Gold, D. T. (1990). Late-life sibling relationships: Does race affect typological distribution? *Gerontologist, 30(6),* 741–748.

Goddard, R. W. (1991). A new vision of work. *Supervision.* April, 14–26.

Gora, J. G., and Nemerowicz, G. M. (1985). *Emergency squad volunteers: Professionalism in unpaid work.* New York: Praeger.

Gould, R. (1978). *Transformation: Growth and change in adult life.* New York: Simon & Schuster.

Green, A., and Boxer, A. M. (1986). Daughters and sons as young adults. In N. Datan, A. L. Green, & H. W. Reese (Eds.), *Life-span developmental psychology: Intergenerational relations.* Hillsdale, NJ: Earlbaum.

Green, J. G., and Cooke, D. J. (1976). A factor analytic study of climacteric symptoms. *Journal of Psychosomatic Research, 40,* 425–430.

Green, J. G., and Cooke, D. J. (1980). Life stress and symptoms at the climacterium. *British Journal of Psychiatry, 136,* 486–491.

Greenglass, E. R., and Burke, R. J. (1988). Work and family precursors of burnout in teachers: Sex differences. *Sex Roles,* 18, 215–229.

Greer, G. (1991). *The change: Women aging and the menopause.* New York: Fawcett Columbine.

Grossman, H. Y., and Chester, N. L. (1990). *The experience and meaning of work in women's lives.* Hillsdale, NJ, Lawrence Earlbaum Associates, Publishers.

Grosvenor, T. (1987). A review and suggested classification system for myopia on the basis of age-related prevalence and age of onset. *American Journal of Optometry and Physiological Optics, 64,* 545–554.

Gutmann, D. (1977). The cross-cultural perspective: Notes toward a comparative psychology of aging. In J. Birren and K. W. Schaie (Eds.), *Handbook of the psychology of aging.* New York: Van Nostrand Reinhold.

Gutmann, D. (1987). *Reclaimed powers: Toward a new psychology of men and women in later life.* New York: Basic Books.

Gutmann, D. (1998). The Paternal Imperative. *American Scholar, 67,* 118–126.

Hagestad, G. O. (1982). Parent and child: Generations in the family. In T. M. Field, A. Huston, H. C. Quay, L. Troll, and G. E. Finley (Eds.), *Review of Human Development.* New York: John Wiley & Sons.

Hagestad, G. O. (1987). Parent child relations in later life: Trends and gaps in past research. In J. B. Lancaster, J. Altmann, A. S. Rossi, & L. R. Sherrod (Eds.), *Parenting across the lifespan: Biosocial dimensions.* New York: Aldine de Gruyter.

Hamon, R. R., and Bleizner, R. (1990). Filial responsibility expectations among adult child—older parent pairs. *Journal of gerontology: Psychological Sciences, 45(3)* P110–112.

Hansen, C. (1989). A causal model of relationship among accidents, biodata, personality, and cognitive factors. *Journal of applied psychology,* 74, 81–90.

Harker, L., and Solomon, M. (1996). Change in goals and values of men and women from early to mature adulthood. *Journal of Adult Development, 3,* 133–143.

Harter, S. (1999). *The construction of the self: A developmental perspective.* New York: Guilford.

Havas, S. (1992). Heart disease, cancer and stroke in Maryland. *Southern Medical Journal,* 85, 599–607.

Havighurst, R. (1953). *Human development and education.* New York: Longmans, Green.

Havighurst, R. (1972). *Developmental tasks in education 3rd ed.* New York: McKay.

Hayflick, L. M. (1996). How and why we age. New York: Ballentine.

Hayslip, B. J., and Panek, P. E. (1993). *Adult development and aging 2nd ed.* New York: HarperCollins.

Hearn, S., Glenham, M., Strayer, J., Koopman, R., and Marcia, J. E. (1998). *Integrity, despair, and in between: Toward construct validation of Erikson's eighth stage.*

Heckman, N. A., Bryson, R. and Bryson, J. B. (1977). Problems of professional couples: A content analysis. *Journal of marriage and the family,* 39, 323–330.

Helson, R., and Wink, P. (1987). Two conceptions of maturity examined in the findings of a longitudinal study. *Journal of Personality and Social Psychology,* 53, 531–541.

Hertzog, C. (1989). Influences of cognitive slowing on age differences in intelligence, *Developmental Psychology,* 25, 636–651.

Hertzog, C., and Schaie, K. W. (1986). Stability and change in adult intelligence: I. Analysis of longitudinal covariance structures. *Psychology and Aging,* 1(2), 159–171.

Hess, B. (1972). Friendship. In M. W. Riley, M. Johnson, and A. Foner, (Eds). *Aging and Society, vol III.* New York: Russell Sage.

Hill, R., and Mattessich, P. (1979). Family development theory and life-span development. In P. Baltes and O. Brim (Eds.), *Life-span development and behavior.* New York: Academic Press.

Hirsch, B. J. (1981). Social networks and the coping process: Creating personal communities. In B. H. Gottlieb (Ed.), *Social networks and social support.* Beverly Hills, CA: Sage Publications.

Hochschild, A. (1989). *The second shift.* New York. Avon.

Hollander, E. R. (1985). Leadership and power. In G. Lindzey and E. Aronson (Eds.), *The handbook of Social Psychology* (pp. 485–537). New York: Random House.

Horn, J. L. (1967). Intelligence—Why it grows, why it declines. *Transaction,* 5(1), 23–31.

Horn, J. L. (1968). Organization of abilities and the development of intelligence. *Psychological Review,* 75, 242–259.

Horn, J. L. (1970). Organization of data on life-span development of human abilities. In L. R. Goulet and P. B. Baltes (Eds.), *Lifespan developmental psychology: Theory and research.* New York: Academic Press.

Horn, J. L. (1982a). The aging of human abilities. In B. B. Wolman (Ed.), *Handbook of developmental psychology.* Englewood Cliffs, NJ: Prentice Hall.

Horn, J. L. (1982b). The theory of fluid and crystallized intelligence in relation to concepts of cognitive psychology and aging in adulthood. In F. I. M. Craik and S. Trehub (Eds.), *Aging and cognitive processes.* New York: Plenum.

Hornstein, G. A. (1986). The structuring of identity among midlife women as a function of their degree of involvement in employment. *Journal of personality,* 54, 551–575.

Horvath, T. B., and Davis K. L. (1990). Central nervous system disorders in aging. In E. L. Schneider & J. W. Rowe (Eds.), *The handbook of the biology of aging.* 3d ed. San Diego: Academic Press.

House, J. S., Robbins, C., and Metzner, H. L. (1982). The association of social relationships and activities with morality: Prospective evidence from the Tecumseh Community Health Study. *American Journal of Epidemiology,* 116, 123–140.

Howard, A., and Bray, D. W. (1988). *Managerial lives in transition: Advancing age and changing times.* New York: Guilford Press.

Hoyer, W. J., & Rybash, J. M. (1994). Characterizing adult cognitive development. *Journal of adult development,* 1(1), 7–12.

Hunter, S., and Sundel, M. (1989). *Midlife myths.* Newbury Park: NJ: Sage Publications.

Huyck, M. H. (1994). The relevance of psychodynamic theories for understanding gender among older women. In B. F. Turner and L. E. Troll (Eds.), *Women growing older: Psychological perspectives.* Thousand Oaks, CA: Sage.

Huyck, M. H. (1995). Marriage and close relationships of the marital kind. In R. Blieszner and V. H. Bedford (Eds.), *Handbook of aging and the family.* Westport, CT: Greenwood Press.

Ingram, G., and Boethel, M. (1979). *Together we can.* Newton, MA: Education Development Center.

Isiugo-Abanihe-Uche, C., Ebigbola, J. A., Adewuyi, A. and Urban, A. (1993). Nuptiality patterns and marital fertility in Nigeria. *Journal of Biosocial Science, 25*(4), 483–498.

Jacobson, J. M. (1995). *Midlife women: Contemporary issues.* Boston: Jones and Bartlett Publishers.

James, J. B. (1990). Women's employment patterns and midlife well-being. In H. Y. Grossman and N. L. Chester (Eds.), *The experience and meaning of work in women's lives.* Hillsdale, NJ: Erlbaum.

James, W. (1890). *Principles of Psychology.* Chicago: Encyclopedia Britannica.

Jensen, L., Olsen, J., and Hughes, C. (1990). Association of country, sex, social class, and life cycle to locus of control in Western European countries. *Psychological Reports, 67*(1), 199–205.

Ji, L. J., Nisbett, R. E., and Su, Y. (2001). Change, prediction and culture. Paper presented at the annual meeting of the American Psychological Society, Toronto.

Josselson, R. E. (1996). *Revising herself: The story of women's identity from college to midlife.* New York: Oxford University Press.

Jung, C. (1933). *Modern man in search of a soul.* W. S. Dell and C. F. Baynes (Trans.) New York: Harcourt, Brace.

Justice, E. M., and Dornan, T. M. (2001). *Metacognitive differences between traditional and non-traditional age college students.* In press.

Kandrack, M. K. R. Grant and Segall (1991). Gender differences in health related behaviors: Some unanswered questions. *Social Science and Medicine, 32*(5), 579–590.

Kannel, W. B., and Belanger, A. J. (1991). Epidemiology of heart failure. *American heart journal, 121,* 951–957.

Katchadourian, H. (1987). *Fifty: Midlife in perspective.* New York: W. H. Freeman.

Kelly, S. (2001). Vacation patterns in Australia. Personal communication.

Kelly, S. J. (2001). Physiological changes in the thalamus. Personal Communication.

Kelvin, P., and Jarrett, J. A. (1985). *Unemployment: Its social and psychological effects.* Cambridge, UK. Cambridge University Press.

Kerckhoff, R. K. (1976). Marriage and middle age. *The Family Coordinator, 25,* 5–11.

Kessler, R. C., Foster, C., Webster, P. S., and House, J. S. (1992). The relationship between age and depressive symptoms in two national surveys. *Psychology and Aging, 7*(1), 119–126.

Kessler, R. C., McGonagle, K. A., Swartz, M., Blazer, D. G., and Nelson, C. B. (1993). Sex and depression in the national comorbidity survey I: Lifetime prevalence, chronicity and recurrence. *Journal of affective disorders, 29,* 85–96.

Keys, C. L., and Ryff, C. D. (1999). Psychological well-being in midlife. In S. Willis and J. Reid (Eds.), *Life in the middle: psychological and social development in middle age.* San Diego: Academic Press.

Kindermann, T. A., and Skinner, E. A. (1992). Modeling environmental development: Individual and contextual trajectories. In J. B. Asendorpf and J. Valsiner (Eds.), *Stability and change in development: A study of methodological reasoning.* Newbury Park, CA: Academic Press.

King, S. (1989). Sex differences in a causal model of career maturity. *Journal of Counseling and Development, 68,* 208–215.

Kirasic, K. C., Allen, G. L., Dobson, S. H., and Binder, K. S. (1996). Aging, cognitive resources, and declarative learning. *Psychology and Aging, 11,* 658–670.

Kotre, J. & Hall, E. (1990). *Seasons of life.* Boston: Little, Brown.

Kroger, J. (2000). *Identity development: Adolescence through adulthood.* Thousand Oaks, CA: Sage Publications.

Labouvie-Vief, G. (1982). Dynamic development and mature autonomy: A theoretical prologue. *Human Development, 25,* 161–191.

Labouvie-Vief, G. (1985). Intelligence and cognition. In J. E. Birren and K. W. Schaie, (Eds.), *Handbook of the psychology of aging.* New York: Van Nostrand Reinhold.

Labouvie-Vief, G. (1990a). Modes of knowledge and the organization of development. In M. L. Commons, L. Kohlberg, R. Richards, and J. Sinnott (Eds.), *Beyond formal operations: 2, models and methods in this study of adult and adolescent thoughts.* New York: Praeger.

Labouvie-Vief, G. (1990b). Wisdom as integrated thought: Historical and development perspectives. In R. J. Sternberg (Ed.), *Wisdom: Its origins, and development.* Cambridge: Cambridge University Press.

Labouvie-Vief, G., Hakim-Larson, J., and Hobart, C. J. (1987). Age, ego level, and life-span development of coping and defense processes. *Psychology and Aging, 2,* 286–293.

Lacayo, R., and Russell, G. (1995). *Time eyewitness collector's edition.* New York: The Time Inc. Magazine Company.

Lachman, M. (1986). Personal control in later life: Stability, change, and cognitive correlates. In M. M. Baltes and P. B. Baltes (Eds.), *The psychology of control and aging.* Hillsdale, NJ: Erlbaum.

Lajer, M. (1982). Unemployment and hospitalization among bricklayers. *Scandinavian Journal of Social Medicine, 10*, 3–10.

Lakatta, E. G. (1990). The heart and circulation. In E. L. Schneider and J. W. Rowe (Eds.), *The handbook of the biology of aging.* 3d ed. San Diego: Academic Press.

Langer, E. (1997). *The power of mindful learning.* Reading, MA: Perseus Books.

Langer, E., and Bayliss, M. (1994). Mindfulness, attention, and memory. Unpublished manuscript.

LaRochelle, G. (1992). The state and the volunteer ideology in Quebec: Issues in a neoliberal context. *Recherches Sociologiques, 23* (3), 69–89.

Larson, R., Mannuell, R., and Zuzanek, J. (1986). Daily well-being of older adults with friends and family. *Psychology and Aging, 1*, 117–126.

Lawrence, R. C., Hochberg, M. C, Kelsey, J. L., McDuffy, M. C., Medsger, T. A., Jr., Felts, W. R., and Schulman, L. E. (1989). Estimates of the prevalence of selected arthritic and musculoskeletal diseases in the United States. *Journal of Rheumatology, 16*, 427–441.

Lemme, B. H. (1999a). *Development in adulthood.* Boston: Allyn and Bacon.

Lemme, B. H. (1999b). *Development in adulthood.* 2d ed. Boston: Allyn and Bacon.

Lerner, R. M. (1982). Children and adolescents as products as producers of their own development. *Developmental Review, 2*, 342–370.

Leu, J., Liu, D., and Nisbett, R. E. (2001). A new age of reason: Exploring age-related enculturation of holistic and analytic cognition. Paper presented at the annual meeting of the American Psychological Society, Toronto.

Levenson, H. (1981). Differentiating among internality, powerful others, and chance. In H. M. Lefcourt (Ed.), *Research with the locus of control construct. (Vol. 1): Assessment methods.* New York: Academic Press.

Levinson, D. J. (1978). *The Seasons of a man's life.* New York: Alfred. A. Knopf.

Levinson, D. J. (1986). A conception of adult development. *American Psychology, 41*, 3–13.

Levinson, D. J., Darrow, C., Kline, E., Levinson, M., and McKee, B. (1978). *The seasons of a man's life.* New York: Knopf.

Levinson D. J. and Gooden, W. E. (1985). The life cycle. In H. I. Kaplan and B. J. Sadocle (Eds.), *Comprehensive textbook of psychology* (4th ed.), Baltimore, MD: Williams and Williams.

Lewin, K. (1931). The conflict between Aristotelian and Galileian modes of thoughts in contemporary psychology. *Journal of Genetic Psychology, 5*, 141–177.

Lewin, K. (1935). *A dynamic theory of personality.* New York: McGraw-Hill.

Lewis, M. (1991). Ways of knowing: Objective self-awareness or consciousness. *Developmental Review, 11*, 231–243.

Lewis, M. (1994). Myself and me. In S. T. Parker, R. W. Mitchell, and M. L. Boccia (Eds.), *Self-awareness in animals and humans: Developmental perspectives.* New York: Cambridge University Press.

Lieblich, A. (1986). Successful career women at midlife: Crises and transitions. *International Journal of Aging and Human Development, 23*, 301–312.

Lock, M. (1986). Ambiguities of aging: Japanese experience and perceptions of menopause. *Culture, Medicine, and Psychiatry, 10*, 23–46.

Lord, A. B. (1982). Oral poetry in Yugoslavia. In U. Neisser (Ed.), *Memory observed: Remembering in natural contexts.* San Francisco: Freeman.

Lowenthal, M. F., and Robinson, B. (1976). Social networks and isolation. In R. H. Binstock and E. Shanas (Eds.), *Handbook of aging and the social sciences.* New York: Van Nostrand.

Lowenthal, M. F., and Weiss, L. (1976). Intimacy and crisis in adulthood. *The Counseling Psychologist, 6*, 10–15.

Lukasik, L. M. (1993). Volunteer environmental monitoring groups: Community-based water monitoring in the Gulf of Maine watershed. Ph.D. diss., *Abstract in Dissertation Abstracts International 32.* University of Michigan.

Luria, A. R. (1976). *Cognitive development: Its cultural and social foundations.* Cambridge, MA: Harvard University Press.

Madigan, T. (1998). Midlife crisis: Two-sided coin for men. *Chicago Tribune,* September 3.

Magnusson, D. (1995). Individual development: A holistic integrated model. In P. Moen, G. H. Elder, Jr., and K. Luscher (Eds.), *Examining lives in context: Perspectives on the ecology of human development.* 1995. Washington, DC: American Psychological Association.

Main, M. (1987). Working models of attachment in adolescence and adulthood. Paper presented at symposium, Society of Research in Child Development, Baltimore.

Male Depression. (2001). Found at www midlifepassage/depressant.

Mallinckrodt, B., and Fretz, B. R. (1988). Social support and the impact of job loss on older professionals. *Journal of counseling psychology, 35,* 281–286.

Mannheim, K. (1928/1952). The problem of generations. In K. Mannheim (Ed.), *Essays on the sociology of knowledge.* London: Routledge & Kaegan Paul.

Maslow, A. H. (1968). *Toward a psychology of being.* 2d ed. New York: Van Nostrand.

May, R. (1975). *The courage to create.* New York: Norton.

McAdoo, H. P. (1993). *Family ethnicity: Strength in diversity.* Newbury Park, CA: Sage Publications.

McCrae, R. R., and Costa, P. T., Jr. (1990). *Personality in adulthood.* New York: Guilford.

McKinney, C. V. (1992). Wives and sisters: Bajju marital patterns. *Ethology, 31*(1), 75–87.

McLoyd, V. (1998). Socioeconomic and disadvantage and child development. *American Psychologist, 53,* 185-204.

McQuaide, S. (1996). Self-hatred, the right to a life, and the tasks of midlife. *Clinical Social Work Journal, 24,* 35–47.

Mead, M. (1978). The new old, struggling for decent aging. In Gerzon, M. (Ed.), *Listening to midlife: Turning your crisis into a quest.* Boston: Shambhala.

Medical Leave Act of 1998.

Memmler, R. L., and Wood, D. L. (1987). *The human body in health and disease.* 6th ed. New York: JB Lippincott Company.

Mercer, R. T., Nichols, E. G., and Doyle, G. C. (1989). *Transitions in a women's life: Major life events in developmental context.* Springer: New York.

Mernissi, F. *Beyond the Veil: Male-female dynamics in a modern Muslim society.* Indiana University Press, Bloomington and Indianapolis, IN.

Merriam, S. (1980). The concept and function of reminiscence: A review of research. *The Gerontologist, 20,* 604-609.

Merrill, S. S., and Verbrugge, L. M. (1999). Health and disease in midlife. In S. Willis and J. Reid (Eds.), *Life in the Middle.* San Diego: Academic Press.

Miller, D. C. and Form, W. H. (1951). *Industrial Sociology.* New York, Harper and Row.

Miller, R. (1990). Aging and the immune response. In E. L. Schneider and J. W. Rowe (Eds.), *The handbook of the biology of aging.* 3d ed. San Diego: Academic Press.

Miller, S. B. (1997). "You can't play that, it's a boy's instrument" After centuries of being stifled, female musicians are sounding a crescendo in the world's top orchestras—and not just on violin, but on trombone and timpani, too. *Chicago Tribune,* 30 March.

Mirowsky, J., and Ross, C. E. (1992). Age and depression. *Journal of Health and Social Behavior, 33*(3), 187–205.

Moen, P. (1992). *Women's two roles: A contemporary dilemma.* Westport, CT: Auburn House.

Moen, P. (1997). Women's roles and resilience: Trajectories of advantage or turning points? In I. H. Gotlib and B. Wheaton (Eds.), *Stress and adversity over the life course: Trajectories or turning points.* New York: Cambridge University Press.

Moen, P., Elder, G. H., Jr., and Luscher, K. (Eds.). (1995). *Examining lives in context: Perspectives on the ecology of human development.* Washington, DC: American Psychological Association.

Moen, P., and Fields, V. (1998). Retirement, social capital, and well-being: Does community participation replace paid work? Bronfenbrenner Life Course Center Working Paper Series #98-10. Ithica, NY: Cornell University.

Moen, P., and Wethington, E. (1999). Midlife development in a life course context. In S. L. Willis and J. D. Reid (Eds.), *Life in the middle: Psychological and social development in middle age.* New York: Academic Press.

Montag, I., and Comrey, A. (1987). Internality and externality as correlates of involvement in fatal driving accidents. *Journal of applied psychology, 72,* 339–343.

Moss, M. S., Moss, S. Z., and Moles, E. L. (1985). The quality of relationships between elderly parents and their out-of-town children. *Gerontologist, 30,* 134–140.

Nash, S. C., and Feldman, S. S. (1981). Sex role and sex-related attributions: Constancy and change across the family life cycle. In M. E. Lamb and A. L. Brown (Eds.), *Advances in developmental psychology.* Hillsdale, NJ: Erlbaum.

National Cancer Institute (1993). *Cancer statistics review, 1973–1990.* (DHHS Publication No. (PHS) 93-2789) Bethesda, MD: National Institutes of Health.

National Center for Educational Statistics (NCES). (1995). *Digest of Education statistics, 1995.* (NCES 95-029). Washington, DC: U.S. Department of Education.

National Heart, Lung, and Blood Institute. (1992). *National Heart, Lung, and Blood Institute fact sheet: CHD morbidity.* U.S. Department of Health and Human Services. Bethesda, MD, National Institutes of Health.

National Institute of Arthritis, Diabetes, and Digestive and Kidney Diseases. (1985). *Diabetes in America: Diabetes data compiled (DHHS Publication No. 85-1468).* Department of Health and Human Services. Bethesda, MD: National Institutes of Health.

National Institutes of Aging, (1992). *Menopause* U.S. Government Printing Office.

National Institutes of Health. (1992). *Menopause.* Washington, DC: National Institutes on Aging.

Neugarten, B. (1968). Adult Personality: Toward a psychology of the life cycle. In B. Neugarten (Ed.), *Middle age and aging.* Chicago: University of Chicago Press.

Neugarten, B. L. (1968). The awareness of middle age. In B. L. Neugarten (Ed.), *Middle age and aging.* Chicago: University of Chicago Press.

Neugarten, B. L. (1969). Continuities and discontinuities of psychological issues into adult life. *Human Development, 12,* 121–130.

Neugarten, B. L. (1970). Adaptation and the life cycle. *Journal of Geriatric Psychiatry, 4,* 50–56.

Neugarten, B., and Hagestad, G. (1976). Aging and the life course. In R. Binstock and E. Shanas (Eds.), *Handbook of aging and the social sciences.* New York: Van Nostrand Reinhold.

New patterns of living arrangements in midlife couples. (2001). *My Generation,* October.

Newman, B. M., and Newman, P. R. (1995). *Development through life: A Psychosocial Approach.* Albany, NY: Brooks/Cole Publishing Company.

Nolen-Hoeksema, S., and Grayson, C. (2001). Why women experience depression more than men do. *Journal of Personality and Social Psychology.*

Norris, K. (1996). *The Cloister Walk.* Riverhead Books, New York.

O. G. Brim (Ed.). *Lifespan development and behavior.* Vol. 3. New York: Academic Press.

Ogawa, N., and Retherford, R. D. (1993). Care of the elderly in Japan: Changing norms and expectations. *Journal of Marriage and the Family, 55,* 585–597.

Oppenheimer, V. K. (1982). *Work and family: A study in social demography.* New York: Academic Press.

O'Rand, M., and Krecker, M. L. (1990). Concepts of the life cycle: Their history, meanings, and issues in the social sciences. *Annual Review of Sociology, 16,* 241–262.

Ornstein, S., and Isabella, L. (1990). Age vs. stage models of career attitudes of women: A partial replication and extension. *Journal of vocational behavior, 36,* 1–19.

Osipow, S. H. (1973). *Theories of career development.* New York: Appleton-Century-Crofts.

Osipow, D. H. (1987). Counseling psychology: Theory, research, and practice in career counseling. *Annual Review of Psychology, 38,* 257–278.

Parlee, M. B. (1974). Stereotypic beliefs about menstruation: A methodological note on the Moos Menstrual Distress Questionnaire. *Psychosomatic Medicine, 36,* 229.

Paul, R. J., and Townsend, J. B. (1993). Managing the older worker: Don't just rinse away the gray. *Academy of Management Executive, 1,* 67–74.

Payer, L. (1991). The menopause in various cultures. In H. Burger and M. Boulet (Eds.), *A portrait of the menopause.* New Jersey: Parthenon.

Peace Corps (2001). Fast facts at www peacecorps.gov.

Peng, Y. (1994). Primary and secondary control in American and Chinese-American adults: Cross-cultural and life-span developmental perspectives. Ph.D. diss., Brandeis University.

Pepper, S. C. (1942). *World hypotheses.* Berkeley, CA. University of California Press.

Perry, A. (1986). Type A behavior pattern and motor vehicle drivers' behavior. *Perceptual and motor skills, 63,* 875–878.

Peterson, D. R. (1992). Interpersonal relationships as a link between person and environment. In W. B. Walsh, K. H. Craik, and R. H. Price (Eds.), *Person-environment psychology: Models and perspectives.* Hillsdale, NJ: Lawrence Erlbaum Associates.

Pina, D. L., and Bengtson, V. L. (1993). The division of household labor and wives' happiness: Ideology, employment and perceptions of support. *Journal of marriage and the family,* 55, 901–912.

Podeschi, R. (1990). Teaching their own: Minority challenges to mainstream institutions. In J. M. Ross-Gordon, L. G. Martin, and D. Brisco (Eds.), *Serving culturally diverse populations.* San Francisco: Jossey-Bass.

Ramseur, H. (1989). Psychologically healthy Black adults: A review of theory and research. In R. L. Jones (Ed.), *Black adult development and aging.* Berkeley, CA: Cobb and Henry Publishers.

Ramu, G. N. (1989). *Women, work, and marriage in urban India: A study of dual and single-earner couples.* Newbury Park, CA: Sage Publications.

Read, K. (1993). 100 years old—and counting. *Chicago Sun-Times,* 27 June.

Reisman, J. M. (1981). Adult friendships. In S. W. Duck and R. Gilmour (Eds.), *Personal relationships: 2. Developing personal elements.* New York: Academic Press.

Repetti, R. L., Matthews, K. A., and Waldron, I (1989). Employment and women's health: Effects of paid employment on women's mental and physical health. *American Psychologist,* 44, 1394–1401.

Rhee, S. (1999). Korean-American outmarriage: Trends and implications. *Arete,* 23(2), 46–55.

Richardson, J. T. E., and King, E. (1998). Adult students in higher education: Burden or boon? *Journal of Higher Education,* 69, 65–88.

Riegel, K. F. Dialectic operations: The final period of cognitive development. *Human Development,* 16, 346–370.

Riley, M. W. (1985). Men, women, and the lengthening of the life course. In A. Rossi (Ed.), *Gender and the lifecourse.* New York: Aldine.

Riley, M. W. (1987). On the significance of age in sociology. *American Sociological Review,* 25(1), 1–14.

Robins, L. N., Locke, B. Z., and Regnier, D. A. (1991). An overview of psychiatric disorders in America. In L. N. Robbins and D. A. Regnier (Eds.). *Psychiatric disorders in America: The epidemiologic catchment area study* (pp. 328–366). New York: The Free Press.

Rodgers, F. A., and Rodgers, C. (1989). Business and the facts of family life. *Harvard business review,* 67, 121–129.

Rogers, C. R. (1961). *On becoming a person.* Boston, MA: Houghton Mifflin.

Rosenberg, S. D., Rosenberg, H. J., and Farrell M. P. (1999). The midlife crisis revisited. In S. L. Willis and J. D. Reid (Eds.), *Life in the middle: Psychological and social development in middle age.* San Diego: Academic Press.

Rosenthal, R., and Rosnow, R. L. (1991). *Essentials of behavioral research: Methods and data analysis.* New York: McGraw-Hill.

Ross-Gordon, J. M. (1991). Needed: A multicultural perspective for adult education research. *Adult Education Quarterly,* 42(1), 1–16.

Rossi, A. S., and Rossi, P. H. (1990). *Of human bonding: Parent-child relations across the life course.* New York: Aldine de Gruyter.

Roth, W. F. (1991). *Work and rewards: redefining our work-life reality.* New York, Praeger.

Rubin, L. B. (1976). *Worlds of Pain.* New York: Basic Books.

Rybash, J. M., Hoyer, W. J., and Roodin, P. A. (1996). *Adult cognition and aging on development role changes in processing, knowing and thinking.* New York: Pergamon.

Ryff, C. D. (1985). Adult personality development and the motivation for personal growth. In D. Kleiber and M. Maehr (Eds.), *Advances in motivation and achievement: Motivation and adulthood.* Vol. 4.

Ryff, C. D. (1989a). Beyond Ponce de Leon and life satisfaction: New directions in quest of successful aging. *International Journal of Behavioral Development,* 12, 35–55.

Ryff, C. D. (1989b). Happiness is everything, or is it? Explorations on the meaning of psychological well-being. *Journal of Personality and Social Psychology,* 57, 1069–1081.

Ryff, C. D., Schmutte, P. S., and Lee, Y. H. (1996). How children turn out: Implications for parental self-evaluation. In C. D. Ryff and M. M. Seltzer (Eds.), *The parental experience in midlife.* Chicago: University of Chicago Press.

Samuels, D. (1997), Mid-life crisis and depression. *Geriatrics, 3,* 55–63.

Sanchez, J. (1997). The status of African American women in U.S. society. Presentation to the Department of Psychology at the University of South Carolina, October.

Sapiro, V. (1999). *Women in American Society.* Mountain View, CA: Mayfield Publishing Co.

Sarason, I. G., Sarason, B. R., and Pierce, G. R. (1989). *Social Support: An interactional view.* New York: Wiley.

Saulter, A. F. (1996). *Marital status and living arrangements: March 1995, PPL-52.* Washington, DC: Bureau of the Census, Fertility and Family Statistics Branch, Population Division.

Scarr, S., and MaCartney, K. (1983). How people make their own environments: A theory of geno-type environments effects. *Child Development, 54,* 424–435.

Schafer, J. (1981). Effects of industrialized goal setting on college biology students' locus of control. *Journal of research in science teaching.* 18(5). 397–401.

Schaie, K. W. (1965). A general model for the study of developmental problems. *Psychological Bulletin, 64,* 92–107.

Schaie, K. W. (1983). The Seattle Longitudinal Study: A twenty-one year investigation of psycho-metric intelligence. In K.W. Schaie (Ed.). *Longitudinal studies of adult personality development* (pp. 64–155). New York: Guilford Press.

Schaie, K. W. (1988). Agism in psychological research. *American Psychologist, 43,* 179–183.

Schaie, K. W. (1989). Individual differences in rate of cognitive change in adulthood. In V. L. Bengtson and K. W. Schaie (Eds.), *The course of later life: Research and reflections.* New York: Springer.

Schaie, K. W. (1994). The course of adult intellectual development. *American Psychologist, 49,* 304–313.

Schaie, K. W. (1996). *Intellectual development in adulthood: The Seattle Longitudinal Study.* New York: Cambridge University Press.

Schaie, K. W., and Hertzog, C. (1983). Fourteen-year cohort sequential study of adult intelligence. *Developmental Psychology, 15,* 531–543.

Schaie, K. W. (1979). The primary mental abilities in adulthood: An exploration in the devel-opment of psychometric intelligence. In P. B. Baltes and O. G. Brim (Eds.), *Lifespan devel-opment and behavior vol 2* (pp. 67–115). New York: Academic Press.

Schaie, K. W. (1989a). Perceptual speed in adulthood: Cross-sectional and longitudinal studies. *Psychology and Aging, 4,* 443–453.

Schaie, K. W. (1989b). The hazards of cognitive aging. *The Gerontologist, 29,* 484–493.

Schaie, K. W. (1990). Intellectual development in adulthood. In J. E. Birren and K. W. Schaie (Eds.), *Handbook of the psychology of aging.* (pp. 291–309). San Diego, CA: Academic Press.

Schaie, K. W., and Willis, S. L. (1986). Can decline in adult intellectual functioning be reversed? *Developmental Psychology, 22,* 223–232.

Schaie, K. W., and Willis, S. L. (1996). *Adult development and aging.* 4th ed. Boston: Addison Wesley.

Schenkel, S., and Marcia, J. E. (1972). Attitudes toward premarital intercourse in determining ego identity status in college women. *Journal of Personality, 3,* 472–482.

Schmich, M. T. (1991). Employee benefit of the 90's. *Chicago Tribune,* 18 October.

Schuessler, D. H. (2000). Love and work in young adult men and women: The relationships among intimacy, mutuality, occupational choice, depression, and ego development. Ph.D. diss., *Abstract in Dissertation Abstracts International 61:* University of Michigan.

Sclar, D. A. (1999). Ethnicity and the prescribing of antidepressant pharmacotherapy. *Harvard Review of Psychiatry, 2,* 45–53.

Sclar, D. A., Ribinson, L. M., Skaer, T. L., Dickson, W. M., Kozma, and Reeder, C. E. (1998). A compar-ison of blacks and whites in a medicade population. *Clinical Drug Investigation,* 26(2), 135–140.

Scott, J. P., and Roberto, K. A. (1981). *Sibling relationships in late life.* Paper presented at the annual meeting of the National Council on Family Relations, Milwaukee.

Setterstein, R. A., Jr. (1999). *Lives in time and place.* Amityville, NY: Baywood Publishing Co., Inc.

Shafer, R. (1980). *Narrative action in psychoanalysis.* Worchester, MA: Clark University Press.

Shannon, L. (1991). Is there a gender difference in locus of control: A meta-analysis. Poster pre-sented at The lives through time: Assessment and theory in personality psychology confer-ence, Palm Springs, CA.

Sheehy, G. (1992). *Passages,* New York: Dutton.

Sheehy, G. (1995a). *Menopause: The silent passage.* New York: Pocket Books.

Sheehy, G. (1995b). *New Passages.* New York: Random House.

Shek, D. T. (1995a). Gender differences in marital quality and well-being in Chinese married adults. *Sex Roles, 32,* 699–715.

Shek, D. T. (1995b). Marital quality and psychological well-being of married adults in a Chinese context. *Sex Roles, 156,* 21–36.

Shek, D. T. (1996). Midlife crisis in Chinese men and women. *Journal of Psychology, 130,* 109–119.

Shek, D. T. (1997). Parent-child relationship and parental well-being of Chinese parents in Hong Kong. *International Journal of Intercultural Relations, 21,* 459–473.

Shibley, K. P. (2000). The revisitation of the psychosocial issue of trust/mistrust in new mothers. Ph.D. diss, The Ohio State University.

Shotter, J., and Gergen, K. (1989). *Texts of Identity.* London: Sage.

Simon, A. F., and Ogilvie, D. M. (1992). *Age, gender, and personal projects: A comparison of college students and middle-aged adults.* Unpublished manuscript.

Simonton, D. K. (1990). Creativity and wisdom in aging. In J. Birren, and K. W. Schaie (Eds.), *Handbook of the psychology of aging.* NY: Academic Press.

Sinnott, J. D. (1984). Post formal reasoning: the relativistic stage. In M. L. Commons, F. A. Richards, and C. Armon (Eds.), *Beyond formal operations: Late adolescence and adult cognitive development.* New York: Praeger.

Skolnick, A. (1991). *Embattled paradise.* New York: Basic.

Sloane, R. B. (1980). Organic brain syndrome. In J. E. Birren, and R. B. Sloane (Eds.), *Handbook of mental health and aging* (pp. 554–590). Englewood Cliffs, NJ: Prentice Hall.

Slocum, J. W., and Cron, W. L. (1985). Job attitudes and performance during three career stages. *Journal of vocational behavior, 26,* 126–145.

Smith, D. W. E. (1992). The biology of gender and aging. In L. Glass and J. Hendricks (Eds.), *Gender and aging.* Amityville, NY: Baywood Publishing Company.

Smith, J., and Baltes, P. B. (1992). A life-span perspective on thinking and problem solving. In M. Schwebel, C. A. Maher, and N. S. Fagley (Eds.), *Promoting cognitive growth over the life span.* Hillsdale, NJ.: Erlbaum.

Smith, J., and Baltes, P. B. (1990). Wisdom-related knowledge: Age/cohort differences in response to life-planning problems. *Developmental Psychology, 26,* 494–505.

Smith, S. D. (1997). Retirement transition and the later life family unit. *Public health nursing,14,* 207–216.

Starling, B. (2000). *Storm.* Hamondsworth, Middlesex, England: Signet Books.

Stein, M. (1983). *In Midlife: A Jungian perspective.* Dallas, TX: Spring Publications.

Steinem, G. L. (1993). *A book of self-esteem: Revolution from within.* Boston: Little Brown.

Stephens, M. A. P., Franks, M. M., and Atienza, A. A. (1997). Where two roles intersect: Spillover between parent care and employment. *Psychology and Aging, 12*(1), 30–37.

Sternberg, R. J. (1985). *Beyond IQ: A triarchic theory of human intelligence.* Cambridge, MA: Cambridge University Press.

Sternberg, R. J. (1986). A triangular theory of intelligence. *Psychological Review, 93,* 119–135.

Sternberg, R. J. (1990). Wisdom and its relation to be intelligence and creativity. In R. J. Sternberg (Ed.), *Wisdom: It's nature, origins, and development.* Cambridge: Cambridge University Press.

Sternberg, R. J. NS Wagner, R. K. (1994). *Mind in context: Interactionist perspectives on human intelligence.* New York: Cambridge University Press.

Stewart, A. J. (1990). Discovering the meaning of work. In H. Y. Grossman and N. L. Chester (Eds.), *The experience and meaning of work in women's lives.* Hillsdale, NJ: Erlbaum.

Stone, R., Cafferata, G. L., and Sangl, J. (1987). Caregivers of the frail elderly: A national profile. *Gerontologist, 27,* 616–626.

Suitor, J. J., and Pillemer, K. (1988). Explaining intergenerational conflict when adult children and elderly parents live together. *Journal of Marriage and the Family, 50,* 1037–2047.

Sung, K. T. (1998). An exploration of actions of filial piety. *Journal of Aging Studies, 12,* 369-386.

Tamir, L. M. (1982). *Men in their forties: The transition to middle age.* New York: Springer Publishing, Inc.

Tamir, L. M. (1989). Modern myths about men at midlife: An assessment. In S. Hunter and M. Sundel (Eds.), *Midlife myths: Issues, findings, and practical implications* (pp. 157–179). Newbury Park, CA: Sage.

Tangri, S., and Jenkins, S. (1992). The woman's life-path study: The Michigan graduates of 1967. In D. Schuster and K. Hulbert (Eds.). *Women's lives through time: Educated American women of the 20th century (pp. 20–35).* San Francisco, Jossey-Bass.

Tannen, D. (1990). *You just don't understand.* New York: Morrow.

Tashakkori, A., and Thompson, V. D. (1991). Race differences in self-perception and locus of control during adolescence and early adulthood: Methodological implications. *Genetic, Social, and General Psychology Monographs, 117*(2), 133–152.

Tesch, S., and Whitbourne, S. (1982). Intimacy and identity status in young adults. *Journal of Personality and Social Psychology, 43*(5), 1041–1051.

"The Aging Mind." (1990). The PBS series *The Brain.*

The State Newspaper. (2001). New trends in cardiac problems in young adults, March.

Tilt, E. J. (1857). *The change of life in health.* London: Churchill.

Toffler, A. (1990). *Power Shift.* New York: Bantam Books.

Toms, M. (1990). *An open life. In Gerzon's* Listening to midlife. Boston, Massachusetts: Shambhala Publications, Inc.

Treas, J., and Bengtson, V. L. (1987). The family in later years. In M. B. Sussman and S. K. Steinmetz (Eds.), *Handbook of marriage and the family.* New York: Plenum.

Troll, L. E., and Bengtson, V. (1982). Intergenerational relations throughout the lifespan. In B. B. Wolman (Ed.), *Handbook of developmental psychology.* Englewood Cliffs NJ: Prentice-Hall.

Two's a crowd. (2001). *My Generation, (July–August).*

U.S. Bureau of Census. (1999). *Statistical abstract of the United States.* 119th ed. Washington, DC: GPO.

U.S. Bureau of the Census. (1992). Population projections of the United States, by age, sex, race, and Hispanic origin. *Current Population Reports,* Series P-25, No. 1092. Washington DC: GPO.

Unger, R. and Crawford, M. (1996). *Women and gender: A feminist psychology.* New York: McGraw-Hill.

U.S. Department of Education. Implications in adult learning in later life. (1999). *New approaches to education and learning.* Washington, D.C. U.S. Government Printing Office.

U.S. Department of Labor. Bureau of Labor Statistics (1990). *Thirty-eight million persons do volunteer work.* Press release USDL 90-154. Washington DC.

US Department of Labor, Employment and training administration. (1993). *Selected characteristics of occupations defined in the revised dictionary of occupational titles.* Washington, D.C., U.S. Government Printing Office.

US Weekly. (2001). "Piano Man" admits to identity crisis. May 28.

Vaillant, G. E. (1977). *Adaptation to life: How the best and the brightest came of age.* Boston: Little, Brown.

Van der Veer, R., and Vlasiner, J. (1991). *Understanding Vygotsky.* Oxford: Basil Blackwell.

Vatuk, S. (1992). Sexuality and the middle-aged woman in South Asia. In V. Kernes and J. K. Brown (Eds.), *In her prime: New views of middle-age women.* Urbana: University of Illinois Press.

Verbrugge, L. M. (1988). Unveiling higher morbidity for men: The story. In M. W. Riley (Ed.), *In social structures and human lives.* Newbury Park, CA: Sage.

Vlasiner, J. (2000). *Culture and human development.* Thousand Oaks, CA: Sage Publications.

Von Drass, D. D., and Siegler, I. C. (1997). Stability in extraversion and aspects if social support at midlife. *Journal of personality and social psychology, 72,* 233–241.

Wagner, D. A. (1978). Memories of Morocco: The influence of age, schooling, and environment on memory. *Cognitive Psychology, 10,* 1–28.

Wagner, D. A. (1981). Culture and memory development. In H. C. Triandis and A. Heron (Eds.). *Handbook of cross-cultural psychology: Developmental psychology.* Vol. 4. Boston: Allyn and Bacon.

Ward, R., Logan, J., and Spitze, G. (1992). The influence of parent and child needs on coresidence in middle and later life. *Journal of Marriage and the Family, 54,* 209–221.

Ward, R., and Spitze, G. (1996). Will the children ever leave? Parent-child coresidence history and plans. *Journal of Family Issues, 17*(4), 524–539.

Warr, P. (1994). Age and employment. In H. C. Triandis, M. D. Dunnett, and L. M. Hough (Eds.), *Handbook of industrial and organizational psychology*, 4, (pp. 485–550). Palo Alto, CA: Consulting Psychologists Press, Inc.

Webb, W. B. (1982). Sleep in older persons. Sleep structures of 50- to 60-year-old men and women. *Journal of Gerontology, 37*, 581–586.

Webber, A. M. (1998). Is your job your calling. *Fast Company,* Feb/Mar.

Weick, A. (1983). A growth-task model of human development as a basis for practice. *Social Casework, 64*(3), 131–137.

Weisz, J. R., Rothbaum, F. M., and Blackburn, T. C. (1984). Standing out and standing in: The psychology of control in America and Japan. *American Psychologist, 39*, 955–969.

Westermeyer, J. F. (1998). Predictors and characteristics of mental health among men at midlife: A 32-year longitudinal study. *American Journal of Orthopsychiatry, 68*, 265–273.

Wethington, E. (2000). Expecting stress: American and the "midlife crisis." *American Sociological Association.*

Whitbourne, S. K. (1985). *The aging body: Physiological changes and psychological consequences.* New York: Springer Verlag.

Willingham, D. B., and Goedert, K. (2001). The role of taxonomies in the study of human memory. *Cognitive, affective, and behavioral neuroscience, 1*(3), 250–265.

Willis, S. L., and Schaie, K. W. (1999). Intellectual functioning in midlife. In S. L. Willis and J. D. Reid (Eds.), *Life in the Middle.* New York: Academic Press.

Wilson, R. A. (1966). *Feminine forever.* New York: M. Evans.

Wohlwill, J. F. (1991). Relations between method and theory in developmental research: A partial-isomorphism view. In P. van Geert and L. P. Mos (Eds.), *Annals of theoretical psychology.* New York: Plenum Publishing.

Wolf, P. A., D'Agostino, R. B., O'Neil, M. A., Sytkowski, P., Kase, C. S., Belanger, A. J., and Kannel, W. B. (1992). Secular trends in stroke incidence and mortality: The Framingham Study. *Stroke* 23, 1551–1555.

Wolfson, C., Handfield-Jones, R., Glass, K. C., McClaran, J., and Keyserlingk, E. (1993). Adult children's perceptions of their responsibility to provide care for dependent elderly parents. *The Gerontologist, 33*, 315–323.

Working Age (March/April 1988). Japanese love of work a lifelong affair 3(5).

Name Index

Subject Index